W9-CUO-920

BARRON'S BUSINESS LIBRARY

Business Law

BARRON'S BUSINESS LIBRARY

Business Law

Christopher Dungan
Donald Ridings

New York • London • Toronto • Sydney

All inquiries should be addressed to:
Barron's Educational Series, Inc.
250 Wireless Boulevard
Hauppauge, New York 11788

Library of Congress Catalog Card Number 89-18300

International Standard Book Number 0-8120-4189-5

Library of Congress Cataloging-in-Publication Data

Dungan, Christopher Wright, 1935-
    Business law / Christopher Dungan, Donald Ridings.
        p.   cm. — (Barron's business library)
    ISBN 0-8120-4189-5
    1. Business enterprises—United States.   2. Business law—United
States.   I. Ridings, Donald.   II. Title.   III. Series.
KF1355.Z9D86 1990
346.73'065—dc20   89-18300
[347. 30665]   CIP

PRINTED IN ITALY

Preface

Picture the situation in which you might find yourself. You have just acquired or started a small company...or purchased a business franchise...or been promoted to a managerial position in your existing company.

You are a businessowner or manager, not an attorney. Legal advice is something you will buy when necessary, you tell yourself. But at every turn you find yourself, as one small businessperson puts it, "practicing law without a license." That is, making decisions with legal ramifications but without the benefit of paid-for legal advice that would make you more comfortable with those decisions. So what do you do? This book will help you decide.

A note of caution: This is not a do-it-yourself law book, although the authors are attorneys. It is designed to provide a framework for understanding some of the legal issues, opportunities, and pitfalls, as well as to help you utilize your attorney more effectively. Indeed, it may encourage you to talk to your lawyer more frequently than you do now.

For example, there may be some legal issues where one visit to your lawyer may provide a roadmap for your future actions, making it unnecessary to consult each time the same issue arises. On the other hand, if you are involved in seeking patents for your products or processes, you will find yourself necessarily spending a considerable amount of time—and probably money—with your registered patent attorney.

The following chapters are meant to be practical and applicable to business situations. You hire and fire employees, borrow money, sign contracts, purchase insurance, pay taxes and deal with the IRS, and plan for your and your employees' retirement. Every day you make decisions that may involve legal issues; this book seeks to arm you with basic awareness of these issues as you deal with your day-to-day problems.

When discussing insurance, for example, the chapter approaches the subject from the standpoint of overall risk management for your company. And when discussing tax obligations and the IRS, the book includes a chapter that deals specifically with how to deal effectively with the IRS.

As an additional aid, throughout the book you will encounter "notes," "cautions," and other signposts to flag your attention to issues that may be especially tricky or important.

Owning, operating or managing a business can be as exhilarating as a ride on a roller coaster. This survival manual attempts to remove some of the danger from that exhilarating experience.

No manual can substitute for good business sense, luck, and being in the right business at the right time. But it can help.

CHRIS DUNGAN
DON RIDINGS

Contents

BARRON'S BUSINESS LIBRARY

Business Law

Starting Up on Your Own

INTRODUCTION

Any start-up enterprise requires careful planning. For example, before you go into any business, you should make some basic internal preparations: development of a business plan, decision on a place of business, targeting of your customers or clients, and selection of employees.

Be warned, however, that you also need to go through an external checklist of legal requirements. Compare it to building a house. Even while you are gathering your building materials, you still have to obtain a building permit, comply with building, electrical, and plumbing codes, and satisfy zoning and subdivision requirements.

You make the business preparations to protect yourself and ensure a profitable bottom line. The legal preparations are to make sure that you stay on the right side of the law and avoid any time-wasting hassles. Keep in mind that legal requirements are not arbitrary restrictions put in place simply to harass entrepreneurs; these laws are intended to protect the public interest and to assure that public needs are satisfied by the way you conduct your business.

After studying the material in this chapter:

▬ You will understand how to check some basic legal requirements for operating a business.

▬ You will know what kinds of licenses may be required for your business and how to check in your area.

▬ You will know how fictitious name statutes may affect your business.

▬ You will be able to evaluate a lease so as to protect your business's interests.

▬ You will know how zoning regulations affect your home-based office or other business.

━ You will be able to determine the extent to which your business is regulated by mail order regulations.

━ You will understand the potential benefits from locating in an enterprise zone.

LICENSES TO DO BUSINESS

States, counties and municipalities all can require licenses to do business. The purpose of such licenses is twofold:

1. To raise revenue for the governmental jurisdiction.
2. To control and monitor individuals and businesses providing certain types of personal services deemed potentially dangerous to the public.

Almost all businesses are subject to licensing for the first reason: Raising revenue. Generally, acquiring such a license is a simple and straightforward process. You might be required to provide your business name, address of the business, type of business, fictitious name if your business uses one, telephone number, number of employees, and names of the partners or stockholders of the business.

You might also be required to certify that your business complies with zoning, fire, plumbing, and other local code regulations.

Under the second category, regulating specific businesses, either state or local government might require special licenses, and some of these licenses might require a test. Examples of local special licenses are a peddler's license, a jeweler's license, an insurance agent's license. Some states require licenses that are granted according to standards of professionalism and ability. Examples are plumbers, barbers, and insurance companies. State licensing and testing requirements may also apply to doctors, attorneys, CPAs, and other workers with specific professional training.

Caution: Wide variation exists among states concerning licensing requirements. Wide variation also exists among local jurisdictions.

For information on local licensing requirements, check the local licensing office, city hall, county courthouse, or the local chamber of commerce.

For information on state licensing requirements, check the state commerce department, state revenue department, or the state agency specifically related to your business (for example, the state plumbing commission).

Licensing Checklist

Before starting to operate your business, ask yourself:

1. Does the business deliver a product or service that could potentially inflict harm on people?
2. Have both local and state agencies been checked concerning license requirements?

FICTITIOUS NAME STATUTES: "DOING BUSINESS AS"

Before you hang your new business sign, remember that some states have fictitious names statutes. A fictitious name, or a trade name, means that the business uses a name other than the surname of the proprietor or the partners. This is commonly referred to as "doing business as," or "dba."

"ABC Plumbing" is a fictitious name and normally would be registered. "George Washington Plumbing" would also need to be registered unless the proprietor's name really is George Washington.

For state registration requirements, check the secretary of state in your state capital. Also, check with the county clerk or business licensing agency in your area, since some local jurisdictions also require registration.

Some states and local jurisdictions also require publication of the fictitious name information in a local newspaper within a certain period after registration. Again, check this with your secretary of state or the county clerk.

Filing for and receiving fictitious name registration is generally relatively simple and can be done by you or your business manager.

LEASING

When you start up a business, you may need a location and you may need equipment. Whether to lease or to buy furniture, automobiles, computers, or other equipment and fixtures needed by your business is an economic decision, not a legal one. The prime advantage of leasing is that it gets you the equipment with the least money paid up front. In the long run, buying may be cheaper, but you don't want to find yourself owning equipment that has become outdated.

Leasing real property as business premises—a shop, store, or office—is chock full of legal complications. Take a look at some of the issues.

Leasing Business Premises

The word to remember in leasing real property for your business premises is *negotiation*. Leases of residential property are closely regulated by law. With commercial leases, you are on your own. The law protects you when you rent the apartment or house you live in. This is not so when you lease an office, store, warehouse, plant, or other business property.

Since the law doesn't look out for you, you have to look out for yourself. You can do this by paying close attention to the lease that you, as "lessee," are signing. The "lessor"—the property owners—will try to get you to sign the lease that *their* lawyer has prepared to protect *them*.

Don't sign a lease right away. Instead, tell the lessor you need time to study it.

After reading this section, you will know much more about leasing than the usual new business owner. Still . . . if the lease is going to involve a substantial amount of money, you may decide to consult an attorney who specializes in commercial real estate law or a reputable commercial broker.

Commercial leases are complex. In every state a long history of court decisions has interpreted lease contracts. These decisions reached by judges in past court cases make up what is called *precedent*. Precedent affects your rights under a commercial lease more so than do statutes passed by your legislators. Below, under the heading "State Law," we describe three legal matters that the precedent of your state may handle in ways that may surprise you. A good lawyer—one who has experience in commercial real property—can study the effect of precedent on your lease.

Should your attorney, rather than the lessor's, draw up a lease? Maybe so, if you have enough bargaining power to bring this about. But here's one legality you may not be aware of: Any unclear or ambiguous parts of a lease will be interpreted by the courts *against* the interests of the party who drew up the contract!

Talk to other business owners about problems they've had with their leases. Ideally, talk to lessees who have signed, and worked with, the very same lease the owner is asking you to sign.

You have leverage *before* you sign the lease, but hardly any afterward. Walk through the premises with the owner (or his agent). Whatever he agrees to paint or install or patch or replace . . . get it in writing before you sign. But don't stop there. It's a fact that many lessors won't do what they've promised, even when they put it in writing. There is a cure for this problem. Insert a clause in your lease that says the security deposit becomes due and payable to the lessor only when the agreed-upon repairs or alterations are completed with first-class materials and workmanship to the lessee's satisfaction. Another clause might say that the lessee has the right, upon giving advance notice to the lessor, to make needed repairs the owner has failed to make, and to deduct their cost from the rent.

State Law

You must understand the way your lease handles three issues. First, look at the paragraph titled ASSIGNMENT in our sample lease on the next page. It says you must get the property owners' permission in writing before you let another person take over your lease.

Suppose the owners don't give permission. Suppose they like the volume of business you bring to their shopping center, or they just dislike the other person's looks. Can they refuse to consent, and do so *arbitrarily*?

There's an important legal issue here. The courts of many states would say the owners may investigate the new lessee but then cannot withhold consent without a good business reason. In other states the owners could refuse consent just because . . . well, they wouldn't have to have *any* reason. If it's necessary to do so in your state, your lawyer will insert a sentence that says, "Lessor's consent will not be withheld without reasonable cause stated in writing. Such consent will be implied 30 days after notice to Lessor."

Here's a related issue. Suppose you've signed a lease for three years, but you must move out after several months. (The reason doesn't matter. You may be ill or you may be going broke.) Can the owner let the property sit vacant and sue you for the rent due? Or, must the owner "mitigate" damages? That is, try to rent to someone else. In most states the owner has no duty to mitigate damages.

Here's one more example. The lease says the lessor must maintain the exterior and roof of the building in good repair. Suppose the roof leaks. Is the lessor liable for the damage to your rug, furniture, business records, or inventory? The answer, if it's not clear under the law and precedent of your state, should be stated in the lease.

Sample Lease

Here is an example of a simple lease. It must not be used without tailoring it to your own situation with the help of your lawyer. It does, however, give you an idea of what to expect to see in the lease you sign (which might be ten or more pages long.) The terms in parentheses, such as (DATE) would not show up in the lease. They are there to call your attention to the basic matters that must be dealt with in any lease. Explanations of terms are given at the end.

LEASE

(DATE)

This lease entered into this <u>twenty-fifth</u> day of <u>October</u>, A.D. <u>year</u>.
(PARTIES)

by and between <u>Acme Properties, Inc.</u> hereinafter referred to as LESSOR and <u>Janet Wagner and Tom Creese,</u> doing business as <u>Newbusiness Sales</u> hereinafter referred to as Lessee.
(DESCRIPTION OF THE LEASED PROPERTY)

In consideration of the rental below specified and of the covenants hereinafter stipulated, the Lessor agrees to lease and demise to the Lessee the premises situated at <u>2384 Industrial Drive, Miramont City, Carpasus County, Texas.</u>
(TERM)

To have and to hold the demised premises unto the lessor, his successors and assigns for the term of <u>five</u> years, commencing the first day of <u>November</u>, A.D. <u>year</u> and ending the <u>first</u> day of <u>November</u>, A.D. <u>year</u>.
(RENT)

The rent for the term of this lease is $120,000, payable without demand or notice in equal monthly installments of $2,000 on the first day of each and every month of the term beginning on the <u>first</u> day of <u>November</u>, A.D., <u>year</u>. Receipt is hereby acknowledged by the Lessor of the first month's installment and of <u>$5,000</u> as security deposit.
(USE)

The use of the premises shall be for <u>a retail store</u> and for no other purposes except with the written consent of the Lessor.
(ASSIGNMENT)

The Lessee may not assign this lease or sublet any part of the demised premises without the prior written consent of the Lessor.
(LESSOR'S MAINTENANCE RESPONSIBILITIES)

Lessor hereby agrees to keep the exterior portion of the premises in good repair and maintenance. The Lessee shall give written notice to the Lessor of necessary repairs and the Lessor shall have reasonable time thereafter to make repairs.
(LESSEE'S MAINTENANCE RESPONSIBILITIES)

The Lessee agrees to maintain the interior portion of the premises in good repair at all times. Alterations, additions, or structural improvements made to the premises shall remain a part of the premises and revert to the Lessor at the conclusion of the term of this lease.

(INSURANCE)

The Lessee agrees to carry adequate public liability insurance with a bona fide insurance company maintaining sufficient protection against any injuries or damages sustained by individuals while upon the demised premises for which the Lessor or the Lessee may be held liable.

(DEFAULT REMEDIES)

Lessee hereby covenants and agrees that if a default shall be made in the payment of rent or if the Lessee shall violate any of the covenants of this lease, then said lessee shall become a tenant at sufferance, hereby waiving all right of notice, and the Lessor shall be entitled immediately to re-enter and retake possession of the demised premises.

(TERMINATION)

The Lessee agrees to quit and deliver up said premises at the end of said term in good condition as they are now, ordinary wear and tear excepted.

(OPTION)

The Lessee shall have the option to renew this lease for a further term of five years beginning the first day of November A.D. year for a total rental of $150,000 payable $2,500 per month. All other terms and conditions of this lease agreement shall remain in full force and effect.

(QUIET ENJOYMENT)

As long as the Lessee performs all of the covenants and conditions of this lease and abides by the rules and regulations he shall have peaceful and quiet enjoyment of the demised premises for the term of this lease.

(SIGNATURES AND WITNESSES)

In witness whereof, the Lessor and Lessee have executed this lease the day year first above written.

Witness:

	By	
_____	_____	
		Lessee
_____	By _____	
		Lessee
_____	By _____	
		Lessee

Leasing Checklist

In addition to the items in our sample lease, here's a list of matters you'll want to pay attention to when you negotiate and before you sign a lease. Don't rely on oral promises of the property owner or leasing agent. Remember the "parole evidence rule" (see the chapter on contracts) that the only promise that counts is the one that's in writing and gives you power to enforce without great cost. Answers to the following questions must appear in the written lease or be omitted only with your lawyer's approval. Be practical: You can't get every clause tilted in your favor, but you can even out the score by careful negotiation.

1. Are you obligated to continue paying rent even if the building can't be used due to a fire or flood?

2. Are the owners prohibited from competing in business against you or from leasing adjacent premises to your competitor? Can they lease space to a tavern right next door to your maternity shop?

3. Are the owners liable for damages to your property caused by a failure or defect in their maintenance routine?

4. Is your rent reduced while the owners' repair or construction work interferes with entry to your business?

5. Are you required to pay for fire and casualty insurance on the owners' building?

6. Who will pay real estate taxes, special assessments, water and sewer bills—or increases in these?

7. Are public toilets provided by the owners?

8. What restrictions are there on signs you may wish to put up?

9. Does the lease allow the owners to change the rules without your consent?

10. Do you understand how your share of common costs (flow-through costs) is determined for such things as electrical service, trash disposal, janitorial, or security services? If the lessees pay all the costs, is there any incentive for the owners to hold these costs in line?

11. Are parking spaces specifically provided for in the lease? Will they be adequate if your business is successful? What is your recourse if other tenants' employees take all the spaces?

12. Is storage space, garage, basement, etc. provided for in the lease?

13. May you make repairs the lessors have failed to make and then immediately recover the cost from them?

14. When your lease is over, can you recover from the lessors the value of improvements you've made?

15. Is the electrical service now adequate? Otherwise, who pays to install it?

16. Do the owners retain a set of keys to the property? For what reasons can they enter your business when you're not there?

17. What's the procedure and how quickly will you get your security deposit back when you vacate? Is it held "in escrow"? Will your deposit draw interest?

18. Do you understand under what conditions the owners can cancel your lease? (If you fail to open on one day, because of sickness or death, can the owners terminate the lease?)

19. In case of dispute, are you and the lessors required to take your case to an arbitrator to avoid a costly court fight?

20. The option clause is one of the most important in any lease. Bargain to make sure it gives you flexibility to renew at a rental price you will be able to afford.

21. If appropriate in your state, do you have the right to mortgage your lease as security for a loan?

22. If you need to move out ("vacate the premises"), can you cancel the lease without great penalty or by paying a stipulated amount? (See the section on liquidated damages in the chapter on contracts.)

23. Multiunit buildings, such as shopping centers, create special problems relating to rules imposed by tenant or merchant associations. Do you have to join? Do the chain stores have to join? Do you understand how your rights will be affected by this group in which you will have only a small voice?

24. Do all lessees have to observe the same hours of operation? Who decides the hours?

25. Does the lease impose restrictions as to when and where on the premises deliveries of merchandise or equipment can be received by you?

ZONING AND OTHER LAND-USE REGULATIONS

The question of *where* certain business activities may take place is most commonly controlled through local zoning and other land-use regulations.

Whether existing zoning is appropriate for your business is the first land-use regulation question you need to address. Check with your local planning and zoning commission or planning department. If you cannot find them listed in the phone book, call the courthouse or city hall.

Warning: Answer this zoning question before you locate your business, not after. It can save you grief and money. Zoning enforcement officers have the power to close you down if you are operating in an improperly zoned area.

You need to address the zoning question whether you plan to operate from your home or from an office or an industrial site.

Working from your home or home workshop has a long and honorable tradition. Before there were any zoning ordinances, people used their homes to give piano lessons, operate barber shops, run boarding houses. So-called "cottage industries" have supported many families, and they sometimes have spawned large corporate enterprises. Small, home-grown businesses constitute a major part of today's economic growth.

But your home is not a castle, free from outside rules, when it comes to business enterprise today.

Zoning originated as a method of separating people's living quarters from the more noxious effects of industrial activities. It has evolved into a complex system of regulations that govern what can be done on a particular piece of property—whether in your house, your garage, your office building, or your industrial site.

For the purpose of your business operations, you need to know that zoning primarily applies to:

▬ the *use* of the property—what is done there.

▬ the *intensity* of the activity—how much business activity is conducted there, and the effects of that activity.

Take the example of an auto repair business that you want to operate from the garage behind your house. Most zoning ordinances prohibit such a business in a residential area because of the noise and unsightliness—period. That is a restriction on use.

Or take the example of a book distributor. If you deal with only a few rare, expensive books, your activities will not cause much of a fuss; you probably would be allowed to do it from your house even if your area is strictly residential in zoning. But if you handle best-sellers and run trucks in and out of your driveway, you probably would be stopped. This is a restriction on the intensity of the use.

Even if you conduct your business from an office building, be advised that most zoning ordinances would prohibit you from activities that might be considered manufacturing or otherwise not compatible with typical offices.

To repeat, *however, zoning is local.* Check out your specific question with local zoning authorities at the planning and zoning commission or the planning department.

Related Local Land-Use Regulations

Zoning has several offspring—related regulations that also restrict or direct land use. The same planning and zoning commission or planning department that handles zoning probably will handle these programs, also. If not, a board of zoning adjustment or zoning appeals board may have jurisdiction. These are also local bodies.

"Nonconforming rights" are provisions that allow you to conduct certain activities on property because they are "grandfathered" into the property (this means those activities were being conducted on the property prior to the adoption of regulations that now prohibit them). *Caution:* This is among the more complicated and touchy areas of land-use control and requires competent advice from a zoning or real estate attorney.

"Variances" provide for certain land-use restrictions to be dropped if such a variance is consistent with the character of the rest of the neighborhood. An example: You might be allowed to build a new garage-office to the alley property line, even though zoning regulations require a setback, because all the other houses in the block have garages built to the alley property line.

"Conditional use permits" may be required in addition to proper zoning for activities considered particularly offensive. Examples: operating a solid waste landfill, even in an industrial zone, or operating a busy day care center in a quiet residential zone.

Caution: If you encounter zoning restrictions that you consider unfair—even in violation of your constitutional rights—do not spend badly needed capital on a lawsuit challenging the basic constitutionality of zoning. That has already been done. Zoning is controversial, but it is legal.

Zoning Checklist
These are some questions that you should ask before moving your business into your home. If you answer yes to any of these questions, consider it a warning flag for you to check with planning and zoning officials or a zoning lawyer.

1. Is your proposed business activity different from what transpires in other houses in your neighborhood?
2. Will your business generate additional traffic in and out of your house?
3. Will the business generate any additional noise, fumes, or other noxious side effects?
4. Will the business require any kind of sign or other identification?
5. Is any kind of hazard associated with your business?
6. Is the business activity substantially different from what transpired in the house before you moved in?

7. Does the business require you to expand your house or construct any additional outbuilding?
8. Will the business require any physical alteration to the grounds?

These are questions that should be asked before moving your business into any area: office building, commercial property, or industrial zone. If the answer is yes to any of these questions, contact the planning and zoning commission, planning department or a zoning lawyer.

1. Is the planned business activity significantly different from others in the same building or area?
2. Are there any hazards or noxious side effects in the operation of the business?
3. Is any expansion of the building or physical alteration of the property required?
4. Does the business generate an unusual volume of traffic?

POSTAL REGULATIONS

If your new business involves selling goods by mail, you need to pay close attention to postal regulations. There are two compelling reasons.

Reason one is the U.S. Postal Service. Its inspectors have police power; they can arrest you and close down your business. Although first offenses of a minor nature might bring only a slap on the wrist, continued and/or serious violations can lead to trial and jail. The inspection division is the oldest federal law-enforcement agency in the country, and it is considered highly effective.

Reason two is the Federal Trade Commission (FTC). False and/or misleading advertising will bring you face-to-face with another set of stringent regulations—and some real trouble for your new business.

The U.S. Postal Service

The Postal Service was chasing violators of postal laws around the country and beyond during colonial days. Today, it boasts a 98 percent conviction rate for cases taken to trial, and regional offices post large gold police shields in their offices to tout their police function.

For you, the point is this: Violating postal regulations and laws can bring you into contact with a very tough law-enforcement organization.

Postal regulations define lotteries as gambling, and that is not allowed through the mails. Since the sweepstakes is a common direct mail marketing device, you need to know how to differentiate between a legal sweepstakes and an illegal lottery. When these three elements appear together, an illegal lottery exists:

1. A payment is required (cash or money order).
2. A prize is offered (money or something of value).
3. A return on investment depends on chance.

Removing the requirement for payment or purchase is the common way of making a sweepstakes legal. That is why you can enter various mail sweepstakes offers without buying the magazine or book or other product.

Confusion between a lottery and a sweepstakes can be an honest mistake, but many other areas prosecuted by the Postal Service constitute more blatant fraud: false billings for products never sent, franchise schemes, fraudulent work-at-home and diploma schemes, charity schemes, promotion of fake health cures and beauty devices, fast-working diets and sex stimulants, and chain letters.

Federal Trade Commission

Before the FTC's Mail Order Rule went into effect in 1976, both the FTC and the President's Office of Consumer Affairs had received thousands of complaints. Compliance is monitored by the FTC's Bureau of Consumer Protection.

An example of the complaints was a letter from a consumer who had not received a stereo component he had ordered with payment in July. By late October, the only communication he had received from the company was an indirect one: his canceled check.

The Mail Order Rule provides that:

1. A business must ship your order when promised.
2. If there is no promise of any specific shipment or delivery time, the merchandise must be shipped no later than 30 days after receiving the order.
3. If the business is unable to ship the order when promised (or within the 30-day limit), the purchaser has a right to cancel the order and receive a prompt refund.

Thus, if you can meet neither the promised shipping date nor the 30-day period, you are required to send the purchaser an "option notice." This notice tells the purchaser the new shipping date; it also gives the purchaser the option of canceling the order with a full refund, or agreeing to the new shipping date. You must provide a way for the purchaser to reply.

There are exceptions to this rule: mail order photofinishing; magazine subscriptions and other serial deliveries (except for the initial shipment); seeds and plants; COD orders; or credit orders where the 30-day shipping requirement applies and the purchaser's account is not charged before the merchandise is mailed.

The Mail Order Rule also applies to orders between businesses, not just to individual consumers. If you sell specialty items (calendars, pens, etc.) as advertising merchandise to other businesses, for example, you must comply with the Rule.

Warning: Your state may have stricter rules than the FTC. Check with the state attorney general's office.

Mail Order Checklist

1. Do you anticipate that delivery of your product will take more than 30 days? If so, have you clearly communicated that to the buyer?

2. If you encounter delivery problems, do you notify the buyer before the expiration of the 30-day or advertised period to provide the option of a delay or a cancelation?

3. Do you use comparative pricing advertising that is misleading by comparing to unrealistic former prices or to generally ignored "manufacturer's suggested list price"?

4. Do you substitute inferior merchandise when offering "two for" sales?

5. When you use endorsements, are the persons making the testimonials paid or do they have a financial interest in the merchandise?

6. Do the persons making the testimonials really use the products? If represented as experts, is that really the case?

7. Is your direct mail sweepstakes incentive carefully crafted so as not to be ruled an illegal lottery?

8. Does your mail order business really deliver an honest product as advertised, or is it a sham that a reasonable person would consider to be a fraud?

PRICING

Problems with deceptive pricing can be tricky; ask the FTC for guidance if you have doubts.

You cannot compare your bargain price with former prices if the former prices are not actual and realistic. The former prices must have been offered to the public on a regular basis. Also, exercise care about comparing prices to such things as "manufacturer's suggested list price" if in reality retailers ignore that advice and routinely sell for a lower price. Do not advertise prices below retail unless they are below or at least equal to retail prices. The FTC has said that you must be selling the same or comparable merchandise, and your price cannot exceed the price at which comparable merchandise is being offered by retail outlets in your market. If you advertise two for one, do not increase your regular price for the article, and do not switch an inferior product for your regular merchandise.

Endorsements also represent legal quicksand for both you and the person making the endorsement. If someone claims to use the product, make sure there is evidence to back that up. If the person is being paid to make the endorsement or has a financial interest in the product, make that clear in the ad or commercial. If the person claims to be an expert with regard to the merchandise, make sure that is true.

If you run into questions about a particular aspect of your business, contact the Federal Trade Commission, Bureau of Consumer Protection. To get an opinion, formal or informal, from the FTC concerning a particular aspect of your business, contact the Enforcement Division, FTC. Or there may be a local chapter of the Direct Marketing Association that you can contact.

ENTERPRISE ZONES

Although they are not for everyone, some businesses can benefit from locating in enterprise zones. These are areas designated in some communities where regulations are waived or eased and where financial incentives are available. They are usually in blighted areas, and therein lies the problem for some businesses. If you plan to open an upscale boutique, an enterprise zone is the wrong spot.

Enterprise zones vary from one jurisdiction to the next. Probably no two are alike, so be sure to check out the specific details in the area where you are locating your business.

The concept of enterprise zones is to revive neighborhoods and at the same time provide jobs.

From a public policy standpoint, government reshuffles the deck of programs, incentives, and regulations to make certain areas more attractive for investment. Instead of offering a single program or incentive, the intent is to create a general climate of opportunity in those areas.

From your standpoint, there may be some aspect of the enterprise zone program that will help jump-start your business. Since programs differ widely, you have to examine your specific locale's program; there is no standard.

Start by checking with the local chamber of commerce. Other sources might be: the local government economic development office; city hall or the courthouse; the state economic development office or commerce department; the local office of the U.S. Department of Housing and Urban Development (HUD).

Nationally, the concept of the enterprise zone is still evolving. Other countries have more experience with enterprise zone–like programs, but a full-fledged national program here has not taken hold.

The federal program mostly encourages such things as tax incentives at the state and local levels; specific actions to reduce, remove, simplify, or streamline governmental regulations at all levels; and improved local services.

Despite federal slowness in establishing a national policy, some local governments have packaged their own enterprise zone programs. Some examples of benefits provided in local programs include the following:

Reduction of city inventory taxes

Preferential treatment for water and sewer hook-ons and reduced building permit fees

Industrial revenue bond financing

Eligibility for city-assisted loans

Construction of various infrastructure projects

Inclusion of companies for special clean-up programs

Establishment of special zoning regulations to expedite business change and expansion

Special agreements negotiated with unions (for example, building trades) to eliminate or minimize work stoppages and construction disruption

Provision of incubator facilities

Provision of state- or city-assisted job training

Exemption from various state sales and use taxes

Writedowns of available land

These examples are weighted toward manufacturing operations, but benefits are also clearly available to some office and service operations.

Just keep in mind that enterprise zones serve a social purpose and may be located in areas you consider undesirable. Physical deterioration, crime, unemployment, and similar characteristics are among the reasons for the area being designated in the first place. If your business requires customer traffic, it is probably not the place for you. The same is true if the location discourages desirable employees from working for you.

Enterprise Zone Checklist

You should be able to answer yes to the following questions before locating your business in an enterprise zone.

1. Have you made a complete list of the benefits of enterprise zone location for your business?
2. Have you made a complete list of the disadvantages of enterprise zone location?
3. Are you aware of specific benefit packages provided in enterprise zones where you are locating? Have you checked them out?
4. Have you considered the possibility of locating a portion of your business (for example, packaging, mailing, or warehousing) in an enterprise zone?

CHAPTER PERSPECTIVE

Starting or running a business requires drive and imagination on your part. It also requires some care and planning. Without checking the kinds of items discussed in this chapter, you can waste vast amounts of energy, time, and money. Always ask questions . . . about the zoning on your property, about the lease that you have been handed, or about any other item about which you are unsure. The only person who places your interest uppermost . . . is you.

Forms of Legal Organization

INTRODUCTION

The legal form in which you carry out your business determines such important matters as the amount of profit you can take home after you've paid taxes; your legal liability to your customers and creditors; the way you share responsibility with your co-owners; and the extent of the red tape you have to cut through for state and federal governments.

In this chapter we will explore the effects of organizing in each of the four major forms of business: proprietorship, partnership, S-corporation, or C-corporation. We'll consider differences in liability, taxation, and ease of formation and operation.

Owners sometimes choose their business structure solely for its tax advantage. This is a narrow approach and is not recommended. You must consider other factors, particularly the threat of personal liability for business debts.

Caution: You can't avoid a decision on legal structure by simply "starting up." Once you open your doors for business, you've automatically formed a proprietorship (or a partnership if you have a co-owner). A different legal structure might be best for you. Study the pros and cons first, and then decide.

After studying the material in this chapter:

▬ You will be able to evaluate the legal effects of setting up your business as a proprietorship, partnership, S-corporation, or C-corporation.

▬ You will know which form of organization maximizes your tax advantage.

▬ You will know when you need to see a lawyer and when you don't.

OVERVIEW

Both sole proprietorships and partnerships subject their owners to personal liability for the debts of the business. (Some owners may qualify as limited partners, thus shielding themselves from liability, but that's a separate issue not relevant to most small businesses.) Neither proprietorships nor partnerships pay federal income tax; instead, profits are taxed on the owners' tax returns at the owners' rates. The same is true for S-corporations. Regular or C-, corporations do pay such taxes.

Setting up and operating a corporation means dealing with government red tape. One of the significant advantages of all forms of corporations is that their owners are shielded from personal liability for business debts.

Regardless of the legal structure of a business, a license to do business may be required by county or municipal governments (see Chapter 1). In addition, most businesses must apply to the IRS for a Tax Identification Number.

Would Incorporation Save Taxes?

To evaluate if taxation as a C-corporation would cut taxes (when compared with a proprietorship, partnership, or S-corporation) you will have to make a careful comparison of personal versus C-corporation tax rates. You need to figure out which rates are lower at the level of income you expect to earn. (This is called the marginal tax rate.) For example, if your marginal tax rate is 28% but the C-corporation rate is 25%, you might pay slightly less tax if you incorporate.

Warning: You must decide on your business form in advance; you cannot wait until the year is over to choose how you wish to be taxed. The choice may not be easy to make, because you have to predict the level of your earnings. At certain income levels the advantage may switch.

PROPRIETORSHIP

Advantages	Disadvantages
No red tape	No limit on liability
No co-owners to answer to	Limited source of capital

You form a proprietorship by opening your doors and beginning operation of a business in which you alone take the risks and own the profits. There are no formalities. (If your spouse helps you run the business and owns a share in the profits, together you have formed a partnership.)

Because a proprietorship is not legally a separate entity from its owner, it is the simplest form of business structure, both to set up and to operate. Even if you are operating under another "dba" name, all you have to do is comply with local regulations and licensing procedures for such name use. Let's look at the consequences of this simplicity.

Legal Liability

A proprietor could face personal liability to customers, suppliers, and, in rare cases, to employees. Suppose a customer slips and falls in a grocery store, and a court holds the business responsible because a beverage spilled by another customer was not promptly wiped up. If business liability insurance is not adequate to cover the money judgment awarded by the court, and business assets are also inadequate, the owner will have to pay the judgment with *personal* assets. Of course, adequate business liability insurance can protect against this "tort" liability, but it may be expensive.

Another kind of liability can't be insured against: debts to business creditors, such as bankers and suppliers. If the business doesn't generate enough profit to pay these debts, the proprietor's personal assets may be sold by a court to pay the creditors.

In most—but not all—cases neither the proprietor nor the business will have to pay a judgment if an employee is injured on the job. Workers' compensation laws provide payment for medical care and lost wages for those employees who are covered. Under certain circumstances, however, a worker may not be covered.

Federal Income Tax

A proprietor reports business income on IRS Schedule "C" and files it with his or her annual Form 1040 tax return. The effect is to tax net profit from the business at the same rate as other earnings the owner receives, such as interest, dividends, and salary from another job. ("Net profit" is what remains after costs of operating the business—such as electricity, employees' salary, and costs of the merchandise that was sold—have been deducted from the revenues or receipts of the business.)

The good side of the tax law is that business losses can be deducted from the owner's other income. This feature might be desirable during the start-up years of operation, before a strong profit pattern has been established.

PARTNERSHIP

Advantage	Disadvantage
"Flow-through" Taxation	No limit on liability

A partnership exists when two or more persons, who have not filed for incorporation, carry on a business together with the objective of making and sharing a profit among themselves. For a partnership to exist it is not necessary that there be a written contract.

Warning: The ease with which a partnership can be formed creates a unique pitfall. Courts sometimes infer that a partnership exists even though one or more of the parties to a lawsuit did not know that they were "partners." If the courts impose partnership status on a business relationship, unless there is a written agreement to the contrary, each "partner" is responsible for the debts of the business and shares equally in the profits or losses. *Moral:* Sign a written agreement with anyone you are in business with. Make it clear whether your associate is an employee or a partner.

In a general partnership, each of the partners can legally bind the partnership to a contract. In some circumstances any one of the partners can be held personally liable for debts and for legal judgments against the partnership.

In a limited partnership, on the other hand, some of the partners are limited in their power to transact business. They also have limited liability for partnership debts—limited to the amount of their capital contribution.

A partnership is a voluntary association of persons, and owners have the right to choose with whom they will be in partnership. Thus, one partner cannot freely transfer an ownership share to another person without every partner's consent. Lack of easy transferability is a disadvantage.

The large amounts of capital needed to operate some types of business may be hard to provide in a partnership. Among the causes of this problem are the awkwardness of transferring ownership, the threat of liability for business debts, and the necessity for partners to pay taxes on their share of the partnership's profits.

Federal Taxation of Partnerships

A partnership, whether general or limited, pays no federal income tax. The business is treated as a conduit. The owners pay tax at their individual (or joint) tax rates on their share of the accounting profits, or deduct their share of the partnership's losses. Tax on the profits must be paid, even if *no cash whatsoever* is paid out by the partnership to the partners.

For income tax purposes, any business having two or more persons sharing in the profits is considered to be a partnership unless it is a trust, estate, or corporation. In general, this means that syndicates, pools, joint ventures, and unincorporated associations are taxed like partnerships.

Warning: Some state laws may allow formation of a business not formally recognized by federal tax law—such as a "limited liability company"—for which the tax consequences are not predictable. If any three of these four attributes are present, the IRS may assess corporate taxes even if state law does not recognize the business to be a corporation:

Continuity of life beyond the death of an owner

Limited liability of the owners

Transferability of ownership interests

Centralized management

Because of the danger of unintended tax consequences, the owners of a small business should stick with one of the four well-recognized business structures.

A partnership must file federal tax Form 1065, U.S. Partnership Return of Income, on or before April 15, to provide information to the IRS but not to compute or pay tax. The partnership sends each partner a Schedule K-1, "Partner's Share of Income, Credits, Deductions, etc.," showing data needed to fill out that partner's individual (or joint) tax return.

A share of operating profit or loss of the partnership is reported on each partner's own Schedule E, Supplemental Income Schedule. Total income from this schedule is transferred to the partner's annual Form 1040. Form K-1 is not filed. The effect is to tax each partner's share of partnership profits at that partner's own tax rate.

On each partner's return the "character" of many items on the partnership return is retained. That is, dividends received by the partnership are reported on the partners' return as dividends and interest is reported as interest. This same flow-through treatment is accorded such items as capital gains or losses, charitable contributions, tax credits, and tax preference items.

The advantage of the flow-through feature is that partnership losses (and tax credits) can be used to reduce the personal tax bill of partners who have other sources of taxable income.

A serious drawback to the flow-through feature must be kept in mind. Since partners pay tax on their share of profits even if they receive *no cash* from the business, they must plan ways to meet their personal tax bills while still leaving enough cash in the business to allow it to thrive and grow.

For many federal tax purposes, partners are not considered to be employees of the partnership. As a consequence, no Social Security tax is paid on their salaries or other withdrawals from the business; instead, they pay the much-higher self-employment tax. Certain tax benefits, including $50,000 of group-term life insurance, accident and health insurance and medical reimbursement plans that are tax-free to employees, are not tax-free to partners.

For tax planning, income can be allocated to partners in lower tax brackets. By this means, income can be shifted to minimize taxes among family members who are partners. This is an area of particular concern to the IRS, however, and the arrangements will be scrutinized to assure that income allocated to a partner is earned by that partner or by the capital attributable to that partner. You should consult a tax accountant or attorney before you attempt to make a gift of partnership shares or income.

How a Partnership is Formed

A partnership can be formed on the basis of a handshake. Such informality can lead to problems in the future. Suppose the partners have a serious disagreement. A partner—or a deceased partner's heirs—may bring a lawsuit to clarify such things as share of profits, amount of salary or drawings, and provision for interest on invested capital. If there is no way to establish the partners' original intent, state laws will govern.

While state law will provide an answer, it may not be the answer any of the partners desire. It is far better that these matters be settled in the partnership agreement at the time the business is formed.

Only in rare instances will an oral agreement be satisfactory. If the partners later disagree, it may be difficult to prove the profit-sharing ratio or other terms of the partnership. In the absence of a contrary, provable agreement, state law usually supposes that profits are to be shared equally, regardless of how much time or capital each partner contributes. The safe course is to put the agreement in writing.

The Partnership Agreement

There are books of legal forms containing partnership agreements; these are available in most public libraries. One of these might be satisfactory, but only if each partner understands and agrees to what is stated in the form *and* is knowledgeable about the provisions that could have been included but weren't. If one partner later becomes disgruntled, he or she can force the partnership to dissolve.

Rather than using a preprinted form, it is wiser to have the partnership engage an experienced business attorney who, after a preliminary conference, will draft and then explain the contract. Before such a conference, the partners should talk over several crucial matters:

1. Name to be used by the partnership
2. Amount of capital to be contributed by each partner, date of its transfer to the partnership, and whether interest is to be credited on capital
3. If property other than cash is to be contributed, describe the property and agree on its value
4. Amount of rent or royalty to be paid for use of a partner's property, such as land, buildings, equipment, patents, leaseholds, copyrights
5. Name of bank in which funds will be deposited, and names of those authorized to sign checks
6. Duties of each partner and whether salaries (called drawings) will be paid during the year
7. Proportion of the business that each partner will own
8. How profits and losses will be shared
9. Whether annual audits of financial statements will be made by a CPA
10. Rights of a partner to engage in other businesses
11. Who will carry out management of the business, and the extent of the manager's authority for such acts as hiring and firing, extending credit, purchasing real estate, and pledging assets
12. Acts that will terminate the partnership, such as a partner becoming physically unable to perform his duties
13. Method of valuing partner's interest and payment to heirs upon death; whether goodwill will be assigned
14. Provisions for resolving disputes—perhaps a clause requiring arbitration
15. Means of terminating the business, securing a final accounting, and distributing assets

Legal Liability

General partners are jointly and severally liable for the debts of a partnership. This means that the personal assets of one or more of the partners can be taken by a court to pay the debts that cannot be paid out of the assets of the business. There is no fail-safe way for a general partner to avoid the dangers of unlimited liability. To protect themselves each partner should stay in touch with partnership affairs to help guide the business out of financial difficulty. On the other hand, a partnership may be formed to limit the liability of certain partners.

Limited Partnerships

In a limited partnership there are one or more general partners and one or more limited partners. The general partners operate the business and have unlimited liability for its debts. Limited partners are not liable for partnership debts. As long as they do not participate in the management of the business—which might cause them to be considered by law to be general partners—they stand to lose only the amount of capital they agreed to contribute. State laws require that limited partnerships be registered with the state in order to warn creditors and customers that certain owners of the business have limited liability.

Limited partnerships are useful if the general partners have the expertise but not the capital to run the business. Limited partners can provide the bulk of the capital but, beyond the amounts contributed, are insulated from the risks of the business. Profits and losses can be shared in any manner agreed upon. This structure is popular where large amounts of capital are needed while retaining the flow-through tax characteristics of partnerships—to buy real estate, for example.

Cost of Forming a Partnership

Most lawyers charge by the hour for setting up a partnership; fees will vary depending on the complexity of the agreement. Figure three hours of legal time for a simple agreement between two or three partners. More complex agreements might require ten hours. To set up a large limited partnership for sale by solicitation to the public requires use of an attorney skilled in securities law. This can be an expensive proposition.

INCORPORATION

Advantages	Disadvantages
Limited liability	Red tape
Transferable ownership	Possible double taxation

A corporation is a legal entity given formal existence by state authority. Each state has its own law that spells out the requirements for setting up a corporation in that state.

Ownership interests are represented by shares of stock. Unless there is a written agreement to the contrary, these shares are freely transferable. Owners are called shareholders or stockholders.

Ownership and profit-sharing is proportional to the number of shares of common stock that are held; ownership of 600 out of 1,000 shares entitles the stockholder to 60 percent of whatever profits are paid out as dividends. Preferred stock may also be issued. It normally bears a stated, annual dividend rate, but it does not carry any ownership rights.

Governance of the corporation is by a board of directors, who are elected by majority vote of the holders of common stock. The stockholders or the directors adopt by-laws that specify rules, such as how many officers the corporation shall have and how often the directors and stockholders shall hold meetings. The board appoints the officers, such as president and vice-president, who carry out the day-to-day operation of the business.

The standard form of corporation, the C-corporation, pays federal income taxes. S-corporations, on the other hand, are flow-through entities similar to partnerships. S-corps are discussed later in the chapter.

How to Form a Corporation

Persons desiring to incorporate a business must apply to the office of the appropriate state official for permission to form and operate a corporation. A public library or county law library can provide the phone number and address of this official, who may be the secretary of state or the director of the state's division of corporations.

In most states, forming a corporation requires nothing more than listing the following items in a notarized letter sent to the appropriate official (along with payment of a small fee):

ARTICLES OF INCORPORATION

Article I—Name

The name of this corporation shall be _____.

(Note: Before filing, check by phone with your state's division of corporations to be sure the name is not already in use.)

Article II—Purpose

This corporation is formed for the purpose of carrying out any lawful business in accordance with the (State) General Corporation Act.

Article III—Capital Stock

This corporation shall be authorized to have outstanding at any one time a maximum of _____ shares of common stock having a par value of _____ per share.

Article IV—Address

The initial address of the principal office of this corporation shall be , .

Article V—Directors

The corporation shall be managed by a Board of Directors, of which there shall initially be one. The number of Directors may be increased or decreased (but not to fewer than one) through procedure provided by by-laws adopted by vote of the stockholders.

Article VI—Name of Director

The name and address of the first member of the Board of Directors is , ,

---

Article VII—Incorporators

The name and address of each person signing the Articles as incorporator is _____, _____, _____.

Article VIII—Duration

The duration of this corporation shall be ___ years. *(Note: Many states allow perpetual existence.)*

Article IX—Date of Commencement of Corporate Existence

The date when corporate existence shall begin is _____.

Article X—By-Laws

The power to adopt, alter, amend, or repeal by-laws shall be vested exclusively in the stockholders.

Article XI—Name and Address of Registered Agent

The undersigned, a natural person and a resident of the State of _____, consents and accepts appointment as Registered Agent for this corporation. *(Note: Either the incorporator or the attorney is usually the registered agent.)*

(Signature)

In witness thereto, the undersigned incorporator executed these Articles of Incorporation the _____ day of _____.

(Signature)

(Statement and signature of notary public) _____

Once the articles of incorporation have been submitted and fees have been paid, the state official will issue a charter or letter of incorporation, in what is essentially a rubber-stamp process. This begins the legal existence of the corporation. An information report must be filed with the state annually. In some states the articles must be filed at the courthouse in the county where the corporation has its principal offices.

Documents must also be filed to qualify the corporation in any other state in which it does a significant amount of business. These documents must name a resident of that other state, referred to as the registered agent, who can receive legal papers in case the corporation is sued in that state. Fees to hire an attorney to serve as registered agent are not excessive.

Legal Liability

The corporation is responsible for its business debts and the torts of its employees. Stockholders' losses are limited to the amount of capital they have agreed to contribute plus loans they have made to the corporation.

Only in rare instances will the legal shield provided by incorporation be pierced by the courts and the owners held personally liable. This result may come about when the corporation is operated as the alter ego of its owner, who freely uses its bank account and other assets as if they were his or her personal property, to the detriment of corporate creditors. In such professional fields as medicine, architecture, accounting, and law, however, individual stockholders retain liability for their personal malpractice.

For a newly formed corporation having few assets and no credit history, however, the concept of stockholder's limited liability for business debts may be illusory. Creditors will often require personal guarantees by the owners before advancing loans or shipping merchandise.

Costs of Incorporating

The use of an attorney to form a corporation may not be necessary but is usually not expensive. Since articles of incorporation are cut-and-dried in their provisions, lawyers often quote a package price, perhaps $300, for the agreement and for presiding at the first meeting of the board of directors. State filing fees, perhaps $50 to $150, will be extra. Do-it-yourselfers should try to examine the articles of incorporation of an existing corporation, sometimes available in the county clerk's office. Libraries and bookstores carry books detailing the mechanics of incorporation, often available in a state edition.

Taxation of Corporations

C-corporations file Form 1120 or 1120-A (a shorter form) to pay federal income taxes. The rates are occasionally changed by

Congress, but in recent years have ranged under a graduated rate scale from a low of 15 percent on small amounts of corporate income to a high somewhat less than 50 percent.

Amounts that remain after corporate taxes have been paid can be retained in the business or can be paid out as dividends. A C-corp is allowed to retain $250,000 plus amounts required to meet the reasonable needs of the business. Larger amounts that the IRS considers unreasonably accumulated are subject to a special tax. Closely held C-corps that pay no dividends and yet make loans to stockholders are particularly in danger from this accumulated earnings tax.

If dividends are paid from the C-corp's after-tax earnings, the stockholders are taxed when they receive these amounts even though such payments are not deductible by the corporation. This constitutes double taxation of corporate profits and can be mitigated by paying larger salaries to stockholders who hold officer or employee positions with the corporation. These salaries will be taxed to the recipient, but they are *deducted* in computing the corporation's taxes. If the salaries are in excess of the value of the services received by the corporation, however, the IRS will claim that they are dividends and disallow the corporate deduction.

Double taxation may also be avoided by having the corporation pay to stockholders rent or royalty for the use of property, or by paying interest on money loaned to the business. The corporation will be allowed to deduct these expenses. If the IRS finds any of these transactions to be a sham, however, deductions will be disallowed.

Caution: Don't set up a corporation merely to hold investments. A corporation that receives more than 60 percent of its income in the form of dividends, rents, and interest, and that meets certain other tests, is subjected to the personal holding company tax on retained profits. In the past this tax rate has been as high as 50 percent.

C-corporations that provide services in the fields of health, law, engineering, architecture, accounting, actuarial science, performing arts, or consulting and where substantially all of the stock is held by employees, retired employees, or their estates are called personal service corporations (PSC). These corporations pay tax at a rate that is adjusted by Congress to discourage use of the PSC by stockholders attempting to shield income from high individual tax rates. In recent years the rate has been set to equal the top C-corp rate; the lower rate structure available to C-corps under the graduated scale is not available to PSCs.

Contrary to the treatment of partners in partnerships, stockholders who are employed by their C-corporation will be considered to be true employees, eligible for many tax-favored benefits.

S-corporations, which have completely different tax characteristics, have become such a popular form of small business organization that they will be discussed separately.

S-CORPORATION

Advantages	Disadvantage
Limited liability	Red tape
Flow-through taxation	

In addition to the C-corporation, federal tax law recognizes the S-corporation. As far as most state law is concerned, an S-corp has the attributes listed above for C-corporations, such as limited liability, allocation of voting power and profit share in proportion to stock ownership, and governance by a board of directors.

Among closely held small businesses deciding to incorporate, the S-corp is favored for two reasons. First, for most purposes S-corps are tax conduits: In this regard, S-corps are similar to partnerships or proprietorships.

Also, as long as its legal identity is preserved (that is, the corporation is not found to be a sham), an S-corp shields its owners from personal liability for business debts and judgments. There is no hiding, however, from responsibility for the owners' professional malpractice nor for debts the owners have personally guaranteed.

Summary of S-Corporation Benefits

Stockholders are shielded from liability for business debts
There is no federal corporate income tax (no double taxation)
Operating losses flow through to the owners and can be deducted from their taxable incomes
Gifts of stock can be used to shift income to family members in lower tax brackets

How to Form an S-Corporation

S-corps and C-corps differ only in the way they are taxed by Uncle Sam, not in their legalities under the laws of most states. (To learn if your state has special regulations regarding S-corps check with a "How To Incorporate" book for your state, or read your state's corporation statutes, available in county law and public libraries.)

You form an S-corp for federal tax purposes by "electing" this status early in the tax year once you have satisfied certain IRS requirements. Begin with a corporation whose charter has been issued by your state. Then, after assuring yourself of the advantages of the S-corp status, you and any other owners may file Form 2553 with the IRS service center where you will be filing the S-corporation's tax return. The form is called Election by a Small Business Corporation. Within three months you will be notified of acceptance of your S-corp election.

There are six important IRS restrictions on an S-corp:

1. It must be a domestic corporation (organized in the United States)
2. There must be only one class of stock, yet loans from stockholders are sometimes considered a second class of stock, disqualifying the S-corp
3. There can be no more than 35 shareholders
4. None of the shareholders can be a partnership or corporation
5. Every shareholder must be a United States citizen or resident
6. No S-corp can be a domestic international sales corporation, a bank, an insurance company, a corporation receiving the Puerto Rico tax credit, nor a member of an "affiliated group."

Taxation of S-Corporations

For federal income tax purposes, operating income or loss passes directly through to the owners, and many other flow-through items such as tax credits, charitable contributions, and deductions for state and local taxes retain their original character and may be deducted pro-rata on each owner's tax return. The S-corp files a Form 1120S for information purposes and reports to each owner a share of profits, losses, and flow-through items on Form K-1, a form similar to that used by partnerships. Owners are taxed on their share of profits even if none are paid out in cash. In other words, an S-corp is treated for tax purposes very much like a partnership, but not exactly. There are significant differences that are likely to make professional tax advice necessary when operating an S-corp. For instance, the S-corp tax status may be lost if care is not used in structuring any loans made by shareholders to the corporation.

Warning: Some states may levy an income tax on an S-corp just as if it were a C-corp.

CHAPTER PERSPECTIVE

The various forms of business organization have advantages and disadvantages that should be explored before choosing one of them for a business. The corporate form protects the owners' personal assets but may lead to additional tax payments. Partnerships are suited to certain service businesses, such as the law.

Getting The Money You Need

INTRODUCTION

In this chapter we help you figure out where to get the money you need to operate your business. We discuss the legal issues you will encounter.

Call it money, cash, funds, financing, or capital. These terms all refer to the wherewithall to pay salaries, taxes, other business expenses and to buy such essential assets as inventory and equipment.

Tip: Pride of ownership has contributed to the downfall of many businesses because of the higher up-front costs involved in owning an asset. Take a serious look at leasing as a way of obtaining the use of the equipment, business premises, or other long-term assets you need.

The first rule of raising capital is to be sure you get enough. There is no such thing as a growing business that has too much cash. Get your accountant to help you forecast what you'll need for the next two or more years. Then make a plan for raising these funds and start negotiating soon to bring home the bacon.

Our plan in this chapter is to discuss the sources most often considered when a business needs funds, covering also the most important legal issues. First we'll deal with borrowing and then move to raising equity capital—selling your stock to venture capitalists or to the public.

After studying the material in this chapter:

▬ You will be familiar with commonly used methods of raising cash for a business, including borrowing from banks and "going public."

▬ You will know the advantages and disadvantages of borrowing money for your business from friends and relatives, suppliers, banks, and other sources.

▬ You will understand the legal arrangements involved in selling stock.

TERMS TO BE FAMILIAR WITH

There are certain terms connected with raising capital that almost everyone is familiar with, including *interest, principal,* and *due date.* Below are explanations of some of the other terms that will come up in our discussion.

Collateral refers to any property that you *pledge* to a lender to give the lender an extra measure of security in case you fail to pay the loan. Whatever property you pledge can be taken by the lender.

If you pledge your house, auto, or other property as collateral for a loan, the possible consequence is that the lender can take legal steps (called *foreclosure*) to take ownership of and sell your property if you *default* on the loan. Default consists of failure to make payments on the loan as they are due, but also occurs if you have made promises that you fail to keep. Example: The lender might ask you to promise not to raise officer's salaries or to pay dividends to your stockholders during the period of the loan. The contract you sign with the lender will specify that a *breach* (break) of these *covenants* (promises) triggers default.

Commercial lenders may ask for pledges of collateral in the form of real estate, vehicles, business equipment, inventory, securities, and practically anything else that is the property of the business or its owner. The term *asset-based financing* is commonly used to refer to borrowing that is secured by either inventory or accounts receivable. Property owned by relatives, friends, or business associates can also be used as collateral, if these persons are willing to sign the necessary papers. In this, as in any other aspect of raising capital, you should try to negotiate the best deal.

The legal form of a pledge of real estate is a *mortgage*, sometimes called a deed of trust. The equivalent structure for a pledge of *personal property* is a *security agreement* that gives the lender a *security interest* in the property.

The phrase *personal property* doesn't refer in legal matters to assets that are used for personal, nonbusiness purposes. It means anything that is not real property—that is, anything that is not land or permanently attached to the land as buildings would be. Autos, photocopiers, bulldozers, and inventory are examples of "personal" property. Stocks representing ownership in other companies, and bonds that are the obligations of other companies can also serve as collateral; both of these are referred to as *securities*.

Both mortgages and security agreements are *recorded* or *filed* at the county courthouse by the lender in order to make them a part of public records. This warns others—*puts them on notice*—that the lender has a *lien* (pledge) on the property. Anyone who buys property that has a lien properly recorded against it will be held liable for paying off the lien.

RAISING CAPITAL FROM FRIENDS AND RELATIVES

There are two times in your business history when you will be most tempted to look to friends and relatives for help: when you're just getting started, and when you are in deep financial difficulty.

Whether they actually become part-owners with you or merely advance you a loan, friends and relatives are more likely to try to tell you how to run your business than would a commercial provider of capital. Also, if the business goes sour, you may lose a friend or bring tension into the family.

Let's consider *separately* the issues related to borrowing and to ownership. First, let's look at ownership.

Particularly when just getting started you may feel generous and want to share your business with people you know and like, even if they can't contribute capital. But remember, by extending to someone a partnership interest or a block of stock, you are giving them *permanently* a part of your profit and the right to have a say in the way you run your operations.

You may be forced to offer up part of your ownership because you desperately need money. Except for this dire need, however, a basic rule in a start-up business is this: Share your ownership only with someone who has an ongoing contribution to make. Look for special technical expertise, management experience, or even important business connections.

The reason you should offer an ownership in your business only to someone whose talent you need is that—at least at the start—you can't afford to pay salaries to get these critical skills. Incidentally, high-priced legal and accounting skills can be hired as they are needed.

The other way of obtaining financing from relatives and friends is by borrowing. The advantages are easy to see. People who know you may be eager to help you out—and they may not insist on a high rate of interest. There are disadvantages, though, attached to loans from friends and relatives. Some of them are:

━ Family and friends are likely to be limited in resources. If you need more money, you'll soon be forced to go to a commercial lender, who won't like the idea that you already have loans outstanding.

━ If you repay the loan on time, no record of your good performance will find its way into your credit history.

Only you can make the decision. Sometimes, friends and family will be your only source of financing. If you choose to give them an ownership interest as partners or shareholders, be sure to protect everyone, legally, by noting the arrangements on paper (see the details in Chapter 17).

If you borrow and agree to pay interest, you will want to deduct the interest expense on your tax return. (If the money is used in your business, the deduction you take is for "business interest expense.") You can do so legally, even on loans from family, but only if there is a "bona fide" debt. This means you must act in a businesslike manner. You should draw up and sign a promissory note that states the terms of repayment and carries a rate of interest appropriate for current market conditions. You will be able to find a form for a promissory note at most office supply stores.

Caution: If you borrow money under an agreement with the lender that does not require you to pay any interest, the IRS will "impute" interest on the loan in certain circumstances, particularly if the loan is over $10,000. If this happens, you will get to deduct interest expense, even though you didn't pay it, and the lender will be taxed on interest income even though he or she didn't receive any.

Following businesslike procedures takes more time but will help assure that you get the tax deduction you are entitled to. You may not like to think about it, but these procedures will also assure that your friendly lender will be able to take a tax write-off if you fail to repay. Without documentation that the debt is bona fide, the IRS will say it's a gift, and gifts that aren't repaid can't be deducted.

If you pledge assets to back up a loan from family or friends, and they record the mortgage or security interest, this public record will further serve to document your tax-deductible interest, though it will of course put other creditors on notice of a debt you might like to keep hidden.

RAISING CAPITAL FROM SUPPLIERS

One of your best early sources of financing will be the firms that supply the goods needed in your business. They won't loan you cash, but under some circumstances they will trust you for payment, even in a start-up business, until you, in turn, get paid by your customers. Typically, however, suppliers will not take a risk for a start-up business unless they get extra collateral, promissory notes guaranteed by others, a line of credit from a bank, or some other incentive.

Sometimes you can parlay your proven abilities into a good deal with a supplier. Here's an example: A manager of a lighting fixtures store decided to set up on her own in a different town. The same suppliers she'd relied upon when buying for her boss's store agreed to stock her new business on credit because they knew her capabilities.

Another example: A young man who had experience as a car salesman decided to open a clothing store. Certain suppliers seemed eager to stock his store with inventory. As time passed, he discovered they had provided him with goods no one else wanted. They were hard to sell because they were out of style or not in popular sizes. And, as you can learn in Chapter 11, once goods have been accepted by a merchant, there is scant possibility of returning them to the supplier.

RAISING MONEY FROM BANKS

As you might guess, banks are the biggest providers of financing for small business. In recent years they have become aggressive in their pursuit of opportunities for lending. They also have greatly increased the ways in which they can help, by making practically any sort of financing arrangement you can find anywhere else, except for deals that would give the bank an ownership interest as a partner or stock owner.

From start-up loans collateralized by personal assets to long-term industrial mortgages, banks are in there pitching for your business. Often, they have subsidiaries that are active in areas that would make a traditional banker blanch, such as asset-based financing and venture capital lending. Be sure to give your commercial banker a call if you need financing.

For loans to smaller or start-up businesses, a bank will probably ask that the owner personally guarantee repayment and may ask that the owner's personal assets be pledged as security, particularly for any loan that runs longer than a few months. Any property can be used this way as collateral, from marketable stocks and bonds to CDs to home equity. Banks are not pawn shops, however, and they will avoid getting into situations where their *only* security is a warehouse full of sofas.

A bank's main business is making loans based on the borrower's credit history and apparent ability to repay the loan. If the borrower has regularly paid past loans, and the business seems likely to earn enough to repay this loan, the bank is likely to give the go-ahead, particularly if the loan is guaranteed by one or more persons.

Two different legal methods can be used to provide a personal guarantee on a loan. The first of these creates "primary liability." Whoever cosigns as a maker on the note or signs after the words "payment guaranteed by . . ." can be sued directly by the bank to get payment. It is not necessary for the bank first to bring a legal action against the business.

The other kind of guarantee results in "secondary liability." Suppose the person signs the note as an "accommodation indorser" or qualifies the signature with the words "collection guaranteed." In that case the bank must first attempt to collect from the business. This difference won't matter if the guarantor is the sole owner of the unincorporated business that borrowed the money. It could make a difference, however, if the guarantor is someone else: a friend or relative, the manager (or any other nonowner) of the business, or one partner or shareholder of a business with several owners. If one of these persons is forced by a lawsuit to pay the debt to the bank, he or she can then attempt to recover from the business or from the other owners of the business, but there is less risk and cost if the secondary liability method is used to make their guarantee.

Traditional *commercial loans* from a bank require repayment in a lump sum at the end of their term, usually three to six months. Such short-term loans can be used for any purpose. A company must have a strong credit rating to get one of these loans. For larger amounts and longer terms, *monthly payment loans* can also be negotiated. These reduce the pressure a business might feel in facing a lump-sum payoff.

A *line of credit* consists of an agreed-upon amount that a borrower can draw upon, as the need arises. Sometimes, in an arrangement called a letter of credit, a supplier can get paid directly by the bank for an order of merchandise shipped to the borrower.

For a credit line the repayment schedule is based upon how the money will be used, but usually requires that the debt be cleaned up periodically. For example, a typical arrangement might require the loan to be fully paid up for 30 days each year.

A revolving line of credit requires no annual clean-up, though the bank will certainly keep its eye on the borrower's performance. Revolving credit lines are usually repaid in monthly installments of interest and principal. They are like revolving charge accounts in that the amount that can be borrowed increases back up to the credit line limit as the old debt is paid off.

It is important to distinguish between credit lines that are committed and those that are uncommitted. You will have to pay an ongoing commitment fee if you wish to be assured that the bank will reserve funds for your use. Otherwise, you might find that your credit has dried up when you need it.

An *inventory loan* is an arrangement to help you put inventory on your sales floor, hence is sometimes referred to as floor planning. The bank will require you to pledge your inventory as collateral. If you don't repay the loan on time, the bank can take your inventory and try to sell it.

Accounts receivable financing lets you pledge the claims you have against your customers' uncollected accounts, thus turning them into cash. To make up for the time and effort the bank must spend in monitoring your books to assure that the accounts are collectible, some banks specify a minimum loan amount, such as $250,000. Some banks now also enter, through affiliated subsidiaries, a type of accounts receivable financing unheard of in traditional banking, that of factoring.

Traditional, old-line factors buy accounts receivables "without recourse." The business gets cash immediately without waiting for customers to pay. Factors initially pay 60 to 80 percent of the value of the receivables, then they collect the accounts and take the risk that some of the customers won't pay. When all accounts are collected, the factor will send to the business a partial rebate of the withheld amount, based on what has been negotiated in advance.

In the usual arrangement, customers will be notified to make payments directly to a postal box controlled by the factor. Some business managers believe this leads to loss of customer loyalty. It may be possible to arrange no-notification factoring; the customer continues to make payments to the business, which then forwards payments to the factor.

There is no free lunch, and factors have to be compensated for the risk they take. Over all, financing from a factor—even one affiliated with a bank—will be more costly than traditional bank or finance company funding. Typically, dealing with a factor experienced in the borrower's type of business will be less complicated and considerably faster than filing for a standard bank loan. Some banks and finance companies have subsidiaries that act as factors.

The single most distressing legal problem we commonly encounter in dealing with a bank is a discrepancy between what the borrower understood would be the terms and conditions of the loan . . . and what actually turns out to be written in the loan agreement.

Sometimes these discrepancies come about because of misunderstandings between the borrower and the loan officer. In other cases someone higher up overruled a negotiated agreement or the loan officer changed his or her mind. Whatever the reason . . . be sure to take the time to read the agreement and promissory note before you sign it.

It is important to be aware of certain legal aspects of the arrangements typically written into a bank loan. *Covenants* are promises that you make concerning the future operation of your business. They serve to extend the bank's control. If you violate a covenant, the bank can declare the loan to be in default and demand immediate payment.

Don't agree to a covenant that is excessively burdensome. If you know in advance the sorts of covenants a bank might request, you may be able to negotiate away one or two that you don't like and offer instead a substitute. Here are commonly encountered covenants:

▬ You are required to use the loan proceeds for the purpose you stated when you applied for the loan.

▬ You must use the lending bank for all your banking needs during the term of the loan.

▬ You must maintain without drawing from it a "compensating" balance equal to 10 or 20 percent of the amount borrowed in an account that pays no interest.

▬ You are limited in your discretion to pay dividends, increase officers' salaries, sell major assets, change lines of business, or make further borrowings.

▬ You must send the bank quarterly financial statements and monthly statements of sales, inventory, and receivables.

Warranties and Representations are promises you make and that the bank intends to rely upon. You will generally have to warrant and represent that your business is operating legally, that there are no undisclosed pending lawsuits, and that your financial statements are accurate. You will also have to promise to notify the bank if significant changes occur in the matters you warranted, for example, in your financial or operating status. If the bank learns that any of your warranties and representations are untrue, they can call in your loan. Even worse: You might be held liable for damages for fraud.

Events (or conditions) of default are occurrences that permit the bank to demand immediate full payment of the loan. They include such events as your failure to make payments on time or a significant decline in the value of the collateral you have pledged. Be sure you understand the events of default.

You should see that the loan agreement you sign requires the bank to give you ample notice of its intent to demand payment and also grants a period of grace during which you are allowed to cure the default. You want this grace period to be long enough to give you breathing room; two weeks to a month might be reasonable.

Warning: Don't rely on what the lender tells you is "policy," when the written agreement is in conflict. We know a borrower who lost his home when he trusted the loan officer who said, "It's the bank's policy not to foreclose a mortgage on a personal residence that we hold as security for a business loan." In all cases read and expect to be held to the terms of the document you have signed.

OTHER SOURCES OF LOANS

Small Business Administration
The Small Business Administration (SBA) is a valuable resource for businesses having a net worth (excess of assets over liabilities) of less than $6 million. There are five major programs offered by the SBA:

1. Program 7A: Loan guarantees to insure up to 90 percent of your bank loan.
2. Program 8A: Covers direct loans available for handicapped, Vietnam veterans, and economically or socially disadvantaged small business owners. The concept of

    social or economic disadvantage covers persons sub-
jected to racial, ethnic, or cultural bias or who otherwise
are impaired when competing in the free-enterprise
system.

3. Disaster loans to help areas the President has declared
   to be disaster areas.

4. Program 503: Certified development company loans for
   up to 40 percent of a firm's capital for the purpose of
   fostering job growth.

5. Program 504: Long-term fixed asset financing.

Small Business Investment Companies

SBICs are licensed by the Small Business Administration to
provide capital through loans or part ownership ("equity participation") in small businesses. The SBA helps fund these arrangements. Contact the National Association of Small Business
Investment Companies, 1156 15th St. NW, Suite 1101, Washington, D.C. 20005.

Finance Companies

Finance companies will assume a greater amount of risk than
will a bank. While a bank may deny a loan to a business that has
a lot of debt on its books, or that seems to be skating on thin ice
financially, a commercial finance company makes asset or asset-
backed loans. (The terms mean the same thing.) They will lend
money on the strength of the assets a firm puts up as collateral,
including not only inventory and accounts receivable but also
land, buildings, or equipment, rather than on the firm's credit
history and repayment potential. Asset-backed loans are more
expensive than credit-based loans from a bank but may be
quicker to get—perhaps a week or two from start to finish.

RAISING CAPITAL BY SELLING AN OWNERSHIP SHARE IN YOUR COMPANY

If you throw open your corporation to ownership by the public,
this is called "going public". You may be years away from making this sort of initial public offering (IPO) of your company's
stock. Because ambitious entrepreneurs so often set this goal,
however, we will give you an overview.

    There are two reasons why business owners are often eager to
make an IPO. First, going public is a recognized sign of success
in business. It proves that the firm has growth prospects sufficient

to attract the confidence and financial backing of the public. It also means that the entrepreneurs who founded the company and have slaved many hours to make it successful are rewarded with a large increase in their personal wealth. Three other advantages of going public are:

Public visibility, which aids in raising more capital in the future

Marketplace valuation for stock, which benefits company officers who have been given bonuses paid with stock

Enhanced prestige among employees and customers

There are two serious drawbacks to transforming a privately held company into a publicly held corporation. First of all, there's the hassle and the cost of conforming to the legal requirements of going public. There are no particular government programs to assist in making an IPO, yet regulation—both federal and state—is strict. The Securities and Exchange Commission (SEC) keeps a sharp eye on the prospectuses that must accompany any IPO but also on the quarterly and annual reports that must be made to shareholders.

Being a public company means the managers have many owners to answer to—most of them strangers. As a consequence, company operations and financial dealings must be conducted under public scrutiny. No longer can special benefits such as cushy jobs and low-interest loans be safely conferred in private on family and friends.

Much management effort goes into taking a company public. Many hours will be spent in conferences with accountants, attorneys, bankers, and publicists. It is an expensive process that exposes the company to the possibility of failure. Some stock offerings fail to sell. Beware of going "too public, too soon."

The rewards of going public may be huge, but there are drawbacks. In reality, almost any other source of capital is easier to arrange and more comfortable to live with. To aid you in deciding if and when to go public, we will cover the mechanics of the process and discuss the risks and costs.

Federal Law

The federal Securities Act of 1933 requires that a document called a registration statement be filed with the SEC Exchange Commission before a public offering of securities is made. (The term "securities" includes stocks, bonds, and limited partner-ships together with a broad range of other types of "investment contracts" that are not of importance to the typical small business operator.)

The purpose of registration is to give the investing public a factual source of information about the securities they are being asked to buy. The SEC gives no endorsement to the securities or to the wisdom of investing in them. The function of the SEC is to say about the registration statement, "Yes, there is enough information here to conform to the law."

The Registration Statement

The registration document filed with the SEC contains two parts. Part I is the prospectus. In booklet format, it contains facts regarding management, business operations, financial condition, and risk factors that face the company. The company going public, or anyone who helps the company sell the securities, must provide a prospectus to anyone who is a prospective purchaser. Among the information that has to be provided is the following:

Audited financial statements

Description of the company's business and the properties owned or leased

Names, business experience, stockholdings, and compensation of management and major stockholders

Description of important transactions between the company and its officers, directors, and major shareholders

Analysis of competitive conditions

Determination of whether there is dependence upon one or a few customers

Listing of pending legal proceedings

Intended use of the proceeds

Plan for distributing the securities

Any significant adverse risk factors

Any other information the SEC's staff asks for.

Part II of the registration statement contains supplemental information that need not be given to a purchaser but is available for inspection in an SEC reading room or by mail for a small fee. Commercial firms—for example Disclosure, Inc., of Bethesda, Maryland—also sell these documents.

Ordinarily, the company making an IPO will make use of the services of a securities attorney, a certified public accountant, a financial publicist, a financial printing firm, and an underwriter. These highly specialized services don't come cheap. Legal and accounting fees for a full registration might be $75,000 to $100,000. To print up the prospectus, other documents, and the stock certificates, a financial printing firm might charge $25,000.

The need for a financial publicity firm may not be apparent, but there are strict federal laws governing the timing of advertisements and news releases once a company has begun the registration process. As to your need for an underwriter . . . well, let's first consider whether you need one.

Going Public by Yourself

Can you go it alone? Can you sell your own securities without incurring the expense of these experts? The answer is: Maybe, but you will at least need the advice of a securities attorney. In no case should you attempt a public offering such as might be made via advertisements and letters to prospective investors. It would usually be OK to sell small amounts of stock to a few friends, relatives, and close, well-to-do acquaintances. Beyond that, check out your plans with a securities attorney. He or she can advise you on the exemptions from federal registration.

Exemptions from Federal Registration

A small business may seek to raise capital through the sale of securities but try to avoid the complications and costs of registration. In some circumstances, full or partial exemption from federal registration is possible. The conditions that have to be met are complex. We can only hint at them.

One type of exemption is that available for private placements. A private placement occurs when the securities are offered or sold without advertising to or soliciting the general public. Another exemption allows sales to a small group of sophisticated, knowledgeable investors.

There is an exemption called the small offering exemption for sales not exceeding $500,000, and one for securities that are sold entirely within the state in which the business has its executive officers and earns the bulk of its revenues. Additionally, there are provisions for a simplified registration for companies that, for example, limit their securities sales to certain dollar amounts specified in the law and also comply with other conditions. Earning exemption from federal registration does not mean that there will not be state laws to contend with.

STATE SECURITIES LAWS

Someone once said that greedy individuals would try to sell the blue sky itself. The term "blue-sky law" has come to refer to state laws governing securities sales.

Although each state has its own statutes, there are some typical aspects to blue-sky laws. For example, intentionally false claims made to promote the sale of securities can be punished as fraud in *all* states. This means you must never misrepresent the facts about your business when selling securities.

Most states have a review process to scrutinize securities offerings within the state to see they comply with criteria such as limits on the size of the underwriter's fees. Some states have an agency that makes a subjective assessment whether the offering is "fair, just, and reasonable." And most states require that securities sales be reported to a state agency since filing fees are based on the amount of sales within the state.

In some states complying with federal requirements will fully satisfy the state's blue-sky laws. In others, the reports you file with the SEC must be submitted to the state commissioner of securities for review. Your securities attorney will know the details, or you can write to your state's commissioner of securities.

UNDERWRITERS

If you are unable to manage an IPO by yourself, you will have to use an investment banker, usually referred to as an underwriter. There are two types of underwriting arrangements: firm and best efforts. In a *firm underwriting* the investment banker presents a check to the company issuing the securities and then turns around and sells them to the public. A firm underwriting by a major investment banker is testimony to the importance of the issuing company.

When the underwriters promise only to use their *best efforts* to sell the securities, the issuing company bears the risk that the securities may not sell. Sometimes the company and the best efforts underwriter agree that no shares will be issued unless a minimum number or, perhaps, "all or none" are sold. This guards against the danger that the company will be stuck with the chores and costs of public ownership while still lacking the capital to operate successfully.

Compensation to the underwriter is in the form of sales commission, expense allowance, and rights for the purchase of additional securities. A ballpark figure is 6 to 10 percent of the money that is raised, plus an expense allowance. State securities commissioners and the National Association of Security Dealers have guidelines for reasonableness of the compensation.

If you decide to go public, choosing an underwriter is a critical decision. The underwriting firm will be your expert advisers on such important matters as timing, price, and number of shares to be offered. After the securities are sold, the business relationship between your company and the underwriters will be close and continuing. They will "make a market" in which your company's securities can be bought and sold, they will provide investment analysis of your company to the financial community, and they will contribute ongoing advice to your company.

When to Go Public

To attract the interest of a "firm" underwriter you will need either a record of steady and impressive growth or a convincing story of the one-of-a-kind nature of your company. Successful IPOs handled by major investment bankers tend to have these features:

A five-year-plus operating history

Annual sales of at least $20 million

Net income of $1 million or more

An historical, annual growth rate of at least 25 percent

A proven need to raise at least $5 million to justify the costs of the offering

A unique product or technological process the value of which can be easily understood

A broadly based management team, including one or two executives who previously have been involved in an IPO.

VENTURE CAPITALISTS

Another way to raise capital by selling an ownership interest rather than borrowing is by dealing with a venture capitalist. This is a firm or a well-to-do individual who provides funds for businesses in exchange for a package of ownership interests.

Most venture capitalists are interested only in businesses that promise very quick growth and substantial financial payback. In the national market for capital they have shown more interest in high-tech firms than in service businesses.

A venture capitalist typically seeks a stock ownership interest in a corporation together with debt that can be exchanged for more stock when the business has proven its success. After the corporation starts to achieve its potential, the venture capitalist helps the company to sell its stock to the public, exchanges the debt for common stock, and reaps the rewards of a high stock price.

Venture capitalists are willing to finance risky ventures that are unattractive as IPOs. They may be willing to take on high-tech projects that are little more than an idea in an investor's head. In exchange for taking risk they insist on the prospect of high rates of return.

They will insist on making a thorough investigation of the businesses they finance. The process will take from four to ten weeks. Once they become investors in a business, they will expect to be involved in management, generally as members of the corporation's board of directors.

Each year the availability of venture capital depends on the condition of the economy and the stock market, and on whether the laws are favorable. Venture capitalists ordinarily are not interested in companies that have already gone public, because at that stage all the big profits have already been wrung out of the stock.

You can get information from *Guide to Venture Capital Sources*, edited by Stanley E. Pratt and published by Venture Economics, Inc., Wellesley Hills, Massachusetts. Also, a non-profit service called Venture Capital Network in Durham, New Hampshire, matches entrepreneurs with investors. You can reach them at (603) 743-3993.

In some localities there are venture capital clubs—investors who have banded together to finance local businesses. Check with your chamber of commerce or ask your accountant, banker, or other financial adviser or check with the small-business development center of the nearest college.

CHAPTER PERSPECTIVE

Securing financing for your company breaks down into deciding, first, whether you will go for a loan or sell away a part ownership of your business. Borrowing creates a debt that *must* be repaid under penalty of foreclosure of the collateral and possible bankruptcy of the business.

Selling an ownership interest doesn't create any obligation for repayment, but permanently gives a share of your profit to another person (unless you are able to negotiate to buy it back). In reality, it's best to sell part ownership if your business is going to fail, and to borrow if it's going to succeed. But who can know which of these alternatives the future will prove best?

Selling part ownership by going public is a creature from a different planet compared with asking a few friends to share in your business. Going public is costly and almost impossible to reverse if it turns out you don't like reporting to strangers.

Whichever route to raising capital you choose, remember to negotiate to get the best deal, insist on taking the time to read whatever documents you sign, and consult an attorney if you don't know the answers to legal questions.

Buying a Business

INTRODUCTION

Unless you receive a business by inheritance or gift, there are only two ways to get into business: Start up on your own "from scratch" or buy a business that's already up and running. There's lots to be said in favor of acquiring a profitable existing business. Probably the biggest advantage is that you can step into the shoes of someone who is successful, and you will probably be able to continue with that success. On the other hand, you will have to pay for that advantage. And a very real danger is that you will overpay.

In this chapter we shall explore the ins and outs of acquiring someone else's business. We'll talk about where to find a business, how to figure out what it's worth, and how to pay for it.

After studying the material in this chapter:

■ You will be able to evaluate the pros and cons of buying an existing business versus starting a new business from scratch.

■ You will know how to determine what a business might be worth.

■ You will be able to protect yourself against a seller who has overvalued a firm's assets.

■ You will understand how "goodwill" affects your purchase.

■ You will know the pros and cons of buying a firm versus buying only the firm's assets.

ADVANTAGES OF BUYING A BUSINESS

There's a lot to be said for buying a business that is already up and running. Such a business is referred to as a *going concern*. Here are the significant advantages:

1. You will be in business quicker than if you started from scratch, because your business will already have a location, equipment, products, customers, experienced employees, and suppliers.

2. Past successful operation of the business increases the chances that you will be successful.

3. You may be able to finance the purchase by paying the owner in installments earned from the profits of the business.

4. The seller may help you by providing you with on-site advice for several months or even a year. And the seller presumably knows how to run the business successfully.

5. In some cases, you may be able to buy the business at a bargain price as a result of, for example, ill health of the owner.

6. Existing records, including tax returns, may give you insight into how the business is best run.

Those are advantages, of course. But notice the number of times we pair those advantages with the word "may." You *may* be able to buy the business at a bargain price. On the other hand, owners know much more about their businesses—from the inside—than do sellers, and what you are eager to believe is a bargain price may be more than the business is actually worth. And you *may* be able to get the owner's continuing advice, but only if you can effectively enforce such an agreement. We will talk more about these aspects later. First, let's take a look at the disadvantages of buying a business that's already up and running.

1. It will be difficult (and maybe expensive) to change the image that customers have of the business. For example, you might want to discontinue X-rated movies from a video store you bought. As a result, you may lose many of your customers while failing to attract more "family" customers.

2. Location of the business may limit its growth.

3. You may not have the flexibility to operate as you wish because of contracts that bind the business, such as contracts with employees, unions, suppliers, customers, and landlords.

4. Substantial expenditures may be needed to modernize, repair, or maintain the building and equipment.

5. The size of the business may be more than you can handle by yourself at first, although you could have started small and made a success of your own start-up business by learning as you went along.

6. The financial burden of paying the owner the purchase price may be burdensome on profits.
7. Because of your lack of familiarity with the business—in comparison with what the seller knows—you may overpay for the business.

Let's explore that last disadvantage first . . . and let's be blunt about it. Unless you run into a very unusual situation—for instance, the seller just inherited the family business and wants no part of it—*the present owner knows a lot more about the business than you do.* If the owner has run the operation for five years, you're negotiating a deal with someone who is five years more experienced in this particular business than you are.

You may be able to do a much better job in running the operation than the present owner. Maybe. Let's hope you can. And, if you are thoroughly familiar with the same *type* of business, you can guard yourself against many of the dangers. But the point is, the present owner has a bigger stock of information about what's actually going on, day to day. He or she knows, for instance, whether the roof leaks or the basement floods, whether the boiler needs to be relined, whether the firm's star salesperson is becoming an alcoholic, and whether the new shopping center is going to pull away all the customers.

Worse yet, owners have been known to out-and-out *lie* about sales and operating costs. (This is known as "cooking the books.") They have also been known to leave the country—after cashing the buyer's check. This matter of misrepresentation—that's a polite word for "lie"—is so important, let's look into a few of the ways in which an unscrupulous seller can inflate the apparent success of a business. These examples are not theoretical. Several of them have been seen in operation recently by the authors of this book.

▬ The tax returns show only a modest profit, but the owner winks and says, "I make more than I report." That may be the truth, but how will you ever know how *much* more?

▬ Family members (including the owner) work in the business but fail to take a salary comparable to what you'll have to pay to hire replacements.

▬ Equipment in apparently good condition is in reality obsolete because competitors using new machines can turn out a better quality product at less cost.

▬ Significant recurring expenses that were paid out in past years have been put on the books as assets that you are being asked to buy. In reality, the payments were for expenses that repeat every year. Examples: costs of advertising campaigns that have to be repeated every year, and costs that have to be paid periodically for retraining employees to keep them up-to-date or technological, legal, or other changes. You're being asked to buy past years' expenses in the guise of assets, and past years' net income was overstated.

■ Necessary business expenses have been paid out of the owner's pocket or out of another business the owner runs, in order to make this business look better than it is. Sales figures, also, can be blown up by transactions that actually occurred in the other business (or were outright phoney).

■ Inventory is full of unsalable goods that have accumulated. After you buy the seller's inventory, you find you can't sell it. Similarly, you buy the receivables and then find you can't collect them.

■ Sales figures have been inflated by transactions that won't recur, such as the sale of an unused parcel of land, or an infusion of cash by the owner is put on the books as a sale.

■ Sales figures are legitimate but are dominated by a very few large customers, any one of which might trade elsewhere (some might even switch to the seller's next establishment).

■ The owner fails to make clear that there are warranties or liabilities associated with products that have already been sold. If you buy the business, you may be stuck with paying these costs. (If you buy only the assets, you may avoid these "contingent" liabilities. Later, we cover buying assets versus the stock of a corporate business.)

■ Maintenance and repairs that have been postponed eventually will have to be paid for out of the buyer's pocket.

■ Significant changes are about to impact the business; the present owner knows about them, but you don't. The changes might relate to new technology, highway relocation, regulation by state or federal law, foreign competition, or the opening nearby of a discount store carrying similar merchandise. Maybe the change is as subtle as a change in customer's tastes. If you are relocating to a new community to buy a type of business you are not thoroughly familiar with, you are particularly vulnerable to the impact of such changes.

There are ways to protect yourself from all the risks involved in dealing with owners who are so eager to sell that they will pull any trick to get you to buy. Let's take a look at the protective steps you can take.

HOW TO PROTECT YOURSELF WHEN BUYING A BUSINESS

Don't pay for—as a going concern—any business that doesn't have a successful operating history of several years. Otherwise, you may step into the uncomfortable shoes of an owner who had big ideas but quickly learned that the business was headed for collapse in a few years.

Try to find out the real reasons why the owner is selling out. Start by asking the owner or the business broker or real estate broker who's acting as the owner's agent. Then, go further. Have a casual chat with the owners of neighboring businesses. Sometimes they will spill the beans about problems the seller is trying to hide.

Get financial statements and schedules that spell out revenues and expenses in the greatest possible detail. For example, get a breakdown of sales per month and by product line for the last two or three years. You or your accountant can study this data for clues as to the likely true profitability of the business and whether the books have been altered. For example, if you were buying an accounting practice, you would want to know how much revenue came from tax return preparation and how much from bookkeeping for clients. If you were buying a funeral parlor, you'd want to know how much was taken in by sales of caskets and other products and how much from chemical and cosmetic preparation services. If you were buying a restaurant, you would want to know the amount of sales from liquor, from private parties, from outside catering, and so on.

Ask for financial statements that have been "audited" by a CPA. You may have to back down on this one, or compromise for statements that have merely been "reviewed," because a CPA's work is costly to the owner if it hasn't been done already. You could negotiate by offering to pay all or a portion of the CPA's fees *if* it turns out that you buy the business.

You will, of course, ask for several years back income tax returns and sales tax returns. Tax returns are better than nothing, but they may understate or overstate income from the business. Typical owner's excuses include: "You won't be able to tell what I've earned because all my businesses are lumped together." Have the owner's accountant separate the figures. Another excuse, "We had a fire and they were burned up." With the owner's permission, get copies from the IRS. Also, "I wish I could show them to you but according to law they are confidential." A taxpayer can show returns to anyone he or she wishes.

When it looks like you are going to cut a deal with the owner, but before it's settled, have your attorney do a "legal audit." This means your attorney will review contracts, statutes and regulations, and public records of lawsuits filed or judgments issued against the business that might have an impact on you. Your lawyer will have to consider what will be your liability for injuries caused by products sold before you took over. If the business premises are leased, it is important to have the lease contract reviewed and to get a written commitment from the owner that you will be allowed to occupy the premises at a stated cost for enough years into the future that you can feel comfortable.

Find out how much a business of this type in this location *should* be making, considering the key factors for profitability in this type of business. By finding out how much the business *should* be making, you may be able to spot a for-sale business that is grossly under- or overpriced.

We can't tell you what these key factors might be for every type of business. The key factor might be the number of square feet of the company's showroom, the number of cars passing in front of the store daily, the number of seniors graduating from high school within a 30-mile radius, population demographics such as age, wealth, and per-capita income, or the number of construction permits issued locally.

If you don't know what the key factor for your business is, you may be able to learn about it from one of your advisors, such as a CPA or a business consultant that you have hired. From your public library you can get the name of trade associations that have information about every business imaginable. Write to them for information.

If you are buying equipment that you're not familiar with, have it evaluated by an experienced appraiser. You can sometimes get a wealth of information by contacting the manufacturer or a distributor (who may maintain a market for used equipment).

Include in your agreement with the owner or owners an employment or consulting contract that obligates them to consult with you for the year after you take over. Sellers are much less likely to misrepresent significant aspects of the business if they will have to be there on the spot to face you when you find out.

Get the seller to take back a note for at least part of the sales price. Generally, the more agreeable the seller is to finance your purchase, the more likely it is that the deal is on the up and up.

Finally, make the exact amount of the purchase price conditional on the performance of the business in the year *after* you take over. The conditional payment could be based on unit volume of sales or dollar volume, or it could even be hinged on net income. For example, suppose the owner wants $70,000 for the business as a going concern. You might agree to pay for the basic value of the assets, say, $50,000. Then, for the going concern value of the business, offer a percentage of next year's net income, calculated to equal the extra $20,000 the owner wants *if* the business is as successful as you think it will be. Your accountant can suggest ways to calculate performance, and your attorney can structure them into the contract.

Most of all, you must adopt the viewpoint that—while you will use advisers such as accountants and consultants—*you* are the one who is responsible for deciding whether or not to buy and what price to pay. Don't depend on someone else, even the most astute of advisers, to evaluate the business. In particular, don't rely on someone who is assisting or being compensated by the owner. A business broker, for example, gets paid only if the deal goes through. *You must rely on your own expertise.* If you truthfully have no expertise in this business, maybe you should step back and rethink the whole deal.

WHERE TO FIND A BUSINESS TO BUY

If you are serious about buying a business, you can find plenty of people to encourage you. Look in the yellow pages of your telephone directory to find business brokers. As noted above, these brokers work for the seller of the business and get paid a percentage of the sales price. You should check with several business brokers because they typically don't handle each other's properties in the "multiple-listing" manner used by real estate agents. Also, when you are dealing with other professionals such as lawyers, accountants, and bankers, ask them who are the well-known business brokers in the community.

Since the sale of a business often includes real estate, real estate brokers may have leads. Other sources of information on businesses for sale include public accountants, business lawyers, bankers, and some chambers of commerce. Also, check classified advertisements in newspapers, including those with national circulation like *The Wall Street Journal.*

Also, ask other business owners. For example, if you are eager to own a pet store in Phoenix, go there and visit pet stores. Talk to the owners and managers of several stores. One of them may know of a store for sale.

WHAT IS THE BUSINESS WORTH?

When you buy a business, you are buying both tangible assets—autos, computers, furnishings, inventory, buildings, and land—and intangible assets such as *goodwill* and *covenant not to compete*. The latter two assets deserve special attention, but let's begin with the tangible assets—those with physical form. Never pay any more for tangible assets than you would have to lay out if you were starting up a similar business from scratch. Remember, you could put together your own business, buying autos, computers, store furnishings, and so forth. The best way to make sure you're not paying too much for these assets, when you buy them in connection with a going business, is to get an appraisal—a written statement from a knowledgeable professional as to what each of the assets is worth.

You may have the expertise yourself to make such an appraisal. As a matter of fact, some advisers say that if you are unable to figure out for yourself what the assets are worth, you shouldn't be buying this particular kind of business. You should, instead, be in a business that you *do* know enough about to estimate what the assets are worth. But that requirement is a bit harsh. Most of us need to take advantage of professional help now and then, and we can't know the value of every piece of specialized equipment that might be used in business or the value of land and buildings in a part of the country that we're not familiar with.

So, get an appraisal. What you are looking for is an appraisal of the *assets*, not of the business as a going concern. If you are buying primarily land and buildings, you need to find a real estate appraiser. Ask your CPA or attorney to recommend an appraiser, or look in the yellow pages. Real estate appraisers are a recognized professional group—but as in all professions, some practitioners are better than others. Try to get references.

Of course, for highly specialized equipment that might be used in the business you're evaluating, such as multineedle sewing machines or ceramic ovens, don't rely on a real estate appraiser. Your best bet will be to find someone with many years' experience in the same type of business. You can find such a person by scanning the pages of trade association journals or by calling the manufacturer or distributor of the equipment.

Be sure the appraiser knows you are interested in the purchase price of the assets as is. This is not the same as replacement value. Replacement value refers to what it would cost to replace the assets with *new* assets. A used car costs much less than a new car, and the same holds true, to one degree or another, for machinery and other business equipment. If you wanted to buy new assets, you would have to pay considerably more than you would to buy assets that have been used, and you wouldn't need an appraiser.

If you will have to move the assets to another location, you should deduct moving costs from the used purchase price. In fact, if used furniture has to be moved to a new location, the appraiser may assign it no value at all.

The building premises may be leased. Leasing can be crucial to business success if *location* is a significant factor. If you're not making a separate deal to buy the premises (land and buildings), you *must* know how long you'll be allowed to stay there. To find this out will take two steps. First, you or your lawyer will read the present lease carefully to see what it says about assignment or subleasing—two different ways to continue the lease. (Remember what we said a few pages back about a legal audit.) Second, you may have to negotiate with the owner of the property to get a lease long enough to allow you to make the business successful. Ideally, you want a three- or five-year lease that is renewable at your option.

Inventory can create special problems. Probably in *no* instance should you be willing to pay the seller the amount he or she has invested in inventory. After all, if you buy the business, you can contact the same suppliers the former owner bought from. They will provide you with fresh, up-to-date products and good advice on what to stock, and they'll do all this on credit.

Be sure you have an accurate count of the inventory on hand. There are firms, called inventory tabulators, that specialize in counting inventory. Find them in the yellow pages, or ask a banker or public accountant. Once the inventory has been counted and listed, you can identify for the seller those inventory items that you do not want to buy.

The owner will also probably want you to buy the uncollected amounts that customers owe the business, known as accounts receivable. The problem is, if they are uncollected they may be uncollectible, particularly if they have been outstanding and unpaid for several months. How are you going to calculate whether you will be able to collect 99 percent or 70 percent or 30 percent of their "book value?" Here's another asset for which you should never pay anywhere near book value. (Book value, also called face value, is the amount carried in the accounting books. Book value is the amount that the business buyer is supposed to pay. Few do. Assets may be listed on the books at amounts larger or smaller than their actual cash value.)

Here are two solutions to the problem of collecting the seller's accounts receivable. First of all, you could refuse to buy the receivables, leaving them for the seller to collect. (Or you might agree to buy only the ones that are current, that is, no older than 30 to 60 days.)

Leaving the receivables for the seller to collect is common enough when businesses are bought, so the seller shouldn't object. Point out to the seller that he or she has a closer relationship with the customer and so should be able to collect more easily than you could.

This arrangement will accomplish the intended purpose, but there are several drawbacks. You would fail to get the inflow of cash that collection of these receivables would provide. Also, you will miss an opportunity to "introduce" yourself to these customers through letters and brochures you could be sending with your monthly statements. Then there's the problem, too, that the seller may be too aggressive in trying to collect, thereby reducing the goodwill of what is now your business.

The other solution is to buy the receivables but pay the seller for them only as you are able to collect them. After a stated period of time, say 90 days, the accounts you haven't been able to collect are turned back to the seller. You won't have to pay for them.

HOW TO VALUE GOODWILL

After you have figured out what the tangible assets are worth, you must take a long, hard look at goodwill. In a sense, the price you pay for goodwill is the price that you pay—over and above the value of the tangible assets—for stepping into the shoes of the owner of a successful, going concern.

The amount you pay for goodwill is completely negotiable between you and the owner of the business. Of course, you want to pay as little for goodwill as you possibly can. *There is no formula used to compute goodwill that is binding on you.*

Don't let the seller or the broker fool you. For some businesses, there will be no goodwill, or it will be a nominal or small amount such as $500 or $1,000. Typically, no goodwill is paid for when the business has one of these features:

▬ Sales are made door-to-door.

▬ Mail order sales, if there is only one product or if the customer is sold only once, such as a water softener to attach to a faucet or an exercise device.

▬ Businesses in which the personality or skill of the owner predominates, such as a small, one-person photography studio.

▬ Businesses operated out of a home.

▬ Mom-and-pop stores and any business in which the whole family pitches in.

In some businesses, where there is goodwill, rules of thumb are used to get a starting point for negotiation. For example, a medical practice might be sold for the value of the tangible assets plus goodwill valued at 20 percent of the previous year's gross receipts. Paint stores and camera sales and service businesses are each said to value goodwill at 10 percent of net income. A veterinary practice is said to be worth, for the entire business including goodwill and tangible assets, 75 to 125 percent of the latest year's revenues. You can learn the rules of thumb for practically all businesses by consulting the trade association appropriate for that type of business.

Warning: Surveys repeatedly show that actual sales prices deviate considerably from the rules of thumb. Rules of thumb give you only a starting point for negotiation.

A supposedly more scientific way to compute goodwill is to capitalize excess earnings. (A CPA hired to value the business would likely determine goodwill in this manner.) To capitalize excess earnings means to figure out how much more the particular business you are interested in is earning, *over and above* what the typical business of that type would earn. For example, suppose the business you are thinking of buying earns $50,000 after all expenses (including the owner's salary). Yet, a typical business of that type and size in that part of the country could be expected to net only $40,000. The amount of excess earnings is $10,000. Once excess earnings has been computed, the question still remains, "What is goodwill worth?"

Actually, the question is better stated, "What's the least I can get by with paying for this business that has $10,000 of excess earnings?" Remember: Putting a pencil against paper to calculate goodwill does nothing more than give you a starting point in your negotiations with the seller.

COVENANT NOT TO COMPETE

After you and the seller have reached agreement on the price you are going to pay for the business, your accountant will be concerned about how you allocate the purchase price. The reason for this concern is that goodwill cannot be deducted as an expense of your business in figuring taxes. On the other hand, you will be able to deduct the cost of the tangible assets, except land. The deduction is called *depreciation*.

While you can't deduct the part of the purchase price that is allocated to the intangible asset, goodwill, there may be other intangible assets that you can deduct. A major asset of this type is called a covenant not to compete. This covenant binds the seller of the business not to reenter the same type of business that you are buying for a specified period of time.

Covenants that obligate the seller of a business not to compete are legally binding as long as they are limited in time and in the geographical area they cover. For instance, a covenant probably would be enforceable that bound the seller not to compete in a named three-county area for a period of three years. The price you pay for such an agreement would be deductible for tax purposes over a three-year period, one-third each year.

Chances are that an attempt to prevent the seller from working in the same trade anywhere in the state for, say, ten years would *not* be enforceable. Your attorney can advise you as to state law on this point.

Liabilities

A final step after determining what the assets, tangible and intangible, are worth, is to list the liabilities that you will have to assume (pay). You will subtract liabilities from the assets to determine the price you'll pay the seller. In a sense, you will be paying the seller's debts. For instance, if the firm's assets are worth $100,000 and there are business debts of $40,000 that you will have to pay, then you will pay the seller $60,000. Later, you'll pay the remaining $40,000 of the purchase price by paying the creditors of the business. This topic is an important factor in the decision whether—when buying a corporation—you should buy the stock or buy the assets.

Buying Stock versus Buying Assets

If the business you are buying is a corporation, ordinarily you will have a choice of buying the owner's capital stock or of buying the assets of the business. If you buy the stock, the corporation continues its legal existence. If you buy the assets, on the other hand, you have to create your own new company, which you might choose to incorporate or run as an unincorporated business.

By far the most frequent arrangement when small businesses are traded is for the buyer to buy the assets. There are, however, pros and cons on each side.

You may decide to buy the stock if the corporation has leases, contracts with suppliers, or contracts with customers. If you want these business arrangements to continue, you will have to buy the corporation. Also, the name of the corporation and its reputation may have some value that would be lost if only the firm's assets were purchased.

On the other hand, when you pay for the whole corporation you may get certain items you don't want. Here are some of the problems you might get that occurred *before* you became the owner, but for which you would have to pay from the corporation's profits:

■ Income tax assessments against the corporation for past years, revealed by IRS audit after you became the owner.

■ Legal claims against the corporation for injuries caused by products that were sold before you bought in, or claims related to claims that the corporation had broken a contract.

■ Legal claims related to discrimination, safety and health, and environmental protection.

The point is that when you buy the stock you get both the assets and the liabilities of the corporation. Of course, you can protect yourself against the liabilities that exist now and that you know about. But you can't do much about claims that are lurking in the shadows, waiting to jump out and take a piece of your business.

The alternative is to buy the assets. You will have to name them and place a value on them individually or by category. You also will have to transfer to your name the titles of such assets as land and motor vehicles. Naming and valuing the assets will present an opportunity for you to allocate a portion of the purchase price to intangible assets such as the covenant on the seller not to open a competing business. Here you'll need to get professional advice from your accountant or attorney as to which assets may be deductible from the firm's taxable income.

The Bulk Sales Act

There are state laws designed to protect the known creditors of a business when the assets of that business are sold. Otherwise, a buyer could avoid debts that creditors entered into thinking they would be able to collect from a going concern. State laws that deal with bulk transfers require that creditors be notified when merchants sell the major part of their business inventory. Equipment is also covered if it is sold together with inventory.

Bulk sales acts protect creditors by holding the transfer of inventory and equipment to be invalid unless proper notice has been given to those transfers. In other words, the creditors retain a claim against the asset you have purchased unless they are notified of the purchase in sufficient time for them to claim whatever interest they have.

To comply with the law, the buyer of the assets requests the seller to furnish a list of existing creditors. The buyer must give notice to these creditors at least ten days before he or she takes possession of the inventory or pays for them, whichever occurs first. The creditors have time to make a claim against the seller's property. If they choose not to do so, they have no further claims against the assets that were transferred. The requirements of the bulk sales act should be handled by your attorney.

CHAPTER PERSPECTIVE

There are significant advantages to buying a going business . . . unless you overpay or go too deeply into debt to make the deal. It's important to use your own common sense and the advice of experienced experts to evaluate the business coolly and objectively. Don't let dreams roll over reality.

Franchising

INTRODUCTION

Not so long ago, we identified franchising only with fast food outlets or a handful of other business establishments in our communities. No longer.

While McDonald's indeed has exploded with success, the franchising wave has been much wider than that, involving hundreds of businesses. The U.S. Department of Commerce attempts to track developments in franchising, listing specific business opportunities and organizing them by business, but admits that keeping current is difficult even with an annual survey. Franchising has become a major influence in American business.

You could start the day by driving your leased car to pick up the laundry . . . pick up your business cards and stationery from the printer . . . make arrangements for some remodeling work on your house . . . file your resume with an employment agency . . . have lunch with business associates . . . stop by the fitness center on the way home . . . call your real estate agent about listing your house after the remodeling . . . start making travel plans for your annual vacation . . . and thus spend your entire day dealing exclusively with franchised businesses.

Franchising is expected to continue to expand as a major force in the economy, as it allows the growing number of small businesses to affiliate themselves with a network of businesses with economic clout.

However, franchising can be complicated, legally dangerous, and fraught with tangles and traps for the unwary. This chapter deals with some of the pros and cons.

After studying the material in this chapter:

■ You will have an understanding of what a franchise relationship is.

■ You will know what to look for when considering a franchise.

■ You will be able to identify some of the advantages and disadvantages of franchises.

■ You will know what the "FTC Rule" is and how it is intended to protect you.

■ You will be able to spot some of the dangers that may be present in franchise relationships.

■ You will be familiar with some typical provisions in a franchise agreement.

WHAT IS A FRANCHISE?

Despite the success of McDonald's and various real estate franchises, the term itself does not refer to a particular product or a service. It refers to a *method* of doing business; it is the process by which a particular business relationship operates.

Franchising arrangements may differ widely, but some common characteristics exist. The franchisee is generally a small independent business providing products or services, with a franchise agreement tying it to a network of other businesses. The knot tying these businesses together is called the franchisor, generally a corporation that distributes its goods or services through the franchise network.

The franchisee has the advantage of being tied to a larger business entity (which may have a respected, recognized name, such as McDonald's); it has the disadvantage of being obligated to pay the franchisor an agreed-upon sum and submit to a potentially wide range of controls.

Two themes run through the franchise relationship: use of a trademark, or service mark, and standardization. Most of us know what the name McDonald's and the golden arches mean; and we pretty well know what to expect when we get inside a fast food outlet graced by the arches.

Since the Federal Trade Commission (FTC) promulgated some strict franchising rules in 1978—providing franchisees with a measure of regulatory protection—you should know how that agency defines a franchise. There are two major categories:

■ Package and product franchising

■ Business opportunity ventures franchising.

Package and Product Franchising

Package franchising includes many familiar businesses, such as fast food outlets and convenience stores. *Package* is an apt description since the arrangement can be comprehensive in governing the relationship between parties.

A first cousin of the package franchise is the *product* franchise, where the emphasis is more on provision of a distribution outlet for the franchisor's product. An example: Lawn care equipment.

Under the FTC's definition, both package and product franchises have these three elements:

1. The franchisor grants the franchisee the right to provide goods or services using the franchisor's trademark or service mark. (Putting up the arches provides an instant credibility that a sign reading "Al's Fast Food Outlet" might not.)

2. The franchisor receives compensation for this right. It can take a combination of forms—for example, up-front franchise fees and continuing royalties. The franchisor's plan of operation is mandatory to varying degree; it can control such things as quality of products, hours of operation, advertising, training and methods of conducting business. The franchisor can provide—in fact, require—various forms of technical assistance.

3. The franchisee must pay at least $500 to the franchisor before or during the first six months of operation.

Business Opportunity Ventures Franchising

A key ingredient of the package and product franchises is missing here: The requirement that the licensor's trademark be used. Businesses handling vending machines and racks fall into this category. In other respects, this relationship looks similar, and, according to the Federal Trade Commission, it is present where these three criteria are met:

1. The licensee (or investor) sells goods or services supplied by the licensor (or seller) or its affiliate or by a supplier with whom the licensee is required to do business.

2. The licensor, or person controlling the supply of goods or services, must provide significant assistance to the licensee. This involves securing retailing outlets or accounts for the goods or services, securing vending racks or machines for the product, or providing the services of someone who performs those acts.

3. The licensee must pay the licensor $500 before or within six months after the business commences.

Typically, the licensor supplies the product and promises to provide a minimum number of outlets. Examples include vending machine routes and distributorships.

What Franchising Is Not

Some business relationships bear a resemblance to franchising, but under the FTC Rule they would not be defined as such. They include situations where:

- No payment of at least $500 is made to the franchisor.
- An established distributor adds products or services from another company (the "fractional franchise" exemption).

   An independent retailer leases space in a larger store (the "leased department" exemption).
- No written evidence exists to support the franchise agreement.
- The business relationship is actually in the form of a cooperative.
- The relationship is actually between employer and employee.
- Organizations authorize the use of their trademark to *all* parties who comply with their standards and pay their fee.

WHAT TO LOOK FOR

Although the FTC and state regulators require franchisors to make certain disclosures, they seldom tell the whole story. For instance, the formal disclosures may not cover all items of interest to you; and they may be incomplete or even inaccurate. A prospective franchisee must make independent inquiries about franchise opportunities.

Start by asking the person who owns a franchise of the type you are considering. No one is more of an expert in that particular franchisor-franchisee relationship.

Another source of information is your local Better Business Bureau. See if it has current information on the franchise you are considering. The BBB will also suggest that you obtain some basic financial data about the franchisor, including:

1. The financial health and history of the company. Does it have a track record to make you comfortable? If the franchisor is financially sick, the franchisee will likely catch the same disease. Have your accountant help you here.

2. The quality of the company officers. They are not just names, they are the persons who have to make the business work. Do their background and experience give you confidence? If not, think twice about the relationship.

3. The source of the company's earnings. Remember that the franchisor can make money from the franchisee in several ways, including front-end franchise fees and royalties from sales. If the bulk of those earnings come from front-end fees, be cautious. Franchisors that make most of their earnings from royalties are more likely to be interested in the ongoing success of the franchisees' businesses.

4. The intrinsic appeal of the product or service. Forget the sales literature here. Think of yourself as a customer: How does the franchisor stack up against the competition? Is this a McDonald's or a Burger Chef?

5. The type and degree of training and field support provided by the franchisor. Since this is one of the primary reasons for affiliating with a franchisor, evaluate this area with a critical eye. Examine the scope, frequency, and quality of training guaranteed. Are additional costs involved?

6. The types and frequency of advertising support. Look especially at national and regional advertising and plans for future campaigns. How much does the franchisee pay as a share for such advertising?

7. The overall operating rules and restrictions on the franchisee. These are a key part of the franchise relationship, designed to ensure uniformity of quality of the product or service. Ask yourself whether they are reasonable and sensitive to market conditions in your area.

ADVANTAGES AND DISADVANTAGES

When you go into business, you basically have three options: Start a new business, buy an existing business, or buy or start a franchised business. There is no "right" answer; there is only an appropriate answer, consistent with your personality, your circumstances and the market.

If you are seriously considering a franchised business, prepare a "balance sheet" of pros and cons. As with most topics covered in this book, that involves looking at a combination of legal obligations and pragmatic business considerations.

Obviously, the time to examine this balance sheet is before you sign a franchise agreement; try to discover and avoid as many potential pitfalls as possible before you are locked into a legal relationship.

Your starting point is to understand the basic advantages and disadvantages of franchising. If you decide that franchising is for you, then get down to specifics—the specific business, the specific franchise agreement.

Here are some of the potential advantages and disadvantages of franchising:

Potential Advantages

1.   You can use someone else's good name, trademark, and credibility. Take the McDonald's example one more time: You are not just in the food business, you are a McDonald's franchisee. There's a big difference, and this is a big advantage.

2.   You have the opportunity to buy not just a business but an established concept with a track record. This can remove some of the risk and guesswork from the process of opening up your own business.

3.   Even if you have only limited business experience, you can get advanced training and continuing business support from a company that can save you from learning the hard way, through trial and error. You have access to management expertise that would not be readily available to you as an independent small business.

4.   With some franchisors, you can expend relatively little capital and still establish a strong credit rating. In some instances, you may also receive financing help from the franchisor. This is not an act of charity on the part of the franchisor; it is one way of preventing failures among the franchise and enhancing the financial reputation of the franchise operation.

5.   You can tap into technical expertise with regard to such things as site selection, facility design, and layout and business operations.

6.   You can benefit from national and regional advertising and publicity campaigns, all of which help presell your product or service.

7.   You may be able to realize savings from quantity purchases of supplies, products, and services by the franchisor.

Disadvantages

1.   You are not your own boss. You have a franchisor partner—maybe a very strong and opinionated partner—who will be involved even in the most minor details of your business. This partner may require you to conform to detailed operating plans;

to handle all his products or services, even though you might not like all of them; and sometimes to make business decisions for the sake of the entire franchise network, even though they may not be best for you.

2.   In addition to sharing authority, you also share profits. That is part of the price you pay for all the potential advantages. Usually, this takes the form of a royalty on *gross* sales; thus, sometimes payment must be made whether or not you make a profit. To get a realistic idea of what the downside may be, prepare financial projections, with an accountant's help, for several sales volume assumptions *lower* than the franchisor's estimates. This helps you avoid potentially burdensome payments under the franchisor's estimates.

3.   Your ability to adjust to local market conditions may be limited. Remember that uniformity is one of the characteristics of franchise products and services. Thus, the franchisor may deny you the opportunity to tweak prices to meet the competition, or to refine your product line to satisfy local tastes.

4.   The franchise agreement may contain many details that favor the franchisor. After all, the franchisor is experienced in this business and understands it better than you. Numerous opportunities exist for the franchisor to gain an edge: required sales quotas, termination of franchise agreement, exclusive territorial rights, mandatory purchases of supplies and equipment from the franchisor.

5.   If the franchisor generates negative public or community relations, you share in it. Management scandal or a health scare are examples.

6.   Extra paperwork goes with a franchise business. Your franchisor partner wants a detailed knowledge of what you are doing and the results.

7.   Enforcing grievances against the franchisor may prove to be burdensome, even impossible. Terminating an unsatisfactory franchise relationship can be extremely time-consuming and difficult.

Caution: You should never sign a franchise agreement in a rush; and never sign it without having an experienced attorney review it in detail with you.

THE "FTC RULE"

This chapter already has made reference to the FTC Rule, formally titled "Disclosure Requirements and Prohibitions Concerning Franchising and Business Opportunity Ventures."

The Federal Trade Commission adopted this rule in response to widespread evidence of unfair and deceptive practices in connection with the sale of franchises. The rule's primary purpose is to require disclosure of essential and reliable information about franchise opportunities to allow prospective franchisees to make informed investment decisions.

Franchisors and franchise brokers must furnish prospective investors certain information about the franchisor, the franchise business, and the franchise agreement. Additional information must be provided if franchisors or franchise brokers have made any claims about actual or potential earnings, either to the potential investor or to the media.

The rule also requires that disclosures must be made *before* any sale is made, and that such disclosures must comply with form and content requirements in the rule.

It is essential to understand that the FTC Rule does not guarantee a fair deal. It merely requires disclosure of information; it's up to you to read or understand that information. You may need help from a knowledgeable and experienced business adviser or an attorney.

The disclosures must be in a single document, and they must be current as of the completion of the franchisor's most recent fiscal year. Revisions must be made quarterly in the event of a material change in the information.

Disclosure documents must be provided at the earliest of either (1) the prospective franchisee's first personal meeting with the franchisor, or (2) ten days prior to the execution of a contract or payment of money relating to the franchise agreement. Failure to provide the disclosure document as required should raise your antennae concerning the franchisor's legitimacy.

The Required 20 Subjects

The disclosure document requires information on the following 20 subjects:

1. Identifying information about the franchisor
2. Business experience of the franchisor's directors and key executives
3. The franchisor's business experience
4. Litigation history of the franchisor and its directors and key executives
5. Bankruptcy history of the franchisor and its directors and key executives
6. Description of the franchise

7. Money required to be paid by the franchisee to obtain or commence the franchise operation
8. Continuing expenses to the franchisee in operating the franchise business that are payable in whole or in part to the franchisor
9. A list of persons who are either the franchisor or any of its affiliates, with whom the franchisee is required or advised to do business
10. Realty, personalty, services, etc. which the franchisee is required to purchase, lease or rent, and a list of any persons from whom such transactions must be made
11. Description of consideration paid (such as royalties, commissions, etc.) by third parties to the franchisor or any of its affiliates as a result of a franchisee's purchase from such third parties
12. Description of any franchisor assistance in financing the purchase of a franchise
13. Restrictions placed on a franchisee's conduct of its business
14. Required personal participation by the franchisee
15. Termination, cancelation, and renewal of franchise
16. Statistical information about the number of franchises and their rate of terminations
17. Franchisor's right to select or approve a site for the franchise
18. Training programs for the franchisee
19. Celebrity involvement with the franchise
20. Financial information about the franchisor.

These are the 20 basic items of information. Additionally, if the franchisor makes any representations about earnings, an "earnings claim disclosure document" must be given to the potential franchisee. These items are required:

1. The earnings claim
2. A statement of the bases and assumptions upon which the earnings claim is made
3. Information concerning the number and percentage of outlets that have earned at least the amount set forth in the claim, or a statement of lack of experience, as well as the beginning and ending dates of the time period covered by the claim
4. A mandatory caution statement, whose text is set forth in the Rule, concerning the likelihood of duplicating the earnings claim

5. A statement that information sufficient to substantiate the accuracy of the claim is available for inspection by the franchisee.

STATE FRANCHISE LAWS

The FTC Rule establishes the basic federal minimum standard of disclosure. Several states also have franchise laws that are intended to provide additional protection to the prospective franchisee.

Examples of provisions in state laws or regulations include:

1. Required registration of franchisors or franchise salespersons
2. Requirements for escrow or bonding arrangements
3. Disclosure requirements that exceed the FTC Rule
4. Franchise agreement provisions, covering termination practices, financing arrangements, and other contract provisions.

SOME BASIC FRANCHISING DANGERS

It is apparent that a considerable amount of *potential* protection and useful information is available—if you take advantage of it. This information is an important resource in sidestepping some of the franchising dangers.

Danger No. 1: Rushing into the deal. It is impossible to know too much, so study the documents thoroughly and talk to other franchisees.

Danger No. 2: Going it alone. Franchising is complicated, so ask for help from an attorney, business adviser, or accountant and from franchisees experienced with the business.

Danger No. 3: Reading the franchise agreement through rose-colored classes. Do not try to put the best light on provisions in the contract; instead, imagine the "worst case" consequences under the explicit terms of the contract. Remember that honeymoons end quickly, even in business, and a happy divorce can be difficult to come by in the franchise business.

Danger No. 4: Dropping your guard. Legitimate franchisors comply with the rules and treat you professionally. Anyone who makes exorbitant promises, holds back on information about the franchisor or its officers, promises profits through chain sales or pyramid schemes, pushes you to "act immediately," promises large income from work-at-home or spare-time efforts, or uses names that "sound like" but are unconnected with nationally known businesses—these franchisors should put you on your guard instantly.

THE FRANCHISE AGREEMENT

The document actually governing the franchisor/franchisee relationship is the franchise agreement. Everything else in this chapter is preparatory to ensure that the agreement is right for you.

Franchise agreements can be quite lengthy, since the relationship has many elements. They should be clearly written. Although your attorney should review the document, you also should understand each provision. Following are typical provisions of a franchise agreement.

Terms of the Agreement

Most franchise agreements have a fixed term, with a provision for renewal. The franchisor wants the opportunity to review the relationship after a certain period of time. The franchisee wants to hold the franchise long enough to preserve his equity—the expenditure of time, effort and expense—and to coincide with his lease term. Of course, renewal is usually conditioned upon satisfactory performance by the franchisee. This point should be clearly spelled out.

Termination of the Agreement

Termination usually comes toward the end of the agreement, but it is discussed here since it can be a condition of the term of the agreement. Franchisors crank out standard contracts that probably favor their interests; a franchisor's bargaining power is usually superior to a franchisee's.

Therefore, detailed provisions under which the franchisor may terminate the agreement are common. Keep in mind that performance by the franchisor in a timely manner is critical to the success of the franchisee. Similarly detailed provisions under which you can terminate the agreement also need to be spelled out.

Franchise Payments

These normally include initial franchise fees, which may be made in a lump sum or installments; royalties, or service fees, which may be based on various factors but are often based on gross revenues; and miscellaneous fees, which can include such things as training fees, required product or service purchases, and advertising fees.

Rights of the Franchisee
The franchisee is allowed to use the franchisor's trademark, or service mark (and concurrently agrees to certain limitations on use of such marks). The franchisor may also stipulate requirements for maintaining the reputation of the trademark. The franchisee is also allowed to use trade secrets (secret recipes or other processes), but agrees to keep them confidential. Exclusive territorial rights for the franchisee may also be spelled out in this section, or in a separate section of the agreement.

Services by the Franchisor
The list can be long and varied; just make sure you understand what realistically to expect once the agreement is signed. Some typical examples:

Standard specifications and plans for the facility, furnishings, decor, layout, and signs

Preopening training programs

Opening supervision and assistance

The franchisor's business operating policies and manuals

Marketing, advertising, and merchandising research data and advice

Consultation and advice from the franchisor's field supervisors

Standardized accounting, cost-control, and other business systems

Site-selection assistance

Group purchasing programs

Continued operating assistance and consultation

Access to new products and services.

Site Selection
Location and specifications of the premises are important in some franchises and may be covered in detail. This section may set out the obligations of both franchisor and franchisee in choosing the site and in completing lease or purchase negotiations. It may also set forth minimum requirements for the site itself and for the property lease.

Premises and Signs

Minimum requirements and uniformity in the appearance of the premises and signs are so important to maintaining the public perception of the franchise that they may be spelled out in some detail. The franchisor may also retain the right to initiate changes or improvements.

Quality Control

In addition to the premises and signs requirements, the franchisor may also stipulate requirements for:

Hours of operation
Accounting and record-keeping
Authorized products and services
Compliance with laws
The franchisee's degree of participation in the business
Employee qualifications, dress, appearance, and behavior.

Training Programs

Training opportunities and requirements are an important part of the agreement. From the franchisee's standpoint, ongoing training programs offer some assurance of continuing business growth and competence. From the franchisor's standpoint, such programs validate the competence of the franchisee. This provision could cover what programs are available and required; specific contents of the programs; costs of the programs; fees for the programs; and whether the franchisor has any recourse in the event of the franchisee's failure to participate or poor performance.

Advertising and Public Relations

The franchisor may want to maintain an active advertising and public relations program to bolster the entire franchise network. To maintain this program, the franchisee may be required to participate in (and contribute funds to) national or regional programs, or to conduct minimal local advertising or public relations.

Purchases of Goods and Services

To help maintain quality and uniformity, the franchisor may require that it be the source of goods and services; or, certain restrictions may be placed on suppliers to be used. This provision may also cover participation in group purchasing programs.

Record-keeping and Reporting

Reference was made earlier to paperwork requirements in operating a franchise, and this is the provision where you probably will find them. The requirements enable the franchisor to assure that the franchisees are holding up their end of the deal, and provide an early warning system if problems develop. These warnings also benefit the franchisee.

Miscellaneous Provisions

Other provisions may deal with: Ability of the franchisee to transfer the franchise; how to handle contract disputes; right of entry and inspection by the franchisor; and noncompetition restrictions on the franchisee.

FRANCHISING CHECKLIST

As you can tell from the foregoing materials, the checklist for evaluating a franchise opportunity can be very long. It should cover the pros and cons of operating a franchised business; the record and reputation of the franchisor; the record and reputation of the product or service; the market area under consideration; and the franchise agreement itself.

Reminder: Have your attorney and business adviser help you review all these areas.

There are 17 key questions to ask about a franchise:

1. Have you checked the franchisor out with franchisees and the Better Business Bureau?
2. How long has the company been in business, and what is its track record?
3. How about the principals in the company? What is their record and reputation?
4. What are the company's financial strengths, and from where does it derive most of its income?
5. What are its plans for future development, and how selective is it in choosing franchisees?
6. What is the product's reputation and quality? Is it a fad, or does it have staying power?
7. How does the product stack up against the competition?
8. Is it priced and marketed competitively?
9. Do you have an exclusive territory? Is it clearly defined?
10. What are the opportunities for growth in the area? What is the competition?

11. Does the franchise agreement seem fair, or is it one-sided? Do both parties benefit?

12. Do you know the full cost of obtaining and operating the franchise?

13. How can the franchise agreement be terminated?

14. Are the operating controls reasonable or burdensome?

15. Are the services you receive from the franchisor adequate and useful? Are they clearly spelled out?

16. What kind of support will you receive in opening and operating the franchise?

17. Is financing help available from the franchisor?

CHAPTER PERSPECTIVE

The franchising phenomenon has opened up wide new vistas for the aspiring businessperson. Franchises allow someone with limited resources and experience to team up with a large, going concern. However, extreme care and meticulous preparation must be exercised in order to avoid the risks and surprises that can be a part of the franchise relationship.

Employment Law

INTRODUCTION

Most entrepreneurs have worked for someone else during their careers, and would probably agree on this: The employer may be the boss, but he doesn't own me. You might benefit by recalling that simple sentence several times a day.

Remembering that your employees are people makes good business sense because your ability to hire and retain the best employees will be enhanced. It also will remind you that failure to plan and define the employer-employee relationship in your business can be energy-draining and costly.

Careful and professional management of employee relations should not only make your business a happier place to be, but it should also help your bottom line.

Employment law originates from two primary sources: so-called common law and statutory law. Common law comes from court decisions and interpretations over many years. Statutory law is based on specific statutes, like the 1964 Civil Rights Act. Taken together, these laws impose significant obligations on you as employer.

After studying the material in this chapter:

— You will know the basic legal requirements in hiring, managing, and firing employees.

— You will be able to identify some major discrimination issues in the employer-employee relationship.

— You will understand some basic requirements concerning pay and working conditions.

— You will know how to avoid problems with the new immigration requirements.

— You will know how to act in a lawful manner when employees launch union organizing drives.

— You will be able to keep appropriate records.

■■ You will understand the requirements for federal and state withholding taxes.

HIRING AND FIRING: YOUR RIGHTS AND THEIRS

Effective employee selection and management can mean the difference between success and failure in your business, so before you interview your first candidate, think ahead.

Even without requirements written into laws or regulations, the courts have provided a "code of behavior" in employer-employee relations. This section briefly explains that code.

Employee hiring, management, and termination are closely intertwined elements. Without developing a careful plan for personnel management, you may find it difficult or impossible to fire an unsatisfactory employee later. And if you do fire someone, it may cost you a lot of money.

Some meticulous employers take as much care in choosing employees as in choosing a spouse. They have learned what you need to know: The record for evaluating both employer and employee performance begins with the application form and the interview.

If the process is done correctly, you will have better employee relations, and you will have the needed flexibility for terminating nonproductive and troublesome employees. Consider an old legal concept, the "Employment at Will Rule." Simply stated, the concept says that without a specific contractual agreement, the employee can quit at any time, and the employer can dismiss the employee at any time. No reason is required. This is not an entirely discarded concept, but any employer who behaves as if it is still the normal way to do business is treading on dangerous ground. Employment at will may not be dead, but it is severely wounded.

The concept was weakened by the rise of the labor union movement in North America, and both courts and legislatures have continued to carve out exceptions to the doctrine.

Three primary areas of exception have emerged from the courts:

1. The "public policy" exception. Under this standard, for example, you as an employer cannot discipline or terminate an employee for refusing to perform an illegal act. Neither can you punish an employee for exercising a legal right or privilege, such as actively participation in

politics (so long as it does not affect the business enterprise), or "whistle-blowing," or reporting illegal or fraudulent activities in the company.

2. The "implied contract" exception. These implied promises can be made in the interview, in the personnel policies, in personnel evaluations, and in various other forms. Later in this section some precautions for avoiding trouble here will be outlined. Keep in mind that contracts do not have to be written; they may constitute obligations on your part even if you were not aware at the time that you were obligating yourself.

3. The "implied covenant of good faith and fair dealing" exception. This is a far more nebulous standard, and it has less currency than the two previous exceptions. Briefly stated, it means that you can terminate an employee only if there is "good cause." This is an approach that strikes fear in the hearts of employers and personnel managers because of its subjective and unpredictable nature.

As stated at the outset of this chapter, thinking through the entire employment relationship is a useful exercise.

Your application form should be straightforward and ask only questions clearly applicable to the job. Some of the discrimination pitfalls will be discussed in the following section. The form should in no way indulge in boosterism or talk about the long and happy work tenure of other company employees. (The mention of tenure of any kind is one of those implied contracts just mentioned above.)

Treat the interview as if it were a formal, written document because enthusiastic oral enticements can also come back to haunt you later as an implied contractual commitment.

Do not promise annual performance reviews, either in the application or the interview. If you discover long before the annual review that the employee is unsuited for the job, you still may be stuck for the full year because of an implied promise.

Make sure that your recruiters and subordinates are sensitive to these considerations; make sure that they make no promises on behalf of your company.

Further insurance might come from this kind of language on the application form, to be signed by the applicant:

I understand and agree that no representative of the company has any authority to promise employment for a specified period of time or to make other representations concerning employment advancement.

Periodically review and revise application forms, job descriptions, personnel policies, company internal communication organs (such as newsletters), training manuals, and any other written documents concerning employment. The purpose of this review is to ensure that current employment law issues are appropriately addressed in your business. The nuances of sex discrimination, for example, have changed dramatically in the past few years, making obsolete many past employment practices.

Establish a fair and equitable system for evaluation and performance reviews. Build a comprehensive file on your efforts to communicate these reviews to the employee. Remember, however: The reviews should contain no implied promises about advancement or tenure.

Routine disciplinary procedures should be carefully considered. For one thing, it is simply good personnel management. For another, it could be important protection against charges of discrimination or other violations of employee rights.

Progressive discipline in accordance with written personnel policies—made available to all employees—is a generally accepted correct form of personnel management. The details may vary in form, but they could involve increasingly severe discipline through an oral warning, written reprimand, demotion, suspension, and discharge. Whatever the details, the rules should be applied uniformly and communicated to all employees. Keep a detailed written file on each disciplinary case, and make its contents available only to the affected employee.

And always remember: Be *consistent* in the administration of disciplinary procedures, and *communicate* these procedures so that employees understand them.

The style of discipline or termination is also important. It should be nonthreatening, without personal vilification of any kind, and private. It should be unembellished with what might be labeled false and misrepresentative charges. It does your cause no good to prompt a lawsuit based on invasion of privacy, defamation, or intentional infliction of emotional distress.

After termination, an exit interview with the employee can be helpful in explaining how to better handle the next job. It might also dampen any ill will felt toward you and your company. If you include severance pay, require that a release from liability and covenant not to sue be required before payment.

Hiring and Firing Checklist

If you answer no to any of these questions, you have some additional work to do.

1. Do you avoid terms like "long term," "guaranteed," "job security," "good cause" and the like in your applications, interviews, personnel policies, and all other company documents?
2. Do you periodically review all of the above?
3. Are all recruiters and subordinate personnel briefed on this policy?
4. Is your discipline and termination process uniformly and privately applied?
5. Do you keep comprehensive and accurate files on personnel matters, including discipline and termination?
6. Do you consider your personnel practices to be essentially fair?

DISCRIMINATION

Antidiscrimination laws have mushroomed during the past 25 years. The civil rights movement and race discrimination provided major momentum for these laws, but employers should be alert to antidiscrimination requirements in other areas, such as sex discrimination. This section will provide an overview of these requirements.

Much of the law banning discrimination has evolved from court decisions over the past few decades, but Ronald Reagan's appointments to the U.S. Supreme Court have signaled a pullback from the broad findings of discrimination that marked the prior quarter century.

In a series of 1989 opinions, the court rewrote long-settled rules of proof and procedure in employment discrimination cases. The decisions set strict time limits on challenges to discriminatory seniority systems and made discrimination suits harder to bring, harder to win, and more vulnerable to attack if successfully concluded.

Prudent employers, however, will continue to exercise care to avoid charges of discrimination.

Although a significant body of federal law sets the framework for antidiscrimination requirements, you need to be aware that a crazy-quilt, varied mixture of state law also exists. Federal laws establish basic requirements; state laws embellish those requirements in some states.

Additionally, some localities—municipalities or county governments—also have their own special requirements (for example, requirements for minority business contractors who do local government business).

In a nutshell, what the antidiscrimination laws require you to do is to deal with your employees without regard to race, color, sex, religion, national origin, or age. There are a few narrow, specific exclusions, but be very careful to understand those exclusions. Antidiscrimination laws have teeth.

Warning: "Discrimination" has a broader definition than many people realize. Examples are given later in this section.

Nondiscrimination requirements apply to advertising, recruitment, hiring, placement, promotion, transfer, training and apprenticeship, compensation, layoffs, and termination.

The primary federal enforcement authority is the Equal Employment Opportunity Commission (EEOC). Major laws administered by EEOC include:

Title VII of the Civil Rights Act of 1964, as amended

The Age Discrimination in Employment Act of 1967, as amended

The Equal Pay Act of 1963

Passage of the 1964 Civil Rights Act set an historic new direction in employment practices. Title VII of that law is the origin of most of the requirements outlined in this section. Specific reference is made to other laws where applicable.

Much of the court-made law stems from Title VII. In the wake of 1989 U.S. Supreme Court decisions that seemed to pull back from earlier civil rights findings, new legislation to supplement Title VII appears to be a possibility.

Your state or local office of EEOC will have brochures, posters, and other information about their programs. Your state EEOC or equal rights commission should also be checked for additional requirements and programs.

Before you brush past the issue of discrimination by saying, "I would never discriminate . . . I'm just looking for the best person," look a bit more carefully at your management practices.

On your application form or in your interview, do you ask health questions that are not directly related to the job . . .

questions that identify an applicant's age (birth date or dates concerning school attendance) . . . questions about handicaps . . . questions about arrests and convictions . . . questions about physical characteristics that could identify the applicant as a minority (hair or eye color) . . . questions about size or height . . . educational questions for menial jobs . . . questions concerning child care requirements . . . or what form of transportation the applicant would use to get to work?

Intentional discrimination for any reason is generally illegal (some of the few exceptions will be listed later). So is *unintentional* discrimination, and the questions above are examples of practices that might be used to make a case of discrimination against you or your company, although the 1989 court decisions make proof of such discrimination more difficult.

If you ask an applicant a question, or if you state a requirement, the court could assume that the question or requirement is a factor in your employment decision. So, do not use any question or requirement unless it is job related. And if it is job related, make sure that omitting it would have an adverse business impact that you can prove.

Before the 1989 decisions, employers could be found guilty of discrimination because of the numerical "adverse impact" of certain employment practices. For example: when white workers hold all the management jobs, while minority employees hold nonsupervisory, low-paying jobs.

In deciding a case that revolved around hiring practices of an Alaskan salmon company, however, the court in 1989 held that employment policies that tend to concentrate nonwhite workers in low-paying jobs do not necessarily violate federal civil rights law. This decision appears to be a move away from the adverse impact rule to an earlier "evil motive" standard that would require a higher level of proof by employees.

Title VII applies if you are in an "industry affecting commerce" and have 15 or more employees for each working day in each of 20 or more calendar weeks during the current or preceding year. However, some states have antidiscrimination laws that cover companies with fewer employees.

Although it is now understood that Title VII has much broader implications, discrimination against racial minorities was a driving force for passage of the law. The civil rights movement leading to passage of Title VII focused on racial discrimination, and its elimination was seen as a prime objective of Title VII.

However, the U.S. Supreme Court has also held that discrimination against all individuals, not just minorities, is forbidden under Title VII. The so-called reverse discrimination suits—in which a "majority" might sue an employer who promoted a "minority" with less seniority or apparent qualifications—are also based on Title VII.

With some exceptions, employment discrimination based on sex is also forbidden. And in 1978, the Pregnancy Disability Amendment to Title VII was enacted to protect the employment rights of pregnant women.

The protection against religious discrimination requires that employers take the affirmative step of accommodating diverse religious beliefs and practices.

Title VII also bans employment discrimination based on national origin. This is tricky, because employment can be refused because of noncitizenship but not on the basis of national origin.

Following are some of the discrimination wrinkles aside from the race issue.

SEX DISCRIMINATION

When Title VII was passed, the ban on discrimination because of sex was not taken seriously. Now there is a large body of evidence of the adverse effects of discrimination because of sex, and enforcement of this aspect of Title VII is taken very seriously.

There is, however, an important exception to the ban against discrimination based on sex as provided in Title VII. It is the "bona fide occupational qualification" (BFOQ) exception. This exception also applies to discrimination because of religion or national origin. Examples of where the BFOQ applies: An actress to play the role of a woman in a play; a male attendant for a men's room. Examples where the court found BFOQ does not apply: A telephone company that would not hire women as switch repairers because of the requirement to lift 30 pounds; airlines that limited jobs as cabin attendants to women.

Some states have gotten very specific in recommending ways to avoid discrimination in the selection and hiring process. For example, one state's regulations include the following discriminatory terms and suggested substitutes:

Discriminatory Terms	Suggested Substitutes
attractive, pretty	well-groomed, presentable
auto parts man	auto parts work

Discriminatory Terms	Suggested Substitutes
bar maid	bar help, bar waiter/waitress
bell boy	bell hop, bell man/woman
body man	body work
busboy, tray girl	busser, dish busser
camera man	camera technician
cleaning woman	cleaning
corpsman	paramedic, medical assistant
counter girl/boy	counter work
doorman	door attendant
draftsman	drafting
farm man	farm hand; farm work
foreman	foreman—man or woman
girl Friday	general office M/W
handyman	handyman or handywoman
host, hostess	host/hostess
janitor, janitress	janitor/janitress; custodian
journeyman	journeyman—male or female
leadman	crew leader, shift leader
maid	domestic help, housekeeper
maintenance man	maintenance work
nurse	nurse—man or woman
phone girls	phone work; phone sales
pressman	pressman/presswoman
repairman	repair work; repairs
stewardess	cabin attendant

Once a woman is employed and working for your company, be alert to two other requirements:

The equal pay requirement for women working in the same jobs as men

The prohibition of bogus job titles as a way of circumventing the equal pay provision.

If you have both males and females filling a job position classified as "manager," pay must be equal regardless of sex. If you have males and females doing the same work, but the male is classified as "coordinator" and the female is classified "secretary"—with the male being paid more—that is an illegal effort to circumvent the law through meaningless job titles. Be sure to look to the substance of the work.

Caution: Eliminate references to "head of household" in job applications and promotion policies. You are not allowed to use this consideration as a method of avoiding the equal pay requirement.

Pregnancy leaves must be treated the same as any other disability leave, regardless of sex. Title VII is supplemented in this area by the Pregnancy Discrimination Act of 1978. Male employers should be particularly cautious not to let old-fashioned attitudes toward pregnancy adversely affect their personnel or employment policies toward female employees.

If the company routinely provides alternative jobs for disabled employees unable to perform their regular jobs, the company must do the same for pregnant employees. The company must not place pregnant employees on leave if they are still able to work, unless they utilize a procedure that is applied to all disabled employees. If the company routinely holds jobs open for disabled employees on leave, the same must apply to females on pregnancy leave. On matters of seniority, pay increases, and vacation time, pregnant females must be treated the same as any other employee on leave because of medical reasons.

A special area of caution concerns sexual harassment. In a 1988 survey of 160 personnel executives at Fortune 500 companies, 64 percent of the sample believed that most sexual harassment charges were valid and almost 90 percent had received a sexual harassment complaint within the 12-month period prior to the survey.

Probably the most important finding, however, was that the most common defense used against sexual harassment charges was: "I was joking."

For you as employer, this is no joke. Keep in mind:

Intent is irrelevant; the effect is the important thing.

The company has a responsibility to correct demeaning work environments or those that promote harassment.

Sexual harassment on the job can range from blatant physical and verbal aggression to gentle patting and subtle coercion by men seeking sexual favors. Women—or men—of any age working at any job can be victims of sexual harassment.

Sexual harassment can be defined as verbal or physical conduct by a co-worker or supervisor of a sexual nature or with sexual overtones, with direct employment consequences.

Since sexual harassment is difficult to quantify, and since charges are sometimes difficult to prove, courts have differed in their interpretations of the law. For employers, the lesson seems to be to include prohibitions in personnel policies and handbooks; to brief all supervisors with regard to the law and consequences for violating it; and to monitor the workplace to assure compliance.

AGE DISCRIMINATION

The Age Discrimination in Employment Act of 1967 makes it illegal to discriminate against persons over the age of 40 on the basis of age. Because of the country's changing age profile, this law now seems well timed for preparing us to use our aging work force.

The law covers workers to age 70, and it removes the mandatory retirement age of 70 for most of the nation's private sector workers. This law applies to employers with 20 or more employees, public employees, employment agencies serving such employers, and labor organizations with 25 or more members.

There are some important exceptions to this law. For example, in some cases age is a bona fide consideration, such as a child actor playing a youngster or if the job entails strenuous physical activity that makes age relevant. There are also exemptions under certain circumstances that apply to bona fide seniority systems; to firefighters and police officers; to executive positions; and to apprenticeship programs.

Employers must offer all employees and their spouses 65 years of age and older the same group health coverage, under the same conditions, as is offered to employees and their spouses under age 65.

RELIGIOUS DISCRIMINATION

An employer, once notified, must make reasonable attempts to accommodate an employee's religious practices. However, the employer may choose the best method for accommodating those practices.

The employee is not allowed to impose accommodations that cause undue hardship to the company or its other employees.

Discrimination Checklist

The employer needs to be able to answer yes to the following questions. If not, some changes in employment practices should be made.

1. Do your applications and interviews contain only job-related questions?
2. Have you eliminated questions that might be statistically linked to a charge of discrimination because of race, sex, religion, or age?
3. Do job descriptions contain requirements that have clear and direct relationships to the needs and responsibilities of the job?

4. Are men and women who perform the same job in your company treated equally in pay and benefits?
5. Is everyone in the company aware of the definition of sexual harassment and the prohibition against it?
6. Does your company prohibit age discrimination in hiring, job retention, and compensation?
7. Do you respect religious differences in your employment and personnel practices? Do you actively try to accommodate religious differences?

FAIR LABOR STANDARDS ACT

The Fair Labor Standards Act has undergone a variety of changes since its passage in 1938—for example, from a 40-cent-per-hour minimum wage to $3.35—but the basic purpose remains: to ensure a fair wage for workers, to protect minors from exploitation and dangerous occupations, and to shorten the work week while spreading the available work among more workers.

The law establishes a minimum wage requirement, child labor standards, and overtime requirements to achieve this purpose. The Wage and Hour Division of the Department of Labor administers and enforces this law with respect to private employment.

Basic Wage Standards

Employers must pay covered workers a specified minimum wage and overtime pay at not less than one and one-half times regular pay after 40 hours of work in a work week. Any deductions from regular pay for such things as uniforms or tools of the trade are prohibited if they reduce wages to below the minimum wage or reduce overtime pay to less than time and one-half.

The law contains some specific exemptions, but they are narrowly defined. Subminimum wage provisions apply to certain student learners and to individuals whose earnings or productive capacity is impaired by age or physical or mental deficiency or injury. Check with the local Wage-Hour office if you think you have employees who fall under an exemption.

Exemptions

The following are exempt from both minimum wage and overtime pay requirements:

Executive, administrative, and professional employees and outside salespersons.

Employees of certain individually owned and operated small retail or service establishments.

Employees of certain seasonal amusement or recreational establishments, employees of certain small newspapers, switchboard operators of small telephone companies, seamen employed on foreign vessels, and employees engaged in fishing operations.

Farm workers employed by anyone who used no more than 500 "man-days" of farm labor in any calendar quarter of the preceding calendar year.

Casual babysitters and persons employed as companions to the elderly or infirm.

Certain other specific exemptions apply to the overtime requirements; in some cases, partial exemptions apply. Check the Wage-Hour office when in doubt.

Some employment practices are not regulated under this law. They include:

Vacation, holiday, severance, or sick pay

Meal or rest periods, holidays, and vacations

Premium pay for weekend or holiday work

Pay raises or fringe benefits

Discharge notices, reasons for discharge, or payment of final wages to terminated employees

Any limit on the number of hours worked by persons 16 years and older

Tipping is a special case. A tipped employee is one who customarily and regularly receives more than $30 a month in tips. In computing minimum wage, the employer may consider tips as wages, but such wage credit may not exceed 40 percent of the minimum wage.

Throughout this book a distinction is made between your employees and independent contractors, and this difference is important here. Wage-hour provisions apply to employees but not to independent contractors.

Each case is examined on the basis of its own facts, but if the company sets the hours of work; dictates the methods by which the work will be accomplished; pays an hourly wage; supplies materials and tools; furnishes space, telephone, or secretarial services; or sets fixed geographic limits on the work—chances increase that the person will be called an employee, not an independent contractor.

CHILD LABOR PROVISIONS

These provisions were designed not only to limit the working hours of minors and thus to protect their educational opportunities, but also to prohibit minors from working in certain hazardous farm and nonfarm occupations.

These three requirements apply to non-farm jobs:

Youths 18 and older may perform any job, hazardous or not, for unlimited hours.

Youths 16 and 17 may perform nonhazardous jobs for unlimited hours.

Youths 14 and 15 may work outside school hours in various nonmanufacturing, nonmining, nonhazardous jobs under the following restrictions: no more than three hours on a school day, 18 hours in a school week, eight hours on a nonschool day, or 40 hours in a nonschool week. Special exceptions apply to approved work experience programs.

Youths of any age may deliver newspapers; perform in radio, television, movie, or theatrical productions; work for parents in their solely owned nonfarm businesses (except in manufacturing or hazardous jobs).

These five requirements apply in farm jobs:

Youths 16 and older may perform any job, hazardous or not, for unlimited hours.

Youths 14 and 15 may perform any nonhazardous farm job outside of school hours.

Youths 12 and 13 may work outside of school hours in nonhazardous jobs, either with a parent's written permission or on the same farm as the parents.

Youths under 12 may perform jobs on farms owned and operated by parents or with parents' written permission outside of school hours in nonhazardous jobs on farms not covered by minimum wage requirements.

Minors of any age may be employed by their parents at any time in any occupation on a farm owned and operated by their parents.

Fair Labor Standards Act Checklist

Check with the local Wage-Hour office or your attorney if you cannot answer yes to the following questions.

1. Have you ascertained whether your business is covered by requirements of the Fair Labor Standards Act?
2. Have you carefully determined that persons you treat as exempt are truly exempt?

3. Are you confident that persons you consider independent contractors are so defined under the law?
4. Do you know how to compute minimum wage when tipping is involved?
5. Are you familiar with your responsibility toward youth workers?

WORKERS COMPENSATION AND UNEMPLOYMENT COMPENSATION

A company's obligations toward its employees extends beyond the work hours—and in some cases beyond the actual time of employment.

Workers compensation deals with accidental injuries, illnesses, and deaths arising from the course of employment. Unemployment compensation deals with involuntary unemployment.

State laws define which employers must participate in these programs, and size of company does not necessarily matter.

Workers Compensation

Prior to the turn of the century, it was difficult for employees to sue their employers because of injuries, and if they did so, proving negligence on the part of employers was even tougher. All that has changed because of workers compensation statutes, which exist in all 50 states. The purpose of these statutes is to provide a minimal level of security for employees.

The coverage and details of workers compensation laws vary from state to state, and they include both hazardous and nonhazardous occupations. The laws have some basic features in common:

They allow injured employees to recover on the basis of "strict liability." This means the employee does not have to prove negligence by the employer.

They eliminate the employer's traditional defenses concerning negligence by the employee or voluntary assumption of risk by the employee.

They make workers compensation the employee's exclusive remedy against the employer.

Because workers compensation is a social compromise, based on strict liability, the statutes generally set the amounts that can be recovered at amounts lower than that which might be obtained in a successful negligence lawsuit against the employer.

Interpretations vary from state to state, but a basic element of workers compensation is that the injury must arise out of the employment, and it must happen in the course of employment. An employee injured by falling boxes in a warehouse would recover; one injured while engaging in horseplay with fellow employees during the lunch break probably would not.

State laws stipulate which companies must participate and which are exempt. Size does not necessarily matter.

The customary categories of damages are:

Hospital and medical expenses

Disability benefits

Specified money awards for the loss of certain bodily parts

Death benefit payments to survivors and/or dependents

As an employer, you must obtain workers compensation insurance. In some instances, you will be allowed to self-insure or to participate in a state fund.

For detailed information, contact your state's department of labor or your insurance agent.

Unemployment Compensation

Most employers are covered by this program, which is financed almost entirely from employer taxes.

State programs vary widely, but the general purpose of unemployment compensation is to pay benefits to persons who have worked a specific number of weeks within the 12-month period preceding the application for benefits. Persons who quit their job without good cause, or are terminated for misconduct, or refuse an offer of appropriate work do not qualify.

Benefit levels vary from state to state, as does the length of time that benefits can be received. During economic downturns the maximum period for receiving benefits may be extended.

Workers Compensation and Unemployment Compensation Checklist

If you cannot answer yes to the following questions, check with your accountant, attorney or insurance agent.

1. Do you know your company's obligations concerning workers compensation and unemployment compensation?
2. Are you properly covered with insurance for workers compensation?

3. Do you periodically monitor premiums and claims under workers compensation and unemployment compensation?

IMMIGRATION LAW AND ALIEN WORKERS

The Immigration Reform and Control Act of 1986 applies to all American employers, although the practical impact is heaviest in areas such as the Southwest and Florida. Because of the relative newness of the law, forms and regulations continue to evolve. For information and forms, call your nearest U.S. Immigration and Naturalization Service (INS) office. Also check your telephone directory for an INS information program called "Ask Immigration."

The INS recommends these procedures to ensure compliance with the law:

1. Hire only citizens and aliens lawfully authorized to work in the U.S. Do this by requiring all new employees to complete and sign a verification form provided by INS and by carefully examining documentation provided by new employees.
2. Continue to advise all new job applicants of your policy to that effect.
3. Retain the form for three years or for one year past the end of employment of the individual, whichever is longer.
4. If requested, present the form for inspection by INS or Department of Labor officers.

Caution: Avoid any temptation simply not to hire applicants who are "foreign looking" or who have an accent. You are then violating antidiscrimination laws.

The employment eligibility form, Form I-9, may be obtained from INS. Instructions list documents that you may use for establishing identity and employment eligibility.

Immigration Checklist

You should be able to answer yes to the following questions. If not, check with your attorney or the local office of INS for the proper procedure and records.

1. Do you fill out Form I-9 on new employees?
2. Do you inform all employees of the company's policy with regard to hiring only U.S. citizens and aliens authorized to work?

3. Do you actually check forms submitted for documentation?

UNIONS

Labor unions emerged as the working man's answer to large industrial companies. They provided a vehicle for employees to present grievances, improve working conditions, and bargain for wages and benefits.

Eventually, some labor unions also become huge, vulnerable to corruption, and subject to intense criticism. In recent years, the percentage of American workers represented by unions has dropped markedly.

The large body of labor law created through this process, however, is still critical to employer-employee relations. It applies prior to the time that employees are represented by a union, or a "bargaining unit."

When a bargaining unit comes into existence, the employer-employee relationship described by the requirements already discussed is supplemented by a contract. Examples of contract provisions include wages, which cannot be reduced below the federally required figure but can be placed at any amount higher by the union contract; and overtime, pay for which cannot drop below the federally required time and one-half, but can be raised to double time or another figure.

Union contracts typically have dealt with pay and benefits, but in recent years—because of the rising tide of imported products in this country—contracts have increasingly dealt with other issues, such as a company's plans to keep a plant open or union representation on the company's board of directors.

The basic labor relations law is the federal National Labor Relations Act (NLRA), and it is administered by the National Labor Relations Board (NLRB).

A variety of factors can lead to union elections, but most commentators seem to agree that poor management of employee relations is always a factor. Fairness, consistency, open communications, and response to employee complaints are critical management responsibilities, and when they are sloughed off or done poorly, they often lead to union problems.

Once you come face to face with the possibility of an election whereby a bargaining unit would represent employees, get some advice from an attorney specializing in labor law. This area of law is technical and precise.

Labor law establishes procedures and protocols that require careful attention. As an employer, you are allowed to argue against representation by a bargaining unit—but only under certain circumstances. There are several activities expressly forbidden. Here are some examples of things you may and may not do.

Things You May Do

■ Tell employees that if a bargaining unit is approved, the company will deal with the union on daily problems involving conditions of employment, wages, hours, and other matters.

■ Reassure employees that you will always discuss problems and requests with them.

■ Outline benefits currently received without union representation—but without any threat that those benefits will be removed with union representation.

■ Inform employees of specific costs and disciplinary measures that may be imposed by the union.

■ Inform employees of the union's rights to call strikes or work stoppages.

■ Compare your company's pay, benefits, and working conditions to other companies in the area.

Things You May Not Do

■ Bribe any employee with pay increases or other special privileges to oppose the union.

■ Threaten loss of jobs, benefits, or income because of the union drive.

■ Favor antiunion employees over prounion employees in any way.

■ Threaten, discipline, or terminate any employee because of union activities.

■ Threaten to close a plant or move it because of union activities.

■ Ask employees whether they favor a union and how they intend to vote in a union election.

■ State that you will not deal with a union.

■ Speak to "captive audience" employees on company time within 24 hours before the opening of the polls for a union election.

■ Present false or misleading information in an effort to influence the election.

■ Spy on employees involved in union organizing activities.

Some Basic Steps in the Process

Employees can initiate union representation by filing a petition at an NLRB regional office. The persons filing the petition must include documentation showing that at least 30 percent of the employees of the proposed bargaining unit support the petition. Authorization cards signed by the employees are typically used.

An NLRB official will determine that an appropriate bargaining unit exists, that the authorization cards or other documentation are valid, and whether any legal obstacles to a representation election exist. The NLRB will also hold a hearing for the union and company representatives to work out the details of the election, and NLRB representatives will count the ballots. Either side may appeal the results of the election or the manner in which it was held.

Union Checklist

You should be able to answer yes to the following questions.

1. Do you and your supervisors stay abreast of employee concerns and complaints?
2. Are you fair, communicative, and consistent in dealing with employees?
3. Are you careful to avoid intimidating or threatening behavior in any way toward prounion employees?
4. Do you avoid spying or other invasions of privacy in order to gain information about union organizing activities?
5. Do you consult with an attorney specializing in labor law with regard to union organizing activities?
6. Do you grant raises and promotions and administer discipline without regard to prounion activities?

KEEPING EMPLOYMENT RECORDS: THE LEGAL REQUIREMENTS

The Internal Revenue Service requires that you keep for at least four years certain information relating to your employees:

Names, addresses, Social Security numbers, and occupations

Dates of employment

Copies of income tax withholding certificates (Form W-4)

Amounts and dates of all wages, annuity, and pension payments you made to employees and the fair market value of any "in-kind" payments (such as groceries given by a supermarket to its employees)

Amount of tips reported to the IRS (Form 8027, Employer's Information Return of Tip Income)

Amounts and dates of payments made to employees while they were absent due to sickness or injury

Records of fringe benefits you provided to the employee, whether taxable (vacations, personal use of company car) or nontaxable (certain kinds of insurance, retirement plans)

Dates and amounts of tax deposits you made. Keep your canceled checks and copies of Form 8109, Federal Tax Deposit Coupon. Keep similar state returns.

Copies of all employment-related tax returns such as Forms 940 (Federal Unemployment Tax Return) and 941 (Quarterly Return of Withheld Income Tax and Social Security Taxes). Keep similar state returns.

Since doubt might later arise about your classification of a worker as an independent contractor (a nonemployee), you should retain information, including your written contract with any contractors, that confirms your understanding.

EMPLOYMENT TAXES

Who Is an Employee?

There are certain taxes you will have to pay because you have employees. Example: state and federal unemployment insurance and the employer's matching portion of the employee's Social Security tax. Not everyone you pay to perform services is an *employee*. The attorney you consult to help you incorporate your business is not your employee. Neither is the public accountant who fills out your tax return. The law refers to these persons as independent contractors.

Let's try another example. Suppose you arrange for a handicapped worker, who has to stay at home all day, to take down and record phone orders for you. Every evening you drive over and pick up the orders. Is that worker your employee . . . or an independent contractor?

The legal issue here is *control* and, to a lesser extent, other factors such as method of pay. If you can control the details of how the work will be done, the worker is more likely to be considered to be an employee. There are other indications of employment: Typically, an employee is paid an hourly wage, while an independent contractor is paid on commission or by the job and bills you on letterhead stationery for the work performed.

The contractor provides his or her own equipment and place of work, pays expenses, and has the right to hire others to assist without asking your approval. It is best to write up a contract specifying how these matters will be handled.

The IRS is aware that some business owners try to avoid liability for employment taxes by calling their workers independent contractors. If you have any doubt about your conformity to the law, study IRS Publication 539, Employment Taxes. It gives examples of the employer-employee relationship. Also, you can request an official IRS decision on how your workers should be handled by filing Form SS-8, Information for Use in Determining Whether a Worker Is an Employee.

Overview of Federal Employment Taxes

Several taxes must be paid by employers. Some of these are the liability of the employee, but the employer must withhold them from the employee's pay and make payments to the government or to a designated bank. Examples are state income taxes and federal income and Social Security taxes. IRS Form 941 is used to report federal tax withheld.

Other taxes are the direct obligation of the employer: state and federal unemployment tax and the employer's matching portion of Social Security tax. Size of the payroll determines how frequently payments must be made, with quarterly payments being the most common for small businesses. Federal unemployment tax (FUTA) is reported on Form 940.

How to Begin Meeting Your Employment Tax Responsibilities

You should apply for an Employer Identification Number (EIN) by filing Form SS-4. You will need to insert this number on all federal and state tax returns. Then, from each employee you should obtain:

> Social Security number. It is safest to record this number directly from the employee's Social Security card.
>
> Form I-9 , Employment Eligibility Verification Form, to verify U.S. citizenship or eligibility of a foreign national to work in this country.
>
> Form W-4, Employee's Withholding Allowance Certificate, to determine how many withholding exemptions the worker claims.

You will also need to set up a calendar of dates at which state and federal tax returns and payments are due. Next, you must secure the state and federal forms on which to file your returns.

The IRS's Circular E (also referred to as Publication 15), Employer's Tax Guide, is the primary source of information about filing returns and paying federal employment taxes. Contact your state revenue office for help with state employment taxes. Some communities have local "occupation" taxes that must be paid.

Tip: The paperwork is time-consuming and the penalties for mistakes are sometimes severe; many small businesses entrust employment tax matters to an experienced bookkeeper or accountant.

Sample of an employment tax calendar:

January 31	Give each employee a completed Form W-2. File Forms 940 and 941. Deposit FUTA tax if more than $100.
February 28	File Form W-3 to report to the Social Security Administration. Report allocated tips on Form 8027.
Other dates	By April 30, July 31, and October 31, deposit FUTA tax and file Form 941.
State tax	Contact state authorities.

Warning: Federal law is rigid in enforcing payment; penalties for late payment can be as high as 25 percent. If income or Social Security taxes are not withheld or are not paid, the penalty can be as high as 100 percent. The responsible officers or employees of the business can be held *personally* liable for these taxes and penalties.

CHAPTER PERSPECTIVE

You do not have to be told how important your relationship to your customers and clients is. Don't forget, however, the critical role of your relationship to your employees. This requires constant attention, from recruiting to termination. Otherwise, you might be paying more attention to employee problems than to delivery of your product—and paying dearly for it.

What You Should Know About Taxes

Our goal in this chapter is to alert you to some of the most common federal tax problems and opportunities for saving federal taxes faced by small businesses. After an overview of tax law as it relates to small business, we begin at the beginning: the tax aspects involved in determining the pros and cons of starting a new business.

After studying the material in this chapter:

▬ You will understand what income is taxed and what business expenses are deductible.

▬ You will see the pitfalls when you investigate starting up a business.

▬ You will know how to choose the cash or accrual methods for reporting income and expenses.

▬ You will know the books and records you must keep for tax purposes.

▬ You will understand the circumstances under which you can take a tax deduction for an office in your home.

▬ You will know how to avoid the hobby loss restrictions.

▬ You will understand deductions for depreciation, travel, auto expenses.

STATE TAX LAW

Businesses are liable for one or more kinds of taxes in most states in which they operate. All states with the exception of Nevada, Texas, Washington, and Wyoming levy a tax on corporate income. Only these four plus Alaska, Florida, and South Dakota omit a tax on unincorporated business income. Without exception, every state imposes one or more sales, use, capital values, real property, or personal property tax. Some municipalities, particularly the larger cities, charge one or more taxes on business. In other words, even if you are able to avoid federal income taxes—and they're the ones that hurt—expect to pay some tax to some authority. That's the price we pay for civilization!

Because of the great diversity of state and local laws, we can't cover them here. Your best sources of information are the forms and manuals available from your state's department of revenue, workshops offered by the Small Business Development Center of a local college, or an accountant who has several years experience keeping books and preparing tax returns in your locality.

OVERVIEW OF BUSINESS TAXATION

Many of the concepts you are familiar with in your individual tax return—such as standard or itemized deductions, personal and dependent's exemption, and adjusted gross income—are unknown in the taxation of businesses. Business income tax is simpler. There are three steps. First, add up all income. Second, add up all ordinary and necessary business expenses. Next, subtract the second from the first to get the firm's taxable income. Apply a tax rate to this taxable income and you have figured out how much you owe Uncle Sam.

There are very few exceptions to this formula. Interest income on municipal bonds is not included in income, for instance. Illegal bribes and kickbacks are not deductible.

A crucial step in this simple scheme of business taxation is determining that an expense is ordinary and necessary to your business.

BUSINESS EXPENSE

You're aware that Congress has created deductions for certain medical expenses, taxes, mortgage interest on your home, and specified other personal expenses. *Only* those few personal expenses that your lawmakers have listed in the tax code are deductible.

With business . . . it's different. *All* "ordinary and necessary" business expenses are deductible from business income. "Ordinary" means customary and usual for that type of business. To be "necessary" doesn't mean that you were forced to incur the cost. All that is required is that the expense be appropriate and helpful to your business.

Example: You pay group life insurance premiums for your employees. You don't have to provide this fringe benefit, but you feel you can get a better company spirit if you do so. These costs are deductible business expenses, because it is helpful to your business to provide these benefits.

Once you have your trade or business up and running, practically every expenditure will be ordinary and necessary as long as it furthers your goal of earning a profit. Just be sure you don't pay any personal living expenses for yourself, friends, or members of your family. (If you're traveling away from home overnight on business, however, your lodging, meals, and transportation costs are not personal expenses; they're business expenses.)

Ordinary and necessary business expenses must also be reasonable. Unless you spend in a truly extravagant manner, however, you're not likely to run afoul of the IRS on this score, except in regard to compensation.

Unreasonable Compensation

Wages or salary paid to yourself or to employees can be deducted from income and thus reduce the tax bill of your business. The same is true for fees you pay to a consultant or contractor. It doesn't matter to *whom* you make the payment, just as long as the work was actually performed. On the other hand, if your business is incorporated, dividends that you pay to your stockholders—representing their share of corporate profits—are not deductible. Uncle Sam treats dividends as being paid with after-tax dollars.

Let's suppose one or more employees are also stockholders of the business. Why not pay salaries instead of dividends? If you and your spouse need $50,000 to live on . . . then make the business pay you that amount in salary. That's a lot better than $30,000 in salary and $20,000 in dividends. (Depending upon the level of your total corporate income, it might take $30,000 taxable income to pay you dividends of $20,000 after corporate taxes.)

The motivation for paying salaries instead of dividends is to get the maximum tax deduction. It doesn't matter a great deal to individuals whether they get salary or dividends; the tax is the same on both. However, since the corporation can deduct salaries paid, its stockholders are better off than the owners of a corporation that pays dividends. The salary-paying business has more money left after taxes.

There is one problem. An IRS examiner may decide that the salary paid to the employee/stockholder is excessive. "It is not really salary," the examiner will say. Regardless of what the payments are called on the corporation's books, the IRS agent will interpret the excess payments as being a dividend. The consequence: The corporation will be denied a tax deduction, yet the employee will still be taxed on the income. Chances are that the owners of the business will wish they hadn't paid that "dividend," because now the money is in the hands of the shareholder, and the corporation has lost the possibility for a deduction.

Tip #1: Include in the minutes of the board of directors a discussion of the good business reasons for the high salary paid to owner/employees or their relatives. Mention whatever factors call for the high salary, such as comparable pay in competing companies, the employee's training and experience, and the nature of his or her responsibilities including the tough business conditions that must be dealt with. Point out that high business profits or tough competition justify rewards for good performance.

Tip #2: To hedge against forever losing a tax deduction, insert a payback agreement in the corporate rules ("bylaws"), obligating an employee to return excessive compensation to the corporation.

Warning: Under no circumstances should you pay compensation to someone who doesn't actually perform work for your company. When you knowingly deduct such payments as compensation, you may be guilty of tax fraud. Other large payments to stockholders—for rent for the use of property or for interest on a loan, for instance—may also trigger IRS skepticism. Be sure that fair value is received by the corporation in exchange for any payments that are made.

INVESTIGATING A NEW BUSINESS

The costs of investigation—whether you are looking to create a new business or to buy an established one—are considered part of what the tax law calls start-up costs. These include expenditures for such things as analyses of markets, traffic patterns, products, labor supply, and distribution facilities. Your travel costs to look over business sites and to line up customers or sources of supply are also part of start-up cost.

Tax law is clear. Unless you are already engaged in the same or a closely related business, you cannot take an immediate deduction for start-up costs. That's because you have no business for which these costs would be ordinary and necessary expenses.

Instead, supposing you do buy or start up the business, you will treat these costs as deferred expenses. This means you will deduct them proportionately and equally over the 60 months beginning with the date you open your doors for business.

Once you have made the crucial decision to go ahead and create a new business or acquire one of a type you are not already operating, chances are that you will incur costs to advertise, train employees, set up an accounting system, and for legal services. These are called preoperating costs and also fall under the 60-month rule, as do the special legal and government fees incurred in setting up a corporation.

Legal, appraisal, and commission fees involved in buying real property, however, will be added to the cost of the property. Also, despite the 60-month rule on start-up costs, any interest and taxes that might be incurred in buying property are currently deductible.

Let's summarize. If you are already operating a business of the type you investigate, you can write off start-up costs as part of the ordinary and necessary expenses of doing business. Example: You can write off the costs of traffic counts, market surveys, and legal consultation in connection with rezoning to open a restaurant *if* you are already, or have recently been, in the restaurant business (perhaps in a different location).

If you enter into a type of business that is new to you, start-up costs fall under the 60-month rule.

If you investigate, but then fail to open a business of a new type, you will generally get *no* deductions whatsoever, in any form. *Example:* The IRS denied deductions for a taxpayer who bought the equipment but failed to follow through with her business plan of videotaping weddings.

If you are already in some form of business, it may be possible to define your present business, or the new one, broadly enough to get an immediate write-off. For example: You are a freelance photographer, reporting and paying tax on your income and expense. You hit upon a plan to open a fine arts gallery for paintings and sculpture. The IRS would probably see this as a different type of business . . . unless you broaden the concept. Investigate opening a gallery devoted to photography as well as other arts. In that way you're incurring expenses that can be seen as ordinary and necessary in expanding your sales of photographs.

111

Also, some existing businesses, such as a business consultancy or real estate brokerage, are broad enough in their activities to allow write-off of the costs of investigation of many different sorts of new business schemes.

Tax tip: In some cases the courts have overruled the IRS and allowed a write-off where the taxpayer investigated and chose a business, expending substantial effort and money in the process, even though the deal fell through at the last moment. In these cases, the taxpayer is considered to have sustained a deductible loss in a transaction entered into for the production of income. (That's another section of the tax law.)

HOBBIES AND BUSINESSES

While business expenses are fully deductible, sometimes the IRS may not believe you're running a *business*. They will say it's a hobby. They are particularly likely to say this if you are moon-lighting—trying to get your own business off the ground while still drawing a salary from your employer—and your activity looks like it provides a lot of fun to you and your family. Raising horses is an example.

There's nothing wrong with having a hobby. It gives you pleasure and may generate income for you. The income is taxable and the expenses are deductible . . . up to a point.

But suppose you pay out more expense than you have income. Certainly, this is often the case in the first year or two for businesses that are just starting up. You would like to deduct these losses from salary income you receive from your employer. The problem is this: If the IRS thinks your activity is a hobby, you are allowed to deduct hobby expenses only up to the amount of hobby income.

Here's an example. Suppose you're trying in your spare time to get your fledgling mail order business up and running, while hanging on to your job at the post office. Suppose your business brings in $13,000 income the first year. But your expenses total $25,000 for stationery, car expenses, and the cost of printing and mailing catalogs. You have lost $12,000 that first year.

If your mail order activities constitute a *business* in the eyes of the IRS, you can deduct the entire $12,000 loss from your post office salary. That will cut your personal tax bill. On the other hand, if the IRS thinks you're just enjoying a *hobby*, they will deny your attempt to deduct the $12,000 loss from your salary income.

How do you convince the IRS that you're running a business? The IRS has two types of tests. One is objective and the other subjective—a matter of judgment.

The objective test says you have a business if you earn a profit in three out of five years of operation. (Only two of seven years are needed if you are raising or racing horses.) This test is not foolproof; it creates a presumption that the IRS could try to disprove. If you had $50 of income in three of five years, but lost $20,000 in each of the other two years, the IRS would be skeptical.

Tip: If you are successful in earning only one or two years of profit in the first three years, you will need to file an election on Form 5213 to waive the three-year statute of limitations on IRS audits. This will reassure the IRS that they can go back and audit these years, even though an audit would ordinarily be barred by law. The IRS will be happy, then, to give you another year or two to prove you can show a profit in three of five years.

The other test is subjective. It considers all the facts and circumstances of your hobby/business. You could incur a loss in five out of five years and still make a believer out of the IRS.

The basic test is this: Are you operating in a businesslike manner with a profit-making intent?

You should structure the facts so they are consistent with a profit motive. Here are actions that you can take to prove you're a business owner and not just a hobbyist:

Seek the advice of an attorney, accountant, consultant

Keep good business records and books of account

Attend how-to-be-successful courses and seminars related to your business

Take steps to reduce your losses

Subscribe to trade publications

Advertise and buy business cards and stationery

Install a business phone even if you operate out of your home

Obtain licenses and permits

Spend considerable time and effort in your business

Tip: Even if it might have been predictable that you'll operate at a loss, you can argue that you expect eventually to earn a good profit through increases in value when you sell your assets (horses, rare coins, etc.).

Caution: Don't expect to win by arguing that your profit motive consists of your expectation of tax savings generated by writing off the business loss against your other earnings. The IRS rejects that reasoning.

One final test: Is your activity the sort that people enter into primarily because it is fun? We picked our example of a mail order business intentionally because it doesn't seem to be something you would do just for fun. However, if your business consists of collecting and trading rare stamps or coins, or of breeding horses or dogs, you'll have to operate in a strict, businesslike manner to convince the IRS that you have a profit motive.

HOME OFFICE

If you operate your business out of your home, you may be able to write off part of the cost of the rent you pay or of depreciation, property taxes, mortgage interest, electricity, water, telephone, lawn care, repairs, and maintenance. (Property taxes and qualified mortgage interest on your home are deductible even if you don't take a home office deduction.)

The rule to qualify for the deduction is simply stated: The space you claim as a business expense must be used exclusively and regularly as your principal place of business or as a place where you regularly meet clients, customers, or patients. (Additionally, you can deduct the costs of a place in your home where you store your business inventory, and you can claim the expenses of a garage, shed, or other building that is separate and apart from your home.)

Exclusively for Business

The space you claim must be used for business and for nothing else. (There is an exception for rooms used part of the time as a day care facility.) Don't deduct the costs of your den as a business expense if you sometimes watch TV there or let guests sleep on the sofa. Don't play games or write personal letters on your business computer. (Buy another computer for these uses.)

Also, don't manage your investments there, or tend to details about your rental property. Why? These are *invest-ment* activities. They would constitute a *business* only if you devote a considerable portion of your time to actively trading securities or commodities or tending to the complex details of your numerous properties.

Regularly for Business

Regularity of use helps to prove that the space is *necessary* to your business. (Remember: No expense can be deducted, whether related to your home or otherwise, that is not ordinary and necessary.) If you use the space only a few hours a month, an IRS agent may decide that's not regular enough.

Principal Place of Business

This test is applied strictly. If you have an office or shop or showroom somewhere else, it is not likely that your home will qualify as the *principal* business location.

This is the test that you will probably fail if you are an employee, whether or not you own the corporation that employs you. There are exceptions—such as when your employer provides no office or work space for you and expects you to work out of your home. But, ordinarily, an employee's principal place of business is the same as the employer's.

How will the IRS ever know? Can't you just pretend you qualify? Don't underestimate the IRS agent's cleverness at finding out the truth from you during an interview. The agents may ask for a floor plan and discuss with you the possible uses of the space. Also, on rare occasion, an IRS auditor has asked to visit the home office area or has suggested a taxpayer bring photos to the audit.

The best course of action is to design an area of your home to conform to the rules. Rearrange the furniture in a room, or part of a room. Buy or convert filing cabinets, a desk, and a computer strictly for business. Use this area regularly as the principal place of your business.

One minor complication you should be aware of. The tax code contains tax benefits for persons who sell their home for a profit. You may be able to postpone paying tax or, if you're 55 years old or older, avoid tax completely. To the extent you've been claiming part of your home as a business deduction, however, you may lose these tax breaks on the business portion of your home. *Tax tip:* Turn your home office back to personal use at least two years before you sell your home. That's enough to satisfy the IRS.

BOOKS AND RECORDS

Tax law requires you to keep books and records that are adequate to determine your income under the accounting method you choose. Books are books of account—accounting ledgers and journals. Records include logbooks, receipts, and diaries.

Only the smallest of businesses can get by with records only; you will probably need books of account. And for those, you may have to consult an accountant, although there are easy-to-use computer programs that can do the trick.

Don't begrudge the cost of setting up a good set of books and records. They help you prove you have a profit motive. Also, the information they provide will help make you a better manager. *Caution:* If you receive a gift or loan to help start your business, or if you sell personal assets to generate working capital, it's particularly important to keep good records of these transactions. Otherwise, if the IRS analyzes your bank deposits, you may not be able to prove the gifts and loans were not taxable income. (Gifts and loans are not taxable, and only the profit on sales of assets is taxable.)

Accounting Method

You must decide whether to use the cash or the accrual method. Your choice determines when you get to deduct expenses and when you are taxed on income. In some cases a hybrid method is acceptable. If you sell merchandise on installments, build construction that takes longer than a year, or operate a farm, there are special rules you'll have to look into.

Under the cash method you don't have to report income until you receive it in cash or in property that has a market value, such as a promissory note receivable. If you work "on account," collecting for it later, you'll not be taxed until you collect. Most small businesses selling services, such as carpenters, painters, auto repair shops, accountants, doctors, maintenance and repair workers, photographers, artists, pest control services, pool maintenance, and authors use this method. Example: You clean, polish, and perform minor maintenance on sail and power boats at your local marina. You decide that it gives a more professional image if you bill your customers at the end of the month. In December you do $2,100 worth of work but don't collect on your billings until January. Under the cash method, the money you earned in December is not considered taxable income to you until you finally receive it.

The advantage of the cash method is that you don't pay tax on income until you receive it. The disadvantage is that you don't get a deduction until you actually pay a bill. (You can use your bank credit card to accelerate deductions. Business expenses charged to a credit card are deductible right away even if you don't pay your card balance until next year, as long as the issuer of the credit card was someone other than the firm you are buying from.) Most businesses will save taxes by using the cash method.

Under the accrual method, on the other hand, you will be taxed for December's profits when you *earn* them in December—not in January or later when you finally collect. The disadvantage is obvious.

Caution: Any business in which the holding and selling of inventory is a substantial income-producing factor must use the accrual method. This also holds true for regular corporations with receipts more than $5 million, tax shelters, partnerships having a corporation as a partner, and certain trusts. Here's a break: If you use the accrual method for purchases and sales of merchandise, you may still use the cash method for other aspects of your business, such as sales on account.

Caution: Uncle Sam likes to get his tax from you when you're flush with cash. If you're in a service business, you must include as taxable income any advance payments you receive from customers. The accrual method allows you to defer reporting income received in advance, however, *if* the income will all be reported by the end of the next year and you will have to perform significant services for the customer in that year.

Example: You sign a contract to rent out a portion of a warehouse you own. In November, you collect a deposit and a full year's rent in advance. The entire year's rent must be reported on your tax return in the year in which you received it, regardless of whether you're on the cash or accrual basis. On the other hand, if the rent was received for a motel room for which you'll provide linen and cleaning services, the income can be deferred until you provide the services. (In any case, the deposit, which may be returned, is not income.)

There are also deferrals for subscriptions received in advance for magazines and newsletters and for membership dues. Deposits from customers who want to buy goods you don't yet have in stock are not taxable until you receive the goods.

Incidentally, the court's theory of "constructive receipt" says you can't postpone paying tax just by putting off taking an income check to the bank, nor can you postpone tax by telling your debtor to "hold off" paying a bill you submitted till the end of the year. That is, you can't turn your back on income and pretend you haven't earned it or received it, when you really have.

Caution: Once you've adopted an accounting method, you must get the IRS's approval to change. If you are starting a business to sell your personal services—interior decorator, yard or pool maintenance, financial planner, etc.—you can safely adopt the cash method. Otherwise, you should consult an accountant when making this decision, because some of the tax traps involve highly technical accounting matters. Also, your accountant can help you set up books that conform to your needs.

DEPRECIATION

In general, a full current deduction is not allowed for expenditures giving rise to benefits that will last beyond a year. For example, the amount paid out for a new building or for permanent improvements or betterments cannot be deducted in full in the year the expenditure is made. These expenditures must be "capitalized," that is, added to your capital assets. Then, the cost of the purchase or improvement is deducted on your tax return little by little each year, as you use the asset. This gradual write-off is called depreciation.

Depreciation is a deduction you get to take on your tax return to "write off " as an expense over a period of several years the cost of business assets. You can depreciate only those assets that have a limited life span, such as automobiles, office equipment, and buildings. Land can't be written off nor can "goodwill."

There are two tax methods for depreciation authorized by the Modified Accelerated Cost Recovery System (MACRS): accelerated and straight-line. The computations for accelerated, or fast write-off depreciation, is built into MACRS tables provided for use with tax forms. This kind of depreciation is available for business assets as long as you don't also make personal use of them 50 percent or more of the time.

In straight-line depreciation you deduct an equal amount each year (except you deduct only one-half this amount in the first and last year). For example, suppose the amount you are writing off—the cost of the asset—is $10,000 and the asset is of the type that tax law lets you depreciate over five years—say, a photocopying machine that you use exclusively for business. That's $2,000 per year. You deduct one-half of this amount in the first year, $2,000 in each of years two, three, four, and five, and another one-half ($1,000) in year six.

In contrast, if you choose to use the MACRS tables to calculate your expense write-off, you will deduct $2,000 in the first year, then in succeeding years $3,200, $1,920, $1,152, $1,152, and in the last year $576. (Yes, that's right: with so-called five-year property you get a deduction in each of six years.)

What's the difference between accelerated and straight-line depreciation? Is it important? The difference is that MACRS gives you more deductions up-front so you save money sooner. Only if you expect higher income in the future, and thus want to save the bigger deductions for those future years, will you choose straight-line depreciation.

Tax tip: If you invest $10,000 or less in equipment, don't depreciate it slowly over several years. Instead, write it off immediately as an expense in the year you make the purchase. You have this option, according to Section 179 of the Internal Revenue Code. Using our photocopier example; your deduction could be $10,000, taken entirely in the first year. Of course, this section may not be perfect for you: You are limited to $2,560 deduction for autos; buildings don't qualify; you can't deduct more than your net income from the business. Also, the deduction is completely lost if you purchase more than $210,000 of equipment.

You can learn all you want to know about depreciation—and more, chances are—in IRS Publication 534, Depreciation.

AUTOMOBILE EXPENSES

The size of the business expense deduction is an issue with car expense just as it is with compensation. No longer will Uncle Sam help you buy and write off the most luxurious stretch limo or the most exclusive sports car. For example, whether you pay $16,000 or $86,000 for a car, the maximum first-year depreciation deduction is $2,560. The rules also spell out limits on how much you can deduct in later years. Since there are too many of these depreciation rules for us to treat in detail, you will have to consult a tax preparation guide, or IRS Publication 917, Business Use of a Car.

You can deduct a "standard mileage allowance" for each mile traveled on business, or you can keep track of and deduct actual car expenses. The standard mileage rate is the easiest and best to use, unless you enjoy keeping records of all your depreciation, repairs, taxes, licenses, insurance, lubrication, and gasoline. Parking and tolls are deductible under each method. You can't use the mileage rate if you lease the car or if your business operates more than one car simultaneously, as in a fleet.

If you take a business deduction for a car but also make personal use of it, you must keep careful records, allocating costs between the two uses. Office supply stores carry forms—"logs," they are called—for recording business and personal mileage.

EMPLOYMENT TAXES

Numerous taxes must be paid by businesses that have employees. Some of these are the liability of the employee, but the employer must withhold them from the employee's pay and make payments to the government or to a designated bank at intervals specified by law. Examples are federal income tax and Social Security tax. IRS Form 941 is used to report federal taxes withheld and the employer's matching portion of Social Security tax. Typically, states and communities that have income or occupational taxes also require these to be withheld by the employer.

Other taxes are the direct obligation of the employer, for instance, state and federal unemployment tax (SUTA and FUTA) and the employer's matching portion of Social Security tax. Federal unemployment tax is reported on Form 940.

Size of the payroll determines how frequently the employer must pay over employment taxes to the government. Small businesses usually have to make these payments at least as frequently as quarterly.

Who Is an Employee?

You pay employment taxes and keep employment records because you have employees. Not everyone you pay to perform services, however, is an *employee*. The attorney you consult to help you incorporate your business is not your employee. Neither is the public accountant who fills out your tax return. The law refers to these persons as independent contractors.

If you try to avoid the hassle of employment taxes by treating an employee as a nonemployee, you will be liable for paying the Social Security and income tax you should have withheld from the employee's pay. Therefore, it is crucial that you know who is and who is not an employee.

Where the employer/employee relationship exists as a matter of law, it doesn't matter what it is called. You can't avoid employment taxes by calling an employee a partner, an agent, or an independent contractor, or by calculating straight commissions. Also, it doesn't matter whether a worker is part-time or full-time.

For purposes of employment taxes there are two kinds of employees, common law and statutory.

Anyone who performs services is a common law employee if the employer can specify the results and the methods for doing the job. The officers of your corporation are employees of the corporation, as are the plant supervisors and the sales clerks. Directors of the corporation are not employees.

Persons whom you pay to perform services, who are in a trade or business for themselves, are not employees. This includes self-employed veterinarians, carpenters, plumbers, pest control contractors, doctors, architects, and lawyers, for example.

Typically, an employee is paid an hourly wage, while an independent contractor is paid on commission or by the job and bills you for the work performed. An employer provides tools and a place to work to his employees. Usually, an employer can discharge an employee, but independent contractors may have a legal right to complete their work before they are "fired."

The contractor provides his or her own equipment and place of work, pays expenses, and has the right to hire others to assist without asking the employer's approval.

But the primary legal issue is one of *control.* If you can establish by the facts of the relationship that the worker controls and determines the means of accomplishing the job, that worker is not a common law employee. You do not have to withhold federal income taxes from his or her pay. Neither do you have to withhold and pay Social Security taxes or unemployment taxes, unless the worker is a statutory employee.

Statutory Employees

Certain persons are called statutory employees and are considered employees for Social Security purposes, even if they are not common law employees. Workers are statutory employees if:

━ It is understood from a service contract that the services will be performed personally by that worker.

━ The worker does not have a substantial investment in equipment or facilities used to perform the services (other than an auto or truck used for transportation).

━ The services are to be performed on a continuing basis.

Following are examples of statutory employees from whose pay you must withhold Social Security taxes, matching these amounts with the required employer's Social Security tax:

━ A driver who distributes meat, vegetables, fruit, bakery products, or beverages (but not milk), or picks up and delivers laundry or dry cleaning, *if* the driver is your agent or is paid on commission. (Federal unemployment taxes must also be paid.)

▬ A full-time insurance sales agent selling principally life insurance or annuity contracts primarily for one insurance company.

▬ A person who works at home on materials or goods that you supply and that must be returned to a person you name, *if* you provide the specifications for the work to be done.

▬ A full-time traveling or city salesperson who works on your behalf and turns in orders to you as his or her principal business activity. (Federal unemployment taxes are also due.)

In addition, the IRS has special employment tax rules governing firms that provide technical service specialists to clients, such as engineers, designers, drafters, computer programmers, and systems analysts. Similarly, there are rules for firms that lease to others the services of secretaries, nurses, and similarly trained workers.

Two IRS publications are essential reading: Publication 15 (also called Circular E), Employer's Tax Guide, and Publication 539, Employment Taxes. You can request an official IRS decision on whether you must pay employment taxes on a worker by filing Form SS-8, Information for Use in Determining Whether a Worker Is an Employee.

Meeting Your Employment Tax Responsibilities

First, you should apply for an Employer Identification Number (EIN) by filing Form SS-4. You will need to insert this number on all federal and state tax returns. Then, from each employee you should obtain:

Social Security number; it is safest to record this number directly from the employee's Social Security card.

Form I-9, Employment Eligibility Verification Form, to verify U.S. citizenship or eligibility of a foreign national to work in this country.

Form W-4, Employee's Withholding Allowance Certificate, to determine how many withholding exemptions the worker claims.

If you are handling the taxes yourself, you will need to set up a calendar of the dates at which tax returns and payments are due. Next, you must secure the state and federal forms on which to file your returns. For federal taxes you can get the dates from Publication 15. Contact your state revenue office for help with state employment taxes. *Caution:* Some communities have local "occupation" taxes that must be paid.

The paperwork is time-consuming, and the penalties for mistakes are sometimes severe; many small businesses entrust employment tax matters to an experienced bookkeeper or accountant.

Warning: Federal law is severe in enforcing payment of employment taxes. Penalties for late payment can be as high as 25 percent. If income or Social Security taxes are not withheld or are not paid, the penalty can be as high as 100 percent (in addition to the tax). And here's the real kicker: The responsible officers or employees of the business—such as those authorized to sign checks—can be held *personally* liable for these taxes and penalties. That's true even if the business is incorporated.

SELF-EMPLOYMENT TAX

Sole proprietors, partners (but not limited partners), independent contractors, and consultants are liable for self-employment tax if they make more than $400 annually from which social security taxes have *not* been deducted (and matching amounts paid) by an employer. This tax pays for social security benefits for persons who are not someone else's employees. The rate approximates the combined employer/employee FICA tax rate. (FICA is a common abbreviation for the Federal Insurance Contributions Act, in other words, social security.)

Dividends, interest, and capital gains received are not subject to self-employment tax. Neither is rental income from real estate unless the owner is a dealer in real estate or is carrying on a business by providing services such as maid services and linens.

CHAPTER PERSPECTIVE

Business taxation is different from personal taxation, generally more complex and, unfortunately, more costly. It is important to be aware of the rights and responsibilities connected with the federal, state, and local tax laws.

How to Deal With the IRS

Most business owners may never have even one run-in with the IRS, and the same may even now be true in your case. Your chances of being audited are higher, however, once you begin operating a business. In this chapter we discuss how to deal with an IRS auditor and how to take your case to Tax Court if you can't get the auditor to agree with you. Also, we discuss why you should apply for an Employee Identification Number, how to seek a refund if you're owed one, and when you should consult a tax professional such as an accountant or attorney.

After studying the material in this chapter:

■ You will know how your tax return is selected for audit and how to handle the audit.

■ You will know how to take your case to the Tax Court.

■ You will have an understanding of IRS organization and thus have an edge when dealing with them.

■ You will know how to file for a refund.

■ You will know when you need a professional and when you can handle the IRS on your own.

Employer Identification Number

One of your first business dealings with the IRS will come when you file for an Employer Identification Number (EIN). Even if you have no employees, you must have an EIN for any business you operate as a partnership or corporation. If you operate a proprietorship, you can use your Social Security number for identification unless you have employees. Even as a proprietor with no employees, however, you will need an EIN if you set up a retirement plan in the form of a pension or a "Keogh" plan (which is the most popular and flexible retirement plan for a proprietor). Additionally, having an EIN is one more piece of evidence to show the IRS that you are operating in a businesslike manner. You may need such evidence—to convince the IRS you are carrying out a business and not a hobby—if you try to deduct your losses from other income you have. You apply for an EIN by filing Form SS-4.

HOW THE IRS IS ORGANIZED

The IRS national office is located in Washington, D.C. The national computer center is at Martinsburg, West Virginia. Taxpayers normally have no contact with the national office except in infrequent instances in which they find it necessary to request a "letter ruling" to learn how the IRS will tax a proposed transaction when tax law is unclear.

There are seven regional offices. They supervise and coordinate the district offices. Disputes arising from an IRS audit of a tax return, if not settled at the district office, may be taken by the taxpayer to the regional Appeals Office.

Taxpayers have most of their dealings with one of the 64 district offices and seven regional service centers. Separate divisions within district offices deal with taxpayer services, examinations, criminal investigation, and collection.

IRS employees a taxpayer might have contact with are:

Tax examiners, also called office auditors, who handle relatively simple tax matters.

Revenue Agents, who have more training in accounting and tax than do tax examiners, and who perform audits at the taxpayer's place of business.

Revenue Officers, who collect unpaid taxes.

Special Agents, who investigate criminal fraud through the Criminal Investigation Division.

Problem Resolution Officers, who intervene, on request, to resolve problems that the taxpayer hasn't been able to clear up through the usual IRS channels.

Problem Resolution Program

The Problem Resolution Program (PRP) gives the taxpayer someone to turn to when normal IRS procedures seem to have failed. If you feel your problem is being ignored or mishandled, contact the Program Resolution Officer (PRO) at the IRS office that is giving you the difficulty. The IRS gives these examples of situations that might benefit from PRO intervention:

━ You have waited at least 90 days for the refund you were due, yet your follow-up phone call did not elicit any action.

━ You requested and were promised information or assistance, yet the IRS has not responded within 45 days.

■ You receive a third erroneous notice, yet you told the IRS of their error when you responded to each of the first and second notices.

■ You believe normal IRS procedures have not been followed, for example, your bank account has been frozen by the IRS but you have received no notice regarding a tax deficiency.

AUDITS OF TAX RETURNS BY THE IRS

The IRS lacks resources to audit every return, every year. Only a very small percentage of returns are given close scrutiny. This is small consolation if your return is chosen. Not all audits result in assessments of deficiency against the taxpayer, however; sometimes errors are discovered in the taxpayer's favor and a refund is granted.

How Returns Are Selected for Audit

A return may be selected for an audit by the IRS based on an informant's tip, a news story suggesting a taxpayer has had a sudden windfall from a merger or other business development, information appearing on a different taxpayer's return, or an investigation by another government agency such as the Drug Enforcement Administration. There is a rule that every business organization must report transactions taking place in *cash* for more than $10,000; this report may trigger an audit. Also, the IRS occasionally targets a certain type of transaction or business believed to be exploited by taxpayers, such as tax-sheltered investments.

A small business is likely to draw audit attention if it:

■ Receives most of its income in cash.

■ Pays large salaries to family members.

■ Earns little profit in relation to type of business and assets invested.

■ Requests a refund related to a transaction for which the IRS has recently proposed a tax deficiency.

Most audited returns, however, are selected by a computer at an IRS service center using the Discriminant Function (DIF) program.

The DIF program analyzes the relationship between items on the return and calculates a "score" for the return. Higher scores send up a red flag. They show that the IRS has more to gain by auditing the return. For example, large out-of-town travel expenses by the owner of a hair salon might result in a high DIF score, but the same expenses wouldn't raise an eyebrow if they were deducted by a free-lance writer of travel articles.

Returns with high DIF scores are forwarded to a local IRS district office. There, an experienced IRS agent makes the final choice.

The IRS's own Classification Handbook says the following items give the agent reason to select a return:

▬ The comparative size of an item compared to the return as a whole.

▬ The nature of the item in light of the rest of the return; for example, airplane expenses claimed on a plumber's Schedule C.

▬ The "beneficial effect of the manner in which an item is reported". This would include payments claimed as fully deductible business expenses when they should be listed as employee business expenses subject to the 2-percent threshold, or gifts to family or friends claimed to be deductible compensation paid to employees on a small business's return.

▬ Evidence of an intent to mislead as shown by missing, misleading, or incomplete schedules or items shown incorrectly.

▬ Relationship among items on a return; for example, business expenses but no business income, or not reporting dividends received when stock ownership is revealed through stock sales.

HOW TO AVOID AN AUDIT

Although an audit can be a stressful and time-consuming process, you shouldn't fret unduly over how to avoid one. You don't want to leave out a legitimate deduction just because you think it looks too large. Instead, fill out your return as accurately as you can according to your knowledge of tax law. Report all income and claim all legitimate deductions. Pay particular attention to these matters:

1. Answer all yes/no questions.
2. Report even small amounts of income that the IRS can verify.
3. Enter expenses on the proper line (to do otherwise may set off a DIF audit).
4. Where schedules are called for, as in "Other deductions, attach schedule," be sure to attach a schedule.
5. Explain and show computations for deductions you think look unusual.
6. Make sure you have and keep documentation as proof of every deduction.

IF THE IRS AUDITS *YOUR* RETURN . . .

An audit, also called an examination, may be one of three types. Correspondence audits request the taxpayer to answer questions by mail. Most originate at regional service centers. The proper response might consist of a written explanation of a transaction or, perhaps, a photocopy of an invoice, paid check, or other documentation. Correspondence audits involve relatively simple matters where the IRS anticipates no great possibility of error or fraud.

Office audits are common for IRS inquiries into the returns of individuals and of very small businesses. They are conducted at an IRS office by tax examiners. The examiner requests the taxpayer to appear at an IRS office, prepared to answer questions and to present proof regarding the subject matter of the audit. Office audits take from 30 minutes to several hours.

Field audits take place on the taxpayer's premises or at the place of business of the taxpayer's accountant or attorney who has the documents the IRS wishes to examine. Revenue agents conduct field audits when they wish to make a detailed examination of accounting records. Often payroll and excise tax returns are examined, as well as the personal returns of the owners of closely held businesses. Field audits occupy from one to several days.

Audits of Partnerships and S-Corporations

If you operate your business as a partnership or an S-corporation, you should be aware of how the IRS audits these entities. Formerly, the IRS had to initiate an audit, propose an adjustment, and assess a deficiency separately on *each* partner's or S-corporation stockholder's return. Now, in a unified proceeding, tax adjustments for businesses with more than ten owners are cleared with one of the owners, called the tax matters partner (TMP). If the TMP agrees to the adjustment, all partners are automatically bound by the agreement. Any partner not wishing to be bound must notify the IRS. Procedures for S-corporations are similar.

Purpose of the Audit

IRS agents look for assurance that true revenues are no greater than what you reported in your tax return and that you have not deducted more expense than you can prove is legitimate.

In a field audit the agents learn what sort of sales records you keep, such as journals and invoices. Then they test these records to see they add up to the amount you reported in your return. They also will examine your bank statements to see if deposits are consistent with the revenues you reported. If you have not kept adequate records, they will look for evidence that your assets, your bank accounts, or your personal lifestyle suggests that you have an income higher than you reported.

Revenue agents become suspicious when they find:

■ Large auto or travel and entertainment expenses that do not seem justified by the nature of the business, or are not properly documented.

■ A level of profit that is very low considering the nature of the business or the amount of assets invested.

■ Repair expenses that look to be out of line with assets.

■ Write-off of unusually large amounts of "bad" debts.

■ Inventory records too informal to allow accurate determination of cost of goods sold.

■ Salary and withdrawals of profits inconsistent with the size of the business or with the owner's lifestyle.

■ Gifts to relatives or friends masquerading as business expenses.

■ Unusual deductions for spoiled, destroyed, or stolen inventory.

How to Survive an Audit

Revenue agents are professionals who know their job and who will be thoroughly prepared to discuss your return. Although policy sometimes changes, the IRS has indicated it normally will not insist that the taxpayer personally be present at the audit, even though the tax code gives them authority to do so.

You may decide it's best to have a tax professional represent you, someone who keeps up with current tax law and is familiar with IRS procedures. An attorney, CPA, or enrolled agent can represent you if he or she has your authorization on Form 2848, Power of Attorney. (An enrolled agent is someone who has demonstrated their knowledge of tax law by passing an IRS exam.) On the other hand, you could ask the professional to go along with you, or you could go it alone.

At a field audit of a small business, the employee who prepared the return will usually be the one to deal with the revenue agent. These tips may smooth things along, while reducing the disruption of your business:

1. Put the agent in a separate room, away from ongoing business.

2. Designate one person to answer the agent's questions and to gather the material that is requested.

3. Request that the agent submit a list at the end of each day of the documents desired for the next day.

4. Keep a record of material the agent inspects and asks questions about (if serious problems arise, this list may help your attorney understand the IRS's suspicions.)

How to Handle an Office Audit

You will receive an audit notice, called Letter 889. Although this notice informs you of the general areas the agent is investigating, you might try to narrow down the issues by telephoning the agent. Also, you may ask to reschedule the exam if you need to.

Then, refamiliarize yourself with the details of your return. Tax law is complicated, and if you now realize you made an honest mistake in an insignificant matter the agent is auditing, you might wish to say, "I inadvertently overlooked this income" or "I mistakenly included this nondeductible invoice."

Warning: These statements constitute admissions that could later harm you in court; make them only if the effect of all such "mistakes" is trivial on your tax return of this and other years. On the other hand, if there are several of these mistakes or if you intentionally omitted income, or intentionally included large amounts of personal expenses on your business return . . . you should consult a tax attorney *before* the audit.

To prepare for the audit you may have to review tax law. You can bone up at most public libraries or at college or county law libraries. There are multivolume looseleaf tax services in which you can research any tax question. Also, the IRS has publications that tell how to handle taxes, and the best way to win is to find your point justified in one of these. (There is a list of valuable publications at the end of this chapter.)

Follow these tips to speed along the audit:

■ Before the audit, sort and organize your material. Let the agent see you are well prepared.

■ Bring photocopies of documents that prove your position.

■ Be on time and be courteous to the agent.

■ Don't try to bully the agent, but do lead off with your most convincing proof in order to establish credibility.

■ Don't volunteer information not immediately relevant. Don't, for instance, say, "That expense must be OK; I deduct it every year."

▬ Don't become angry, don't lie, and, particularly, don't insult or abuse the agent.

▬ Don't offer lunch or personal favors. Keep the session on a business level.

▬ Don't try to hide your nervousness by idle chatter that may alert the agent to problems with your return.

▬ Even if you think the agent is right, don't immediately agree to an adjustment; wait to see the extent of other proposed adjustments, then be prepared to negotiate and compromise.

Caution: When you go alone to an office audit, two points are critical:

1. Keep the agent focused on the matters you came prepared to discuss. Don't volunteer information and don't chat idly about such things as travel, inheritances, large purchases, children in college, or problems meeting payroll. (If you say the word "bankruptcy," the IRS may put a lien on your assets, just to protect itself.)

2. To protect your rights, be alert for the possibility the agent suspects you of fraud. (Fraud consists of intentional misstatement or omission; the penalties are severe. You could go to jail.) Be sure you understand the role of each person who is present at the audit. If an IRS "special agent" appears, call off the audit and find yourself a tax attorney.

Tip: The IRS instructs its own examiners to immediately stop their audit whenever they suspect fraud. So, if the examining agent suddenly calls off the audit, without explanation . . . call your attorney.

How the Audit Is Concluded

Usually, the revenue agent will propose adjustments to the return that result in a money deficiency being assessed against the taxpayer.

The agent will ask if you wish to sign a Form 870, Waiver of Restrictions on Assessment and Collection of Deficiency in Tax. On the good side: Signing this form will stop interest from accruing against you. On the bad side: You lose the right to take your case to Tax Court (you can still appeal within the IRS). Since it is only in the small case procedure of Tax Court that you can realistically defend your own case without hiring a lawyer, you should not immediately sign this consent form.

If You Disagree with the IRS Agent

At an office audit, ask for a conference with the examiner's supervisor. This is desirable if the examiner indicates that your proposal for settlement is beyond his authority, or if you are strong in your belief that the examiner is disregarding important facts or misapplying tax law. Compromise settlements are possible at this time because the IRS likes to wrap up office audits on the spot.

Alternatively, you can wait for the "thirty-day letter" spelling out the deficiency and proposed assessment. At that time you may file a protest with the appeals office. A formal, written protest may be made if the amount at issue exceeds $2,500 and originated in a field examination. The facts, law, and arguments must be spelled out. Instructions accompany the thirty-day letter.

Tip: Don't omit from your protest facts that contradict your position; instead, deal with them directly and tell why they are not important or not relevant. In addition to the law and facts, argue that "fairness and equity" support your position. The appeals officer will make a decision on the basis of your letter, or you can request a conference. A conference is almost always a good idea.

Thirty-Day Letter

A few weeks after the audit, the IRS will send the taxpayer a "thirty-day letter," which is official notice that the IRS proposes to make changes to a tax return. It is an invitation to appear at a hearing before the appeals office, and there is a thirty-day period in which to file a formal response, known as a protest. The IRS is not adamant about the thirty days; request an extension for a short period, if needed. If the IRS receives no response to this letter, they will issue a ninety-day letter. Payment before receipt of the ninety-day letter precludes the taxpayer from litigating in Tax Court.

Ninety-Day Letter

The ninety-day letter constitutes a notice of deficiency. It states the amount of tax the IRS believes is due. If the taxpayer does nothing, the IRS will assess the tax, setting it up as a receivable on the government's books and beginning collection efforts. The ultimate collection tool used by the IRS is seizure of your property; pay attention when you get a ninety-day letter.

One good point about the ninety-day letter: It creates Tax Court jurisdiction. This means that the Tax Court will hear your case if you wish them to, but only if you have received the ninety-day letter. If you want to go to court but you wait until the ninety days have passed, you will have to pay the deficiency and then sue for a refund in a U.S. district court or the U.S. Claims Court.

THE COURT SYSTEM

Taxpayers who have tried but can't get their case resolved to their satisfaction within the IRS can take their case to court. Final recourse is to the U.S. Supreme Court, of course, but only a very small number of tax cases—several a year—go that far.

Only 15 percent of all proposed deficiencies become the subject of court proceedings. Of these, most disputes are ended in trial court. (If an error of law is made in a trial court, the taxpayer's attorney may decide to take the case to an appeals courts.) There are three different trial court systems.

U.S. Tax Court

This court hears only tax cases. The judges, who have expertise in tax matters, "ride circuit" and hold court at various locations throughout the country. Cases are heard by one of the judges; there are no juries. A taxpayer can take his or her case to Tax Court without first paying the deficiency assessed by the IRS.

Small Tax Case Procedure

Within the Tax Court there is a small tax case procedure that can be used if the tax plus penalty is not more than $10,000. The taxpayer—referred to as the petitioner—chooses where the trial will be held from among available locations throughout the United States. In Pennsylvania, for example, there are two: Pittsburgh and Philadelphia.

Procedures are informal; taxpayers who are well-prepared can represent themselves. The case will be heard by a "commissioner" rather than by a judge. No appeal to a higher court is allowed from the small case procedure.

If you are considering personally taking your case to Tax Court, send for the booklet *Election of Small Tax Case Procedure and Preparation of Petitions*, available from:

Clerk of the Tax Court
400 Second Street, N.W.
Washington, D.C. 20217
Phone (202) 376-2754

U.S. District Court

District Courts are organized within circuits; the United States is divided into 11 circuits. The seventh circuit, for example, covers Illinois, Indiana, and Wisconsin. Taxpayers whose attorney takes their case to a District Court must first pay the deficiency assessment and then sue the IRS for a refund. Trial by jury is available. Since District Courts hear all sorts of cases, the judge may not be as expert in tax matters as would be a Tax Court judge. Technical details of law, such as those governing the admission of evidence, are stricter than in either Tax Court or Claims Court.

U.S. Claims Court

This court is based in Washington, D.C., but judges travel to other locations, which can be a convenience for witnesses. Claims Court judges typically become knowledgeable by hearing more tax-related cases than do District Court judges, but fewer than Tax Court judges. A jury trial is not available. Taxpayers must pay the deficiency assessed against them before this court has jurisdiction.

Choosing a Court System

If the case does not fit the Tax Court's small case criteria, most experienced attorneys would choose the court system. (Recall that only the Tax Court will hear a case before the taxpayer has paid the deficiency assessed by the IRS.) The decision is usually made on the basis of the court's history of favorable decisions in similar cases. Split decisions carrying some benefit to the taxpayer are more common in Tax Court but, overall, one court system is not clearly preferable to another.

ASSESSMENT

An assessment is an account receivable on the books of the U.S. Treasury showing the tax, interest, and penalty due from a taxpayer. When a taxpayer files a return, the IRS becomes authorized to assess the tax.

The IRS assesses additional tax by determining there is a deficiency for the tax year and giving notice to the taxpayer (the ninety-day letter). The taxpayer has three courses of action:

1. Wait ninety days, at which time collection procedures begin.
2. File a petition with the Tax Court, thus delaying assessment until the case has been decided.

3. Consent to immediate assessment of the deficiency by signing one of the waiver forms (870, 870AD, or 4549) and paying the tax.

Which action should you take? Here are some of the matters you should consider.

You can stop interest from accumulating by paying the deficiency. Payment of the tax *before* receipt of the ninety-day letter cuts off access to the Tax Court, but a suit for a refund can be taken to a District or Claims Court. Payment *after* receiving the ninety-day letter stops the accumulation of interest but preserves Tax Court jurisdiction.

IRS COLLECTION PROCEDURES

Within sixty days after the ninety-day period referred to above the IRS will assess the tax and issue a notice and demand for payment. (This must happen within three years of the due date, or filing date if later, of the return.) The taxpayer must pay the tax within ten days. Then he or she may file for a refund from the IRS. This refund claim will ordinarily be denied, and the taxpayer must then either give up the case or file a legal action in a U.S. District Court or in the U.S. Claims Court.

If the taxpayer fails to pay, the IRS can use its powers of "levy and distraint" to collect the tax, interest, and penalties. Levy and distraint is a legal concept meaning that the government has a lien on the taxpayer's property and can ultimately seize and sell it. The levy covers all property owned or later acquired. The IRS has six years to force payment of the debt.

Although the news media recount scandalous tales of IRS's seizure of bank accounts and cars, sometimes from the wrong person, in all but rare occasions taxpayers have adequate warning that a deficiency has been assessed and that they must act to protect themselves.

Warning: Never ignore a communication from the IRS. The IRS very rarely forgets about a case. In case of IRS error, respond promptly in order to begin what may be a lengthy process of straightening things out. If you don't understand what the notice requires of you, phone the IRS directly or request an appointment with a tax professional such as a CPA, enrolled agent, or tax attorney.

The IRS computer seems to have a purpose of its own. Once it starts sending you notices, it is hard to get them stopped. Here's what you should do if you are pestered by notices from the IRS computer yet you have already settled the matter. Send a written reply if one is requested. Keep a copy. Expect to do this twice. If this doesn't work, try phoning the Problem Resolution Officer.

The surest way to get relief from a runaway computer—although it will require you to spend effort you will not think is justified—may be to personally take all the IRS notices, together with your responses, into a local IRS office. (If you receive a refund check you don't deserve, don't cash it. Take it into an IRS office.)

Levy Against Property

Before the IRS can legally take property, a notice of levy must be given to the taxpayer in person, left at the taxpayer's business or home, or sent by registered or certified mail. If the property the IRS wants to seize is being held by another person, the notice is legal if given to the holder of the property. This means the law allows the IRS to tell your banker to freeze your bank account. A notice of deficiency, if not already sent, must be sent within sixty days.

Jeopardy Assessments

The IRS has authority to make an immediate assessment without going through the thirty-day and ninety-day procedure whenever a district director believes collection of the tax would otherwise be in jeopardy. Once the assessment has been signed by the IRS official, the taxpayer has ten days to pay or to post a bond. At this point the taxpayer's failure to pay will cause the IRS to begin collection efforts through levy and distraint.

The IRS resorts to jeopardy assessment when it gets information that the taxpayer is about to leave the country, file for bankruptcy, or attempt to sell or conceal assets. A taxpayer's casual remark to an IRS agent that he or she may have to file for bankruptcy may trigger a jeopardy assessment. Unfortunately for a few taxpayers each year, the IRS sometimes initiates jeopardy assessments on the basis of erroneous information.

FILING FOR A REFUND

You can file for a refund if you realize you have overpaid your income taxes. This might happen for several reasons:

1. You discover you made an error in the government's favor,

2. You sustain a net operating loss (NOL) that can be carried back to reduce taxes for one or more of the three prior years,

3. You earn a tax credit that can be carried back to a return of an earlier year.

The IRS will automatically credit you with a refund if they discover upon audit of your return that one is due. They are prohibited by law from doing so after the three-year statute of limitations, however, unless you filed a claim for the refund before the period expired. Filing the claim puts the IRS on notice of the overpayment and preserves your claim beyond the statute of limitations. Filing also protects your right to go to court to sue for the refund should that be necessary. You might have to sue if the IRS slips up and loses your file or otherwise fails to pay. The IRS must pay you interest if they improperly delay your refund beyond an interest-free period specified by law, in most cases thirty or forty-five days. (You can call 800-554-4477 for information about your refund.)

Refund claims must be put in writing. There are several alternative formats to use:

■ An amended return, Form 1040X for individuals and Form 1120X for corporations.

■ The same income tax form originally used to file the return, marked "Amended," showing and explaining the change that causes the refund claim.

■ Form 870 requested by a revenue agent, signed by the taxpayer, showing a refund.

■ Form 4466 for a corporation desiring a quick refund for overpaid estimated taxes.

■ A Tax Court petition, or protest, stating the refund claim and reasons therefor.

■ A letter to the IRS District Director including the necessary information.

"Speedy" Refund Procedures

Form 1045 (individual) or Form 1139 (corporation)—Application for Tentative Refund—can be used to request a "speedy" refund in certain cases. It must be used within twelve months of the close of the tax year that generated the refund. The IRS will act within ninety days. Technically, this procedure does not satisfy the statute of limitations referred to above.

The speedy procedure can be used for adjustments to a prior year's tax return arising from this year's net operating loss, or corporate net capital loss, or from a general business credit, such as from the research, targeted jobs, alcohol fuels, low-income housing, or rehabilitation credits.

Time for Filing

The general rule is that the refund claim must be filed within three years from the date the original return was filed (or the due date if the return was filed early). If the tax, including the overpayment, was paid later than the filing of the return, two years from that date is acceptable. Refunds resulting from bad debts, worthless securities, and foreign income tax credits have longer filing periods.

Following are some of the most important cautions to observe:

▬ A separate refund claim must be filed for each taxable period and each type of tax.

▬ Particular attention must be put to describing the facts of the basis for the refund. Additional arguments for the refund cannot be brought up if the case later goes to court. Taxpayers are not bound to a single theory as to why they deserve a refund. Two or more reasons can be stated, even if they are inconsistent.

▬ While the claim should demand a specific sum of money, it should add the phrase, "or such greater amount that may be found to be refundable."

▬ The refund claim should be signed by the person who signed the original return, or by a legal representative who attaches a form showing authority to sign.

▬ The claim should be filed with the regional service center for the district where the tax was paid.

HOW LONG TO KEEP TAX RECORDS

There are two reasons to keep tax records: to prove the entries on a past tax return and to fill out a future return.

You must keep records of a long-lasting business or investment property until you dispose of it. You need these records to determine taxable gain or loss when you finally sell or exchange the property. You also need these records to prove you are deducting the correct amount of depreciation. Keep canceled checks, work orders, contracts, invoices, and contractor's statements. Also, hang on to property tax bills and interest expense statements if the property qualified for these two items to be added to its cost.

For securities such as stocks and bonds, keep brokers' statements, canceled checks, and records of any stock dividends or splits. If you sell part of your shares in one company's stock, you have to keep data showing how you figured the cost of the shares you sold and the cost of the shares you keep. For your share of partnership or S-corporation earnings and losses, you should retain the K-1 forms that annually report to you the amount of earnings and losses. Under laws enacted during the 1980s, you must keep track of nondeductible contributions you've made to an Individual Retirement Account (IRA).

The other kind of records you need to keep relate to your annual tax return. Here, you must pay attention to the statute of limitations.

The Internal Revenue Code specifies that your return can be audited and a deficiency assessed against you within three years from the *later* of the date the return was due or the date the return was actually filed. To be able to defend your return if it is audited you must keep not only your tax return but also all accounting records, invoices, travel logs, canceled checks, and other documents that prove the accuracy of your return.

The audit and assessment period is extended to six years if the IRS can show that the taxpayer omitted from the return more than 25 percent of gross income. Gross income includes the total amount received as business revenue without reduction for cost of goods sold or any other expenses. It also includes dividends, interest, and gain on sale of assets. No deduction is allowed on account of capital losses.

It is not necessary that the IRS prove the taxpayer was attempting to evade taxes or even that he was negligent. An honest oversight can extend the period of vulnerability for six years.

Warning: Small business owners sometimes get so wrapped up in managing their businesses that they fail to file a return. But there is no statute of limitations for a taxpayer who either files no tax return at all or files one that is false or fraudulent.

Extending the Statute of Limitations

On occasion the IRS will request that a taxpayer extend the assessment period. If the three- (or six-) year period is about to expire the IRS may feel, otherwise, that it must act quickly to issue a deficiency notice. In those circumstances the notice of deficiency may cover issues the IRS hasn't had time to study fully or those that an appeals officer might be willing to compromise. Both the IRS and the taxpayer may benefit from an extension. Professional tax advice should be sought before agreeing to an extension.

PROFESSIONAL TAX ASSISTANCE

Anyone can prepare a tax return for anyone else. With a few exceptions, the person who represents a taxpayer in an interview or hearing before the IRS must be an attorney, CPA, or enrolled agent. These persons, also, may represent the taxpayer:

▬ Full-time employees may represent the individual, partnership, or corporation that employs them.

▬ An immediate family member can represent an individual.

▬ A partner may represent a partnership.

▬ An officer may represent a corporation.

▬ The person who prepared the return may represent the taxpayer on matters concerning the tax liability covered by that tax return.

How to Find a Tax Professional

Look in the yellow pages of your local telephone directory under Accountants or Tax Advisors. Your state's Society or Institute of Certified Public Accountants can provide the name of a CPA. For an attorney, contact the referral service of your County Bar Association. The National Association of Enrolled Agents has a toll free number, (800) 424-4339. The cream of the crop, the American Association of Attorney-CPAs, can be reached for referrals at (800) 272-2889.

FURTHER SOURCES OF INFORMATION

The IRS has publications to help the business taxpayer. Particularly useful are the following publications:

15: Employer's Tax Guide
17: Your Income Tax
334: Tax Guide for Small Business
541: Tax Information on Partnerships
542: Tax Information on Corporations
589: Tax Information on S Corporations
910: Guide to Free Tax Services

These relate to audits and refunds:

5: Appeal Rights and Preparation of Protests for Unagreed Cases

556: Examination of Returns, Appeal Rights, and Claims for Refund

586A: The Collection Process (Income Tax Accounts)

594: The Collection Process (Employment Tax Accounts)

1383: The Correspondence Process (Income Tax Accounts)

HOW TO GET INFORMATION FROM THE IRS

In addition to the phone numbers that may be listed in your local telephone directory you can reach the IRS at:

(800) 424-1040 for information on relatively simple personal or business tax matters,

(800) 424-FORM (3676) for forms and instruction booklets.

The IRS conducts Small Business Tax Workshops. You can learn times and locations from your local IRS office or from the information number listed above.

CHAPTER PERSPECTIVE

The IRS is a vast governmental organization charged with collecting revenues and enforcing one of the world's most complex systems of taxation. In dealing with the IRS the business person must rely upon knowledge and professional advice, not personal feelings and emotions.

Negotiable Instruments

INTRODUCTION

Certain written documents have a quality about them that the law refers to as *negotiability*. These documents are called *negotiable instruments*. Checks and promissory notes are examples of negotiable instruments.

Anyone who signs a negotiable instrument is said to have *issued* that instrument. The person who receives a negotiable instrument and gives something of value in exchange for it is said to have *accepted* the instrument.

Business firms often accept negotiable instruments issued by their customers. They may also be on the issuing end of a negotiable instrument when they buy goods from a supplier or borrow money from a bank. Other examples of negotiable instruments are sight and time drafts and trade and bank acceptances, which will be explained below.

Negotiable instruments are so important that it's likely you won't be able to transact business a single day without coming in contact with one of them. In the great majority of instances such transactions are routine; you won't have time to consult your lawyer before accepting (or issuing) the instrument.

In this chapter we will first take a look at what turns a written document—such as a check or a promissory note—into a negotiable instrument. Second we will focus on certain examples to illustrate how you can protect yourself when confronted with a bad check or a note that your customer refuses to pay. That will lead us to the nature and use of legal judgments and how to take advantage of your community's small claims court to enforce your rights.

After studying the material in this chapter:

▬ You will be able to recognize if a check, promissory note, or other document is negotiable.

▬ You will know how to protect yourself against a worthless check.

▬ You will be aware of your rights when you accept or sign a promissory note.

▬ You will know what to do when a check or note turns out to be bad.

▬ You will understand what you can and cannot expect to recover when you take a debtor to a court of law (in general) and Small Claims Court (in particular).

BACKGROUND

Our ideas regarding negotiability came to us from the English colonists and merchants. When they bought goods from another country, they didn't want to take the risk of sending a shipload of gold to pay for the cargo they wanted to bring back. Pirates were active, and captains and crewmen were not always honest. Thus it was safer to send a document that would be accepted as readily as would gold. Together with European bankers, the merchants developed the negotiable instrument. Before negotiable instruments came along, the only ways to transfer value (money) were to ship it (gold) or to assign the rights to a contract.

What is this quality called negotiability? Why is it so important? In a sense, negotiability is important for the simple reason that you can be a *holder in due course* of an instrument *only* if the instrument is negotiable. But that's getting ahead of the story. It is best to view negotiability by contrasting it with another legal concept called *assignment*.

Assignment

When two persons have signed a contract, each has rights and responsibilities. In many cases, one party to the contract agrees to take an action—deliver merchandise or perform services—as the other party agrees to pay money in exchange for the action.

Ordinarily, the rights one party has under the terms of the contract can be transferred to someone else. Often it is the right to receive money that is transferred, in a transaction that is referred to as *assignment*.

Suppose Richard Retailer agrees to buy a number of TV sets from Joan Jobber. Richard pays $10,000 today and promises to pay the remaining $10,000 next month, after his big holiday selling season. Since Joan needs the cash now, she *assigns* to Arthur, another party, the right to receive next month's $10,000. Arthur, the assignee, then gives $8,000 to Joan now for the right to receive $10,000 next month—that's a whopping 40 percent discount, but Joan needs the cash to purchase more merchandise from manufacturers.

Arthur has the right to receive $10,000, but this right is said to be "subject to the defenses" Richard Retailer would have had against the original seller, Joan Jobber. If the TVs are defective, the buyer has a claim against the seller that arises because of this "failure of consideration." In such instances Richard Retailer *doesn't have to pay Arthur.* There might be other defenses based on fraud or duress (force).

Recall from our chapters on contracts and on leases that an assignor (Joan in this case) can assign only the rights given to her by the contract. The person to whom these rights are assigned, the assignee, takes these rights subject to any of the defenses that could have been exercised against the assignor. In other words, the assignee "stands in the shoes of the assignor" in enforcing the claim against the obligor and has no greater rights than did the assignor.

Also, when Joan assigned her remaining rights under the contract the law says she made certain implied warranties. Among these are a warranty that the right that was assigned actually exists, that the right is not subject to a defense or counterclaim, that the assignor will not hinder the enforcement of the rights given by the assignment, and so on. The warranties extend only to the assignor's immediate assignee, however. If the assignee, in turn, assigns the right to a third party, the original assignor is not liable to the person for any breach of implied warranty.

We won't bother with other minor and unlikely legal complications relating to assignment. The point is: if you *assign* your contract rights to receive money, you are still tied into the contract. And the person who bought your contract rights also bought your contract duties. Questions about the validity and the performance of the contract continue to affect the right to receive money—the right that Joan Jobber tried to transfer. Thus, assigning a contract right to receive money is a very awkward way to transfer the right to receive money. Negotiability is a big improvement over assignment. Let's see how it works.

NEGOTIABILITY

Suppose when Joan sold the TVs she got $10,000 cash and a promissory note for $10,000. She could then *negotiate* the note by endorsing it over to Arthur in exchange for $8,000. Ordinarily, and making some further assumptions that aren't important at this point, Arthur would then have a claim against Richard for $10,000. Richard would have to pay, *even if the TVs were defective*.

Also, Arthur could negotiate the note to anyone else who was willing to pay for it. Arthur would do this by endorsing (signing) the note on the back and receiving value in exchange for it. Neither Arthur nor the party he endorsed the note over to would have to worry about whether the TVs worked.

Arthur would be in this enviable position because he is a *holder in due course*.

Holders in Due Course

Negotiation of an instrument is its transfer in such a manner that the recipient (referred to as the transferee) becomes a *holder*. Arthur, in our example, is a holder.

If the instrument is payable to "bearer," negotiation is accomplished by delivery to the transferee. The danger of a bearer instrument is that if it is lost or stolen, the finder or the thief may negotiate it to an innocent third party merely by delivering the instrument.

If the instrument is payable "to the order of" a specified person, negotiation is accomplished by endorsement plus delivery. Ordinarily, checks and promissory notes are written "Pay to the order of" a designated person. In order to transfer such an instrument, the designated person—the payee—must sign and deliver the instrument to the transferee.

There are several types of endorsement. *Endorsement in blank* is accomplished when the payee signs the back of the instrument without adding any qualifying words. For instance, if the instrument is payable to the Whitworth Corp., writing or stamping the words "Whitworth Corp." on the back constitutes an endorsement in blank. After being endorsed in blank, the instrument becomes a bearer instrument. It can be negotiated by delivery only and requires no further signatures; however, as a matter of fact, most subsequent transferees would be wise to require the signature of the transferor. If you endorse a check in blank, you are in effect expressing a willingness that anyone who gets possession of the check should be allowed to cash it.

A *special endorsement* specifies the person to whom the instrument is being negotiated. It becomes payable only to the person named in the endorsement and can be further negotiated *only* by this person's endorsement.

A *restrictive endorsement* limits further transfer of the instrument. Example: an endorsement with the name of the payee, Whitworth Corp., and the words, "for deposit," "for collection only," or "pay XYZ Bank." Use of one of these phrases gives a warning to a transferee that the funds (represented by the check or note) must be used consistently with the endorsement.

The best policy to follow when you receive a check in the course of your business dealings—or in your personal affairs—is to endorse it immediately with your signature or company name and one of these phrases: "Pay to XYZ Bank," "Pay to any bank," or "For deposit only." The result is the same with any of these endorsements. The person or institution next receiving this check must apply the funds consistently with your endorsement. In other words, if the check is stolen before you have a chance to deposit it, there is very little chance that you will stand a loss.

Now that we can identify a holder, let's take a look at a holder in due course. Here's why the concept is important: If the transferee is a holder in due course, the person who created the instrument—the drawer of a check or the maker of a note—cannot raise a number of defenses that might be raised against the assignee of a contract or against a mere holder of a negotiable instrument.

A holder in due course (HIDC) is a holder who has taken the instrument for value, in good faith and without notice that it is overdue or has been dishonored and also without notice of any defense against or claim to it. Thus, when you receive a negotiable instrument, it's a good idea to be sure that you are a holder in due course.

Ordinarily, when you receive a check or note you will give value in the form of merchandise or a service. As a general rule, however, an unexecuted promise doesn't constitute value. You can't be a holder if you promise to pay, or to perform work, in the future in exchange for the instrument.

When accepting a negotiable instrument, you must pay attention to the requirements relating to good faith and notice of a defense or defect. There are three danger signals to watch out for when you accept a negotiable instrument, if you want to have the status of HIDC—and you definitely do want this status.

First, the instrument must not be overdue. If a promissory note is written so as to be payable on July 15, no one who becomes a transferee on July 16 or later can be a HIDC. This provision does not apply if it is only the *interest* on the note that is overdue. As to checks, there is no clear time period after the date of the check that becomes its due date. The Uniform Commercial Code (UCC) creates a presumption, however, that 30 days after the date of the check it becomes "stale," and no one can become a HIDC after that date. There are exceptions to this presumption relating to the surrounding circumstances, but the 30-day rule is a good one to follow. You should always deposit or otherwise negotiate a check well before the 30 days are up, and you should never accept a check dated anywhere near 30 days prior to the present date.

Second, the UCC sets out a number of instances that are supposed to signal to you a notice of a claim or defense. For example, any indication of alteration of the date, dollar amount, interest terms, or due date should put you on notice of the probability of a defense that the maker or drawer might have. These alterations suggest forgery.

Third, an instrument that is incomplete in an important respect—called a "material" respect—should also put you on notice. An instrument is materially incomplete if it leaves blank the amount to be paid, the name of the payee, or the time when it was due.

Exception: You can be a HIDC if a blank portion of the instrument is filled in, in your presence, if you have no reason to believe the act of filling it in is improper. For example, suppose the secretary to the president of a small company comes to your store to stock up on office supplies. The president has previously signed the check, and all the secretary has to do is fill in the dollar amount. You will acquire the status of HIDC when the agent (secretary) of the principal (president) properly fills in the check in accordance with the principal's instructions and intentions, as long as you have no reason to doubt the proprieties of the transaction.

Forms of Negotiability

Certain formalities have to be followed for an instrument to be negotiable. These formalities are governed by Article III of the Uniform Commercial Code. All states have adopted this Article, so there is nationwide uniformity.

For an instrument to be negotiable the UCC requires that it

▬Be in writing and be signed by the maker or drawer

▬Contain an unconditional promise or order to pay a certain sum of money (and contain no other promise or order)

▬Be payable either on demand (that is, whenever the holder wishes) or at a definite time

▬Be payable to "bearer" or to the order of a designated person.

We'll take a quick look at some of these requirements before we focus in on checks and promissory notes. First of all, consider the signature. No one can be liable to pay a negotiable instrument unless his or her signature appears on it.

The UCC says that an instrument is signed when it includes *any* symbol executed or adopted by the maker or drawer with the present intention to authenticate the instrument. Marks, stamps, or symbols have been accepted in court as signatures when the evidence indicated that they were placed on the instrument by the maker or drawer intending to sign.

You don't want to have to go to court to prove that your customer intended to sign by drawing a skull and crossbones on a check, so you should ordinarily insist that the maker or drawer sign by hand with his or her name. Of course, when you receive a check by mail, you might as well go ahead and deposit it, regardless of the means by which it is signed.

It is not a forgery for one person to sign another's name, as a representative of that other person, as long as the signing is authorized. The person signing may be *personally* liable, however, if the representative capacity is not made clear.

If you feel you have to accept a check or note signed by one person for another person, the preferred form of signature is, for example, "Lisa Long by Rex Mathers, Agent." This format discloses the principal/agent relationship. It is up to you to verify whether Rex has Lisa's authority to sign for her. If you accept a check, and the bank refuses to pay because Lisa has not okayed Rex to sign, your only recourse is to try to collect from Rex. Lisa is off the hook.

If the instrument bears the "signature" of a corporation the corporate name should be signed together with the name of the person actually doing the signing and his or her title, such as "Snowbird Corporation, by Leigh Spinks, President."

The signature on a negotiable instrument is usually in longhand and placed at the bottom right of the instrument, but it could be elsewhere. For example, a promissory note might begin "I, Wilma Weaver, promise to pay . . . "

If you accept a promissory note that is signed by two (or more) persons as makers of the note, each one is personally liable for the full amount of the instrument. Cosigners can be important. If you have any doubts about the ability of willingness of the maker to pay, be sure to get a cosigner.

Now, let's take a look at the requirement that the order or promise be unconditional. Suppose you accept from a customer a note saying, "I owe My Merchant $500." This is a mere acknowledgement of debt and does not obligate anyone to pay. Thus, the note is not a negotiable instrument. The note should say "I promise to pay."

Suppose you, Lonnie Lender, loan Marsha Pringle $100. Marsha gives you a piece of paper saying, "Received of Lonnie Lender the sum of $100." This is merely a receipt and does not constitute an unconditional promise to pay. Thus, this paper cannot be a negotiable instrument. To reiterate the words you want to see are "I promise to pay" (on a note) or "Pay to . . . " (on a check).

For an obligation to be unconditional, there can be no necessity to examine other documents or to investigate if a contract has been performed. Avoid instruments that contain words such as "subject to our contract," "as per our agreement," "as governed by the deed," and similar qualifying phrases. If the signer wishes to tie together or relate the contract to the check or note, the way to accomplish this is to refer in the contract to the check or the note.

An instrument that says "Pay only from royalty funds" is not negotiable. Any instrument that states it is to be paid only from a particular fund or source of moneys is open to question—but there are two important exceptions. If a *government agency* specifies that payment is from a particular fund or from proceeds from specified taxes, the instrument is negotiable. If the instrument is issued by an unincorporated business entity such as a sole proprietorship, partnership, trust, or estate, negotiability is *not* destroyed by a statement that payment is limited to the assets of the entity.

Courts have held that the maker or drawer can indicate the fund or account that is to be charged and still be unconditionally liable for payment. For example, the phrase "Pay to order of Sam Spud and charge the payroll account" would be negotiable because the general credit of the drawer is behind the transaction.

AVOIDING BAD CHECKS

If a customer promises to pay but then fails to do so, you have a right of civil action against the customer. You can try to enforce your rights in court, as we'll discuss later in this chapter.

There are few people in business who have not taken a check that turns out to be worthless. Such checks are returned from the bank with a notation such as "no such account" or "insufficient funds." If a customer pays you with a check that turns out to be worthless, you may be able to initiate a criminal action. Anyone who passes a bad check with the intent to defraud is guilty of a crime. Thus your local police or other law-enforcement authorities should be able to assist you. The pressure exerted by a notice from the police may be enough to convince the check writer to make it good. You can also make a bad check claim in court.

About the only way you can *completely* avoid bad checks is by selling only for cash and credit card charges. (Incidentally, this is not such a bad idea to consider, depending on the nature of your business.) However, there are ways to reduce the incidence of bad checks. Let's take a look at what you can do.

Suppose a customer presents you with a check that is made out by a third party, not to you but to the customer. The customer wants to endorse the check (sign it on the back) and transfer it to you in exchange for cash, merchandise, or services.

There are multiple risks in accepting this check, principally related to the fact that you can't investigate the drawer (the person whose bank account will make payment). The drawer is not standing there in front of you with the endorser. You probably don't even know the drawer. The signature might be forged, or if the signature is valid, the account might be empty. The endorser (the drawee on the check) may be perfectly honest but may have been duped by the drawer, just as you will be if you accept the check.

Some businesses make a practice of accepting certain kinds of endorsed checks. Typically, these businesses find it profitable to deal with customers who do not have bank accounts. A customer without a bank account must have some way to get cash for the payroll, Social Security, tax refund, or welfare check that he or she receives. However, in some areas of the country theft of government checks, which are then fraudulently endorsed, is so widespread that even banks refuse to accept them except from someone who has an account at the bank.

Payee checks are checks payable to you and signed by the customer as drawer of the check. You should adhere to certain standard practices when you accept payee checks. In addition, these practices should be more stringent the larger the amount of the check. For example, if your average sale is $65, you might tell your employees to get the approval of a supervisor (or you) for any check that is more than $100. Of course, sharp operators can find out the limit you've set and write checks below that amount. (It is said that the most popular amount for a bad check is $35.) Retailers are most vulnerable to people who pass bad checks. Wholesalers, manufacturers, and others who deal not so much with the public but with a relatively small, known customer base are of course less vulnerable but will also run into trouble from time to time.

When you are accepting a check in person, it should be filled out and signed in your presence and it should bear today's date. The name signed to the check should be the same as the name of the account imprinted on the check. You should avoid taking a check that is already signed, with the customer merely filling in the amount, unless you know the parties involved.

Sometimes, particularly with elderly or handicapped persons, all items on the check except the amount will have been filled out in advance. It is a simple matter, in cases where the signature already appears on the check, to ask the customer to sign the check *again*, in your presence, immediately below the first signature. Then you can compare the signature against the customer's ID and continue with your regular procedures.

Your state law may spell out the points of identification necessary if you later want to prosecute someone for passing a worthless check. You might check with your local police department to find out their requirements. Regardless of state law it is wise to get the following information and jot it on the face of the check:

▬ Full name, address, and phone number. Put a check mark by the imprinted information if it is correct.

▬ Name of employer, address, and business phone number.

▬ Sex, date of birth, approximate height, and race (for purposes of identification).

Typically, the information on a state driver's license— together with the license number—will provide sufficient ID if you also get the name, address, and phone number of the employer. You may decide to record less information, but you're not likely to need more.

Some businesses make it a policy to see a second ID, too. Be sure the secondary ID is valid and is properly signed.

Warning: The possibilities for fraud are endless. Anyone can buy a machine for less than $100 that will heat-seal an instant photo and a preprinted ID in a plastic sleeve. And, of course, wallets filled with all kinds of ID are stolen every day.

In no case should you take a check if the customer asks you to hold it for a few days before depositing, nor if you have previously received a bad check from the same customer.

Safe Practices for Merchants

▬ Accept only preprinted checks on a local bank that show a local address for the drawer.

▬ Don't take a check from someone who seems drunk or drugged.

▬ Don't take a check that has any erasures or mistakes written over.

▬ Don't accept a check drawn payable to your customer, who then endorses it over to you.

▬ Be particularly careful during holiday seasons.

▬ Be wary of the customer who seems to pick a random collection of merchandise without considering size or color.

What to Do When a Check Is Returned

If you get a check returned for "not sufficient funds" (NSF), or if the check is marked "account closed," or "no such account," here's what to do. First, send the customer a certified letter (return receipt requested) stating that the check has been dishonored and demanding that the customer immediately pay the amount of the check together with the authorized service fee. Retain a photocopy of the letter. If the customer comes in to pay you, accept only cash. An example of such a letter is reproduced on the next page.

NOTICE AND DEMAND FOR PAYMENT

Date: _____

TO _____

_____

_____

You are hereby notified that a check numbered _____ issued by you on _____[date]_____, drawn upon __[name of bank]__, and payable to _____, has been dishonored. You have 30 days from receipt of this notice to tender payment in cash of the full amount of the check plus a service charge of $10 or 5 percent of the face amount of the check, whichever is greater, the total amount due being $_____ and _____ cents.

Unless this amount is paid in full within the 30-day period, the holder of the check or instrument may file a civil action against you for three times the amount of the check, but in no case less than $50 or more than $2,500, in addition to the payment of the check plus any court costs, reasonable attorney fees, and any bank fees incurred by the payee in taking the action.

(Note: The service charges and penalties are those provided by Florida law, as is the 30-day period. The clerk of your county small claims court should be consulted for the fees in your locale.)   If the certified letter comes back undelivered, you have good reason to believe the customer has tried to defraud you. Take the unopened letter, the check, and your copy of the letter to your police department, who will help you proceed further with criminal proceedings, if you desire.

If you get back the receipt showing the certified letter was delivered, but you don't hear from the customer, take the receipt, your copy of the letter, and the bad check to the police.

If the bank reports that the signature is not authorized for that account, the check is a forgery. As in the case of returned checks, you should contact the local police department.

Occasionally, but rarely, you will be so busy that you later find you have accepted a check that was not signed by the drawer. The remedy is to contact the customer to sign the check or to give you cash in exchange for it.

Sometimes a customer will stop payment on a check. It is legal to do so if the goods or services bought from you turn out to be defective. (The legal term for defective goods or service is "failure of consideration.") Your police department will *not* be able to help you with stop-payment checks. The drawer of a check who then stops payment has committed a crime only if he or she issued you the check *intending* to stop payment. If you can't work things out with the customer, you'll have to consult an attorney or take the matter to small claims court.

There are state statutes relating to worthless checks. It's not a bad idea to post a small sign that refers these statutes: "Passing a worthless check with intent to defraud is a crime under [name- of your state] statute number _____." Also, post a sign stating that you charge a fee when a check is returned. (The amount you can charge is regulated by state law.)

SMALL CLAIMS COURT

Small claims courts exist to provide a low-cost way of taking legal action. Rules of court procedure are simplified so that you will often be able to take your case to court without an attorney.

Small claims courts hear questions of law where the remedy sought is money or possession of personal property. For example, if you sell a set of fine dinnerware and the buyer won't pay, you can go to court asking for your money or for the return of the dinnerware. There is a ceiling amount determined by state law, perhaps $2,000, $3,000, or $5,000. If your claim is greater than that, you'll have to see a lawyer about taking your case to another court.

The small claims court won't pay you the money owed to you. What you will get from the court, if you are successful, is a money judgment. Later, we'll discuss how to collect on a judgment.

Most small claims courts charge a small filing fee and a fee for "serving" (delivering) papers on the person you're suing. And, of course, you will also "pay" by losing time away from your business. Consider carefully whether the amount of your claim is worth the time and money it will take.

A good starting point is to pick up a claims form at the court. Read the form and instructions and talk to the clerk about what is required. (Don't "bad mouth" the debtor; he or she might then have a right of legal action against you.) If you decide to sue there is one technicality of the legal system you must be alert to. You have to provide the correct name of the party you are suing; otherwise, you'll end up with a judgment that is worthless because no property is owned by the nonexistent party. If there is a person with the name that you put down as defendant in the lawsuit—but it's not the right person—you may be liable for his or her legal fees. It turns out to make a difference, sometimes, whether the name is XYZ Company, Inc. or The XYZ Corporation. These may be two completely different business entities.

If it's a corporation you're trying to sue, you will have to determine from state records whether it is incorporated in your state or is just licensed to do business there; in the former case you'll want to get the proper address of the corporate headquarters, in the latter case you need the name and address of the registered agent, the person on whom the legal papers must be delivered. The clerk of the court can give you assistance in getting information from the proper state agency.

If the contract you have with your customer says that the loser of a lawsuit has to pay attorney's fees, you might consider hiring an attorney to represent you. Before proceeding, however, you should try to find out if the debtor has any nonexempt assets from which your judgment and legal fees can be paid. Two sources of information: a credit reporting agency, which will charge a small fee, and the public records file at the courthouse of the county where the debtor lives. Public records will tell you if the debtor owns real property and whether there is already a long line of judgments against the debtor.

Small Claims Court Procedure

Although procedures vary from state to state and, to some extent, from county to county within a state, here's the way the system usually works. First, you go to the court clerk's office and pick up a claims form. The nature of your claim will determine which of several forms you should use. For example, there may be different forms for claims for unpaid rent, to recover on a promissory note, and for breach of contract. For some courts you may have to make up your own form. If you are suing a corporation, it may be necessary for you to send an inquiry to the state's division of corporations. The court clerk will be able to assist you.

After you fill out the claim form and pay the filing fee, you have a choice of having the papers served by registered letter or delivered by the sheriff or by a private process server. Since the defendant can refuse to accept a registered letter, it's probably best to try the sheriff. In any case you will have to provide an address for the defendant. If you don't know the address, you may have to hire a private process server or a private detective to find it.

When you file the papers, you become the plaintiff. If you are lucky, the threat of trial will motivate your defendant to agree to a settlement. It may be wiser for you to settle, at this point, for partial payment of what you believe you are owed. When you think you deserve $250, it's usually better to settle for, say, $150 before trial than to take a chance on collecting nothing while incurring additional cost and lost time. The $100 in your pocket is worth more than a judgment for $250 that you may not be able to collect. Never go to court seeking justice or vindication of some principle. The risk is too great that, regardless of the righteousness of your claim, you will lose on a technicality, or perhaps the judge will feel sympathy for the other side.

If you don't settle, a pretrial hearing may be scheduled to determine if a trial is necessary. If there is a trial, you must have witnesses and documents in the courtroom to prove your case. Of course, you may have to pay the witnesses or arrange for them to get time off from their work. But the trial will be your only chance to gain restitution, and you should be fully prepared.

At trial, you will make opening remarks, and then the defendant will make opening remarks. Next, you and the defendant will take turns presenting your witnesses and your evidence. Finally, you and the defendant will make your closing arguments, and then the judge will render a decision. Most small claims courts like to keep the cases moving. You may be surprised at the speedy disposition of your lawsuit.

Here are a few tips: Dress neatly and conservatively, (use the dress of the people you see behind the counter in the clerk's office as a guide). Treat the judge as if he or she were a grandparent who was trying to decide whether you deserved a million-dollar inheritance. In other words, be respectful. Listen carefully to what the judge says, and answer all questions truthfully and directly, and don't argue with the judge. In the courtroom, *the judge rules absolutely*.

If you fail to answer a question, the judge may not ask you again. He or she may simply conclude that the reason you don't respond is that the answer is unfavorable to your case.

If the judge decides in your favor, there may be an opportunity for the defendant to pay prior to entry in the court records of a formal judgment. Or you might be offered installment payments. It is probably better to accept installments than to try to collect under the judgment.

How to Collect a Money Judgment

A money judgment is nothing more than a finding by a court that the debtor owes you money. You still have to collect it. If the debtor is not willing to pay you, the first thing to do is record the judgment in the courthouse of a county in which the debtor lives, has family ties, or owns real property. The judgment will become a lien against property, to be collected when the property is sold.

There will be other enforcement procedures available to you. These procedures differ from state to state but typically involve levy (seizure of property owned by the debtor) or garnishment (seizure of property held for the debtor, such as a bank account or wages payable). The enforcing agency, such as the county sheriff's office, will be able to provide further details.

Don't get your hopes up. Many debtors turn out to be "judgment proof." Either they have no assets of any meaningful value or the only assets they have are exempted by state law from creditor's actions. (Disability benefits, for example, may be exempt, as is a "homestead" allowance.)

CHAPTER PERSPECTIVE

Many business people deal less in cash than in pieces of paper that represent—or should represent—money. But these negotiable instruments are governed by legalities that can serve as traps for the unwary. Know your rights—and the rights of your payors—before accepting any negotiable instrument.

How to Extend Credit and Deal With Bankruptcy

Few businesses operate for long without facing credit problems. Either some of their customers can't pay the amounts they owe or, what is worse, the business itself can't pay its debts. A bit of forethought and planning can reduce some of the risks.

Many of the problems with customers can be prevented if credit is not extended too generously. We will discuss methods of screening credit applicants and of collecting overdue accounts.

We also will suggest sources to turn to if *yours* is the business that is having trouble paying its debts.

When other techniques fail, bankruptcy is the last resort, the only solution to unpaid debts. Bankruptcy is a court-supervised procedure the purpose of which is to help those who owe money (debtors) and those to whom they owe it (creditors). Generally, debtors come out of bankruptcy better than do creditors. Debtors have their debts discharged (forgiven), and creditors must make do with less money than they were owed.

The last half of this chapter discusses the ins and outs of bankruptcy. First, however, we will cover how you can reduce the problems you have with collecting from your customers.

After studying the material in this chapter:

▬ You will know how to screen your credit applicants and decide whom to accept.

▬ You will be able to design a credit application that will aid you if you later have trouble collecting the debt.

▬ You will know how to find assistance when you have difficulty paying *your* debts.

▬ You will understand the basic ins and outs of bankruptcy.

RULES FOR EXTENDING CREDIT

Require a Credit Application

The information you get on a customer's credit application can make a big difference in whether or not you can collect a high percentage of the debts you're owed. You should insist on a comprehensive credit application that

▬ Fully identifies the applicant

▬ Demands credit references

▬ Sets reasonable credit limits

▬ Requires the debtor to pay interest, costs of collection, and attorney's fees

At the very outset you must ask for more than the applicant's name and address. It's a good idea to inquire of a credit reporting agency what information they will need to help you check on the applicant. They will send you a sample of a credit file that shows what information is included.

From the Correspondence Branch, Federal Trade Commission, Washington, D.C. 250580 you can get information helpful in designing credit applications that do not ask questions that violate federal law. For example, you cannot ask questions about the marital status, spouse, or ex-spouse of a person who is applying for credit on the basis of his or her own creditworthiness.

Typically, for an individual, you will need to get person's Social Security number, current and former address, employer, and name of nearest relative. These items will help you make a credit check and aid you in finding the person if they move.

It seems strange that it could be so, but some business applicants will indicate they don't know the legal form of organization of their company. They will tell you that they are a "company" and that their lawyer (or accountant) took care of all those details. You must verify, however, whether you are dealing with a corporation, a partnership, or some other form of organization that might be authorized in your state.

The form of organization will determine who you can "go after" in the event of nonpayment of the debt. If your customer is a partnership, for instance, you will ultimately be able to look to the assets of the individual partners if the business can't pay.

If your applicant is a corporation, you should learn the state of incorporation, the date of incorporation, and the name of the local registered agent. The application should be signed by an officer of the company. You can verify this information for a company incorporated in your state by making a phone call to the appropriate state agency (your county law library can tell you where to call).

The registered agent is the person on whom you or your attorney would serve legal papers, if that should become necessary in trying to collect a debt. For large accounts it's not a bad idea to phone or write the registered agent, just to confirm his or her status.

If the corporation is not a "domestic" corporation—that is, not incorporated in your state—you should verify that the corporation is registered to do business in your state. You do this by contacting the state agency referred to in the previous paragraph.

If the corporation is not registered to do business in your state, the likely legal effect is that the stockholders are doing business—and are liable for debts—as individuals, but this could vary depending on your state. In any case, you might be better off not dealing with an unregistered corporation.

You may want to keep credit low for a recent start-up. By learning the date of incorporation you will get an idea how long the company has been in business.

For a credit applicant identified as a partnership, be sure to get a list of names and addresses of all the partners. They will be liable to you for debts if the partnership assets are inadequate, provided that the person who signs the application on behalf of the partnership has the authority to do so. It's a good idea to send a letter to the business address of partnership, confirming that you have received the credit application, naming the person who signed it, and indicating that you will notify them when you have approved the application. Ordinarily, there will not be a state agency where you can check on a partnership, but there will be a record identifying the names of the partners on file in your county courthouse.

Obtain References

You should get a list of credit references with whom you can check to learn how long they have had a business relationship with the applicant and whether the applicant pays bills on time or has ever presented a check that was later dishonored by the bank. *Contact several of the references.*

Be sure to ask the references what is the nature of their relationship with the applicant, and then carefully evaluate the response. You want to avoid being taken in by persons who may be in collusion to defraud you. Be wary of purported business references with addresses, phone numbers, or greetings upon answering the phone that indicate residences.

Use a Credit Reporting Agency

Refer your application to a credit reporting agency to which you have paid a membership fee. Look in the yellow pages for "Credit Reporting Agencies." The most prominent nationally are the Credit Bureau Inc. (CBI), Trans Union, and TRW. Ask other business people in your community which agency they use.

Although most of the information you require will be available from the credit agency, you might choose to hire a real estate title company to search county public records to see what real property is owned by the applicant, and whether there are mortgages, liens, or legal judgments against the applicant. Get the name of a title company from your yellow pages.

Set a Reasonable Credit Limit

You have to use your business judgment on this one. It's better to start off with a low limit. Customers understand this. Remember, also, that after a few months of satisfactory payments by a customer, you can always raise the credit limit.

Beware of bad credit risks who flock to the site of a new business. They hope that in your eagerness for business you will be lenient. Extending easy credit can get your business started with a bang. The bang can become bankruptcy. After all, what you really want is *cash*, not a big list of customers who are *promising* to pay.

Get Personal Guarantees When Extending Credit to a Corporation

Beware of extending credit to a corporation just because you know it is "backed by" a prominent person. Shareholders of a corporation are *not* personally liable for the corporation's debts, regardless of whether the business is a "C corporation" or an "S corporation." When dealing with a corporation, particularly one that does not have a long and successful record, you would be wise to get a personal guarantee of payment of debt by one or more solvent stockholders.

Provide for Interest, Attorney Fees, and Collection Costs

Your agreement with a customer—as expressed in your credit application—should provide for payment to you of interest on customer's debts that go unpaid for longer than a period of time that you specify—perhaps 30, 45, or 60 days. Be sure you don't charge more than a "legal" rate of interest. The legal rate varies from state to state. Also, be sure you provide in the application for reimbursement by the debtor for legal and other costs you might incur in collecting the debt. You might specify in your application that 20 percent of the amount of the debt is the agreed amount. Not only will this reimbursement partially compensate you if you have to hire an attorney, but it will also further motivate the debtor to pay your bills on time.

Get Security for the Debt

To "get security" for a debt means to require that the debtor pledge to you property that he or she owns. If the debt isn't paid, you automatically own an interest in the property. You can then go to court and take advantage of a legal procedure to cause the property to be sold to pay you off. Even if the debtor attempts to sell the property that was pledged, your interest in the property continues. In the event of the bankruptcy of a customer or client, being a *secured* creditor is much better than being unsecured. *Warning:* Ordinarily you must acquire your status as a secured creditor 90 days before any bankruptcy procedure begins.

As examples of security, you might ask for a mortgage (also called a deed of trust) on real estate the debtor owns, or a lien on the debtor's auto or truck. (The terms "mortgage" and "lien" mean essentially the same thing.) Practically any property can be the subject of a "security agreement" that will be recorded at the courthouse as a "financing statement." This is easily done, and does not require a lawyer. All you need is the debtor's okay.

There need be no relationship between the product or service you are providing the customer and the property that is pledged to you. If the customer refuses to pledge any security ask what other guarantee of payment is available.

Depending on the nature of your business, you may discover that the law grants you a labor or materials lien on the debtor's property without very much action on your part. (You may still have to record the lien at the courthouse, but it's not necessary to get the debtor's approval.) In many states, for example, you have a lien on the property you worked on or materials you furnished on construction or repair work on a building, boat, or motor vehicle. Bookkeepers and public accountants in some states are given liens on the client's books of account.

Don't let the various terms, such as mortgage, lien, or security interest complicate the picture. If the amount of credit you are allowing the debtor is large enough to justify it—and state statutes don't grant you a materials or labor lien—*ask the customer for security.*

Make Vigorous Collection Efforts

You should establish an unvarying sequence of steps to take whenever a debt goes beyond a certain number of days without payment. For instance, if you specify payment within 30 days of the invoice date, at the conclusion of this period you might send a letter advising the debtor that the debt is overdue and requesting immediate payment or that the debtor immediately contact you. (If the debtor does contact you, be prepared to extend the due date for another week or two.) *Be sure* your sales staff is notified that no more credit can be extended until payment is received.

Then, on the 45th day—if you've had no response—you might write (or phone), warning the debtor that you are placing the debt in the hands of a collection agency if you don't receive the amount due within five days.

If the collection agency can't collect, they will refer the matter to their attorney. You might save time by regularly referring uncollected debts to your own attorney. Remember, your agreement with the debtor requires that he or she pay your attorney's fees.

The collection schedule we've just outlined is admittedly harsh. You may wish to be more lenient, depending on the nature of your business and the competitive conditions in your community. In any event, you need to have a set of collection procedures to follow that you *rarely* deviate from.

BANK CREDIT CARDS

Many businesses choose to avoid problems with debtors by having none. That is, these businesses sell only for cash or for charges against a credit card that someone else has the burden of collecting. (In this context "cash" includes checks.)

Increasingly, the use of credit cards is accepted by merchants and customers alike. The most recent trends is for credit cards to be accepted by service business (for example, car washes) and professionals (for example, dentists and attorneys).

There is a cost connected with shifting your credit problems to a bank. Charges to the merchant vary depending upon the credit card, issuing bank, and the nature and size of the merchant's business.

There are initial set-up costs and continuing costs. Typically, credit card costs run in a range of 3-5 percent of the amount that a customer buys from you. This means that for a $100 purchase you will be able to collect $95 to $97 from the bank the day after the sale.

For most small businesses the cost of accepting credit card is probably less than the cost of running credit checks, billing customers monthly, and maintaining a credit and collection department. Of course, credit card costs are not subject to control by the merchant, as the merchant's own costs would be. You can try to cut corners and reduce your own, in-house costs, but you are pretty much at the mercy of the bank as to what they charge you.

Some business owners decide that the extra cost of handling their own credit arrangements is made up for by a feeling of increased closeness to customers and an enhanced business image. There are other advantages. For instance, mailing a monthly statement gives an opportunity to enclose promotional offerings. Other owners simply resent the credit card charges.

If you are starting a new business, you might want to begin by accepting cash, checks, and credit cards only. Then, as you grow and learn the size of your success, you can consider starting your own credit department.

Warning: Don't let your own management time be eaten up by credit and collection problems. Marketing and planning are more important uses of the small business owner's (or manager's) time.

WHAT TO DO WHEN *YOU* HAVE DEBT PROBLEMS

We hope the only debt trouble you have is with customers who are slow in paying. Sometimes, however, your business slows down, cash is tight, and you may find it difficult to pay your bills. Here are several tips to help you through the bad times.

Keep in Close Touch with Your Creditors

If creditors don't hear from you, the chances are greater that they will band together and force you into bankruptcy. You may be able to prevent this *if* you can convince them you will make payments that leave creditors better off than they would be in Bankruptcy Court.

When you encounter serious financial difficulty, you should sit down with your accountant and your attorney to try to devise a workable plan for making regular payments to all your creditors. Then bring your creditors together, lay out your financial position honestly, present your plan, and ask for their cooperation.

Dealing with your creditors individually is unwise. If it becomes known that you are making payments to some creditors but not to all, those creditors being left out will attempt to force you into bankruptcy. They won't let much time go by because if your debts exceed your assets, payments made by you within 90 days prior to the filing of a bankruptcy petition can be recovered and shared among all creditors. (Transfers that benefit one creditor over others and are made during the 90-day period prior to bankruptcy and while the debtor is insolvent, are called "preferential transfers.")

If you can't devise a workable plan with the aid of your accountant and lawyer, don't wait for miracles to pull you out of the hole. File a petition for voluntary bankruptcy. We will discuss bankruptcy later in this chapter, but choosing the type of bankruptcy is a job for an experienced attorney.

Get All the Professional Advice You Can

Getting into financial difficulty can sometimes be a good thing . . . if it makes you look at your business with the kind of scrutiny that leads to new concepts, better marketing, and stronger financial controls.

Inability to pay debts may indicate that you are undercapitalized and need additional financing. The pricing structure you have set for your products or services may be unrealistic. Your marketing plan may be ineffective. Get someone to help!

Sources of advice when you are in trouble include business consultants, certified public accountants, bankers, the Small Business Administration, the business development center of a local college or university, and organizations of retired executives that you can learn about from your chamber of commerce. In some cases, the creditors that you bring together to discuss your problem will be able to offer valuable advice.

Don't Be Afraid of Bankruptcy

Slipping into bankruptcy may be embarrassing, but the process offers an end to past troubles and promises a new start free from most debts. Bankruptcy carries less stigma than it once did, and you will be able to begin over again.

Warning: Despite what you may hear, you will have more trouble getting credit if you have recently been a debtor in Bankruptcy Court, particularly in a Chapter 7 proceeding. For example, if you start a new business you may have to prepay for merchandise.

Some bankruptcy procedures, such as those under Chapter 11, don't put a debtor out of business. Instead, they provide for payments to creditors while the debtor's business continues to operate.

BANKRUPTCY

Bankruptcy is a court-supervised procedure that helps both those who owe money (debtors) and those to whom they owe it (creditors) make the best of an unfortunate situation. There is a federal law that governs bankruptcy: the federal Bankruptcy Act.

The Bankruptcy Act preempts (overrides) state laws dealing with debtors who can't pay their creditors. Bankruptcy legal actions, therefore, are supervised by *federal* Bankruptcy Courts.

The primary purpose of the Bankruptcy Act is to relieve honest debtors from the burdens of debt in order for them to make a fresh start. This is known as a "discharge."

Once a debtor comes under the protection of the Bankruptcy Court, creditors have to withhold further efforts at collecting the debt. Instead, under the oversight of a bankruptcy trustee a court-supervised procedure begins that is designed to pay off as much of the debts as is possible.

We will begin with a few definitions relevant to bankruptcy and then discuss the most commonly encountered portions of the Bankruptcy Act.

Definitions

Automatic stay. The commencement of a bankruptcy action by filing a petition with the court prohibits ("stays") certain acts against the debtor and the debtor's property. Examples of prohibited acts are attempts by a creditor to take a mortgage or lien on the debtor's property, to repossess secured property, or to talk the debtor into repaying the money owed to one creditor while slighting others. The purpose of a stay is to maintain the status quo.

Avoidance. A bankruptcy trustee appointed by the court has the power to set aside ("avoid") certain prebankruptcy transfers of property made by the debtor. For example, property a debtor sold to his brother six months before the bankruptcy for half its value can be brought back into the debtor's ownership.

Chapter 7. The most frequently used section of the Bankruptcy Act, involving appointment of a trustee who will sell ("liquidate") the debtor's nonexempt property and pay off the claims. Chapter 7 is available to individuals and to most business debtors.

Chapter 9. Provides for adjustments of debts of a municipality. A plan of reorganization is created. There is no provision under this chapter for sales of assets.

Chapter 11. Provides for reorganization of a business while the debtor devises a plan for full or partial repayment of debts usually by revising the terms—interest rate and payment schedule—of debt and modifying the financial structure of the company. Debt holders are often paid off in shares of company stock. The business continues to operate while under Chapter 11, but if operating losses continue, the court will step in and begin procedures to liquidate the company.

Chapter 12. A plan under which a family farmer can continue ownership and operation of a farm while repaying debts according to a plan that will be overseen by a trustee.

Chapter 13. Individuals with a regular income, whether wage-earners or business owners, are allowed to tailor a plan for the eventual repayment (or discharge) of their debt. Chapter 13 applies only if the unsecured debt is less than $100,000 and secured debt less than $350,000.

Claim. A right to receive payment from the assets of a bankrupt person or business. Persons who have claims are creditors of the bankrupt. If they expect to share in the debtor's estate, creditors must file with the bankruptcy court a "proof of claim," which consists of an official form together with documents that prove the existence of the debt.

Confirmation of a plan. Approval by the bankruptcy court of a plan for reorganization and repayment under chapters 11, 12, or 13. Creditors will receive notice of a confirmation hearing from the Clerk of the Court; they should attend this hearing if the size of their claim justifies it.

Cram-down. The process by which a plan to reorganize a debtor is forced into effect by vote of a sufficient number of creditors, even though some creditors may not agree.

Creditor. The person or business who lent money or sold goods and is now trying to collect from the debtor—the person or business the creditor lent or sold to.

Debtor. The person or business who borrowed money or purchased goods.

Discharge. A discharge by the Bankruptcy Court releases the debtor from any legally enforceable obligation to make payments on unpaid balances of most—but not all—debts. Some debts, such as taxes and alimony, cannot be discharged.

Discrimination. The Bankruptcy Act prohibits governmental agencies from taking actions—such as refusing to renew a license—that discriminate against a debtor who has been bankrupt. Similar prohibitions prevent employers from firing bankrupt debtors.

Exempt property. Certain property owned by a debtor cannot be used to satisfy creditors in a bankruptcy proceeding. Both state laws and the federal Bankruptcy Act contain lists of exempt property.

Foreclosure. A court-ordered procedure to sell a debtor's property by auction. Foreclosure is considered to be a last resort for both debtor and creditor because a forced foreclosure sale is not likely to bring top dollar for the assets.

Fraudulent conveyance. Transfers of property by the debtor in the year prior to the filing of a petition in bankruptcy may be voided (set aside) by the bankruptcy trustee if the transfers hindered creditors or were made for less than fair value.

Garnishment. A debt-collection procedure in which the court orders a third person to withhold from the debtor money that is owed. The money is paid instead to a bankruptcy trustee, who in turn pays the creditors. An employee's pay is garnisheed by notice to his or her employer.

Insolvency. A financial condition in which debt exceeds assets. *Equitable insolvency* refers to a debtor's inability to pay debts as they become due.

Involuntary petition. A petition filed by creditors, under chapters 7 or 11, forcing a debtor into bankruptcy court. The debtor has 20 days in which to file an answer to the creditor's petition, that is, to object to being forced into bankruptcy. If the court grants judgment against the creditors, they have to pay court costs and the attorney's fees for both themselves and the debtor.

Lien. A legal interest in property to secure the payment of a debt. A mortgage against real property is a lien, as is a security interest such as might be retained by the seller of an auto.

Liquidated debt. A debt that is undisputed in dollar amount.

Liquidation. As used in bankruptcy, this term refers to the conversion of a debtor's assets into cash. Liquidation of debt means payment of the debt.

Order for relief. An order for relief admits a debtor into supervision by the Bankruptcy Court. Generally, an order for relief goes into effect at the time a voluntary petition is filed, but in the case of an involuntary petition, the debtor is granted time to object to the order.

Personalty. Property that is tangible but is not real property. Personalty includes such varied items as clothing, dishes, automobiles, horses, office furniture, and computers. A basic classification exists in law between real property (primarily land and permanent attachments to the land such as buildings) and personal property: *realty* versus *personalty*.

Proof of claim. Once a bankruptcy procedure has begun, creditors are invited to submit proof of the debt they are owed by the bankrupt. See also *claim*.

Proof of interest. Stockholders of a bankrupt corporation must file a proof of interest to document their claims.

Reorganization. Restructuring of a business so that its debts can be paid while it continues to operate. For example, creditors of a corporation might be asked to accept preferred stock in lieu of repayment of amounts owed them. A reorganization can take place outside of bankruptcy proceedings, or inside, in which case Chapter 11 of the Bankruptcy Act governs.

Secured claim. A creditor's claim for repayment that is backed by an ownership interest (a lien) on the debtor's property.

Security interest. An interest in a debtor's personal property or fixtures—in effect, a lien—that operates as security for the debt.

Statutory lien. A lien that comes about by operation of law rather than by court action or by consent of the debtor. A mechanic's lien is a statutory lien.

Trustee. A person appointed by the court to oversee the process of a debtor's bankruptcy.

Unsecured creditor. A creditor who does not hold a security interest in a debtor's property. Generally, unsecured creditors in a bankruptcy proceeding are paid after secured creditors.

Voluntary petition. A bankruptcy proceeding that is voluntarily initiated by the debtor. A voluntary petition operates as an *order of relief*, putting the debtor under the protection of the Bankruptcy Court and prohibiting collection efforts by creditors.

The first step in bankruptcy consists of the filing of a petition that, in effect, asks the Bankruptcy Court to take over supervision of a debtor's estate. Petitions must indicate which chapter (section) of the Bankruptcy Act is relevant. Petitions that are filed under chapters 7 or 11 may be either voluntary (filed by the debtor) or involuntary (filed by creditors).

A petition under Chapter 13, relating to an individual debtor who has a regular income, must be filed by the debtor. Creditors cannot force a Chapter 13 proceeding. Chapters 11 and 13 allow for the debtor to propose a plan for the payment of debts.

LIQUIDATION: CHAPTER 7

The essence of Chapter 7 is this: A trustee liquidates (sells) the debtor's nonexempt property and uses the cash to pay debts. Exempt property is retained by the debtor, and most remaining debts are discharged (excused). Some debts such as those for taxes and alimony are not discharged.

Chapter 7 is the least complicated form of debt relief and generally the least expensive. It is also the most frequently used bankruptcy procedure: About 70 percent of all bankruptcy filings are made under Chapter 7.

Debtors themselves voluntarily file for Chapter 7 bankruptcy when they are overwhelmed by debts to the point of having no prospects of reorganizing or otherwise repaying. Sometimes, even a debtor who appears to be in acceptable financial shape— one whose assets exceed liabilities—will file a voluntary petition.

Filing a voluntary petition immediately positions the Bankruptcy Court between the debtor and his or her creditors. A voluntary petition filed under Chapter 7 constitutes an *order of relief* that operates as an *automatic stay*, which prevents creditors from making further collection efforts.

Filing a Chapter 7 petition is sometimes used by a debtor as a quick way to stop a creditor from foreclosing on secured property. The creditor must hold back from foreclosing, giving the debtor time to study the alternatives. The debtor can later convert to either a Chapter 11 or a Chapter 13 procedure.

Any "person," including individuals, partnerships, or corporations, can file for Chapter 7 bankruptcy. However, railroads, insurance companies, banks, savings and loan associations, and credit unions—although they are considered to be "persons" for many legal purposes—cannot use Chapter 7. There are special rules, beyond the scope of this book, for these entities and for commodity brokers.

When the owner of a sole proprietorship files an individual petition, both business assets and nonexempt personal assets are subject to liquidation for the benefit of creditors. Husband and wife can together file a joint petition.

You won't be happy to learn that one of your debtors has filed under Chapter 7, because these cases tend to be "no-asset" cases, particularly for an individual debtor. You would be very lucky if you were to collect 75 percent of the amount owed you by a business bankrupt. If it is an individual who files Chapter 7, you might be lucky to get 10 percent.

A typical Chapter 7 liquidation case proceeds in five stages:

1. Filing of a Chapter 7 voluntary petition commences an automatic stay of debt collection efforts. An interim (temporary) trustee will be appointed. The clerk of the court will notify you and other creditors of the filing. The notice also schedules the first meeting of creditors, often called the "341 meeting," after the section of the Code that authorizes it. A typical form is reproduced on the next page.

The debtor or the debtor's attorney often notifies creditors immediately upon filing the voluntary petition, without waiting for the clerk to do so. Once notified, creditors must hold back from further efforts to collect from the debtor. That is, the debts are "stayed" by the court.

Only debts created prior to the filing are automatically stayed. Certain types of prepetition debts, such as taxes, alimony, and child-support payments, are not stayed.

A creditor may be held in contempt of court who—having knowledge of the stay, whether from the debtor or the court—tries to collect money from the debtor, take possession of or sell the debtor's property, or improve his standing in relation to other creditors. You must avoid even such low-key efforts as making phone calls or sending letters to the debtor in an effort to get payment or obtain security for the amount owed to you.

Within ten days of filing the petition the debtor must file a schedule showing amounts owed and to whom they are owed, a statement of assets, and information about income and expenses. There is a small filing fee that must be paid.

A Chapter 7 petition may also be filed by a group of creditors. The end result tends to be the same, whether the petition is voluntary or involuntary.

2. A meeting of creditors is held, a trustee is elected, and the period begins for filing proofs of claim. The debtor must be present at the "341" meeting of creditors and will be put under

oath for questioning by the trustee and by creditors. Creditors will pool their knowledge to inform the trustee of any property they know the debtor has failed to list or about any property he might have transferred fraudulently.

If you know the debtor has no assets, it may be a waste of time to attend the meeting. It's a good idea, however, to talk to a creditor who was present.

Creditors vote on the selection of a permanent trustee. Usually, in Chapter 7 cases, the interim trustee becomes the trustee.

The trustee and creditors try to determine the value of nonexempt assets, if there are any. They also seek to learn whether the debtor has made any conveyance or transfer of property that can be set aside—that is, taken from the person now possessing the property and returned to the bankrupt's estate.

Creditors have 180 days in which to file proofs of claim against the bankrupt's estate. In the typical no-asset case, an unsecured creditor may decide it is not worth the trouble to file a proof. On the other hand, sometimes assets are discovered that creditors did not expect.

If you are a *secured* creditor, you should file a proof of claim. Otherwise, you will lose your security interest and find yourself standing in line with the unsecured creditors, slated to receive little or nothing.

3. In order to prevent individual debtors from being left destitute, certain property is retained by them. This property is known as exempt property.

The federal bankruptcy law provides a set of exemptions but also allows the debtor to choose between taking the federal exemption or the exemptions that are provided by the state of domicile. Some states, however, have legislation to prohibit debtors from taking the federal exemptions.

We will list the federal exemptions, the only law uniform throughout the country. State laws generally follow the same pattern, but with different dollar amounts. Federal law allows these amounts:

■ Homestead exemption: $7,500 equity in a residence used by the debtor or by a dependent. For husband and wife there is a joint exemption of $15,000. As an example of a different approach: Florida allows a homestead exemption of 160 acres outside a municipality or one-half acre within a municipality; value is not taken into account.

▬ $1,200 excess in value over the loan balance in a motor vehicle. Typically, this exempts most autos because the loan balance does not decline as quickly as does the value of the vehicle, and there is no excess value.

▬ $200 equity in each item of household goods, furniture, musical instruments, appliances, books, clothing, animals, crops. State laws often limit the total amount subject to this exemption. In one state, for example, personal property exemptions are limited to $1,000.

▬ $500 of jewelry for personal or family use.

▬ $400 in any other type of property. Any unused homestead exemption, up to $3,750, can be added to this category.

▬ $750 in tools and professional books.

▬ $4,000 in cash-surrender, loan, or dividend value of an unmatured life insurance contract.

▬ Health aids, if professionally prescribed for the debtor or dependent, such as dentures and eyeglasses.

▬ Right to receive benefits such as Social Security, unemployment compensation, veteran's benefits, disability, alimony, pension plan payments.

▬ Right to receive crime victim's awards, payments on account of the wrongful death of another, payments from life insurance contracts, and payments on account of bodily injury not exceeding $7,500. The exemption extends only to the extent necessary for the debtor's support. The excess is distributed to creditors.

Filing a petition automatically creates an estate in the debtor's assets. The estate consists of *all the debtor's nonexempt property* at the commencement of the case. The trustee takes possession of this estate in a procedure called "marshalling."

Certain property acquired by the debtor after the petition has been filed also becomes part of the estate, including:

▬ Property the debtor becomes entitled to by bequest, devise, or inheritance within 180 days after filing the petition, or by property settlement or divorce decree.

▬ Life insurance proceeds received as a policy beneficiary.

▬ Earnings from the estate property, such as rents.

▬ Property received from the conversion of estate property, such as insurance payments for property that suffered a casualty. The trustee attempts to collect debts due the estate. He uses his powers of avoidance to recover property that was recently transferred by the debtor, and he converts all assets to cash.

If it is a business that is bankrupt, the trustee may operate the business until he can choose the best time for a close-out sale. He may list real property with a broker or sell it at auction.

Trustees are motivated to do their best in realizing the most they can for the estate's assets. The more the trustee collects, the higher is his fee and the more the creditors receive.

4. Trustees have a duty to pay only legitimate and legally binding debts; therefore, they are legally obligated to "defeat" (find fault with) claims. Trustees scrutinize the proofs of claim presented by the creditors. They will also attempt to defeat secured claims, making secured debts into unsecured ones.

Claims are ranked into classes representing their priority, that is, the order in which they will be paid. (Satisfaction of each secured claim is attempted from its security. Any unsatisfied, secured debt becomes an unsecured debt.)

Claims in each higher category are paid first in full (or proportionately, if funds are inadequate). Only if the creditors in the higher categories are fully paid will the next lower category be given any return. The order of categories is as follows:

▬ Administrative expenses, such as court fees and taxes, and fees of professionals such as attorneys, incurred by the bankruptcy procedure.

▬ Claims created after an involuntary petition was filed but before the court has entered an order of relief.

▬ Debts to individuals for unsecured claims of wages, salaries, and commissions earned within the earlier of 90 days prior to the filing or prior to the date the bankrupt ceased business.

▬ Amounts of contributions the debtor should have made to employee benefits plans arising from services performed for the debtor within 180 days before the petition (or the date the debtor ceased business). Value of the contribution must not exceed $2,000 for each covered employee.

▬ Certain claims by one who raises grain against a debtor who owns a grain storage facility and by commercial fishermen against the operator of a fish storage or processing facility.

▬ Claims of individual consumers up to $900 each for deposits made with the debtor for goods not delivered or services not performed.

▬ Most types of federal, state, and local taxes.

▬ Other unsecured debts for which proofs of claim have been filed within the allowed period.

▬ Unsecured claims that were filed late.

━ Secured and unsecured claims for fines, penalties, forfeitures, or punitive damages arising before the earlier of the order for relief or appointment of trustee.

━ Interest from the date of the petition on the preceding classes of claims.

5. A debtor who is an individual is forgiven remaining nonexcepted debts. In some circumstances a discharge can be set aside within one year, upon the petition of a creditor or the trustee. The Bankruptcy Court might revoke a discharge if, for example, it became known that the debtor had concealed non-exempt property that should have been listed.

Corporations and partnerships are *not* discharged of their remaining unpaid debts. After the assets are sold, typically the owners of a corporation or partnership will dissolve it, or it will be dissolved by operation of state law. Federal law does not apply to dissolution of these entities.

Discharge bars enforcement of most debts that arose prior to the order for relief. It doesn't matter whether the creditor had filed a proof of claim or whether the claim was allowed or disallowed.

There is no discharge for the debtor who has:

━ Within one year prior to filing, transferred or concealed property with the intent to hinder or defraud a creditor or the trustee, or has knowingly made a false oath, presented a false claim, or withheld information from creditors or the trustee.

━ Concealed or failed to keep documents or books of account by which financial condition and business transactions can be determined.

━ Failed to give satisfactory explanations for losses of assets.

━ Refused to testify or to obey a court order.

━ Performed one of these stated acts in connection with another bankruptcy filing case within one year prior to filing this present Chapter 7 petition.

━ Received a discharge under Chapter 7 (or Chapter 13) within the last six years.

6. The trustee files a final report with the Bankruptcy Court and the case is closed.

The trustee files with the court an accounting report of the completed liquidation of the debtor's estate. From the accounting the court orders the distribution of the funds collected according to the schedule of priorities and rules of distribution provided by the Bankruptcy Act.

Discharge is granted by a written document issued by the Court. The discharge will be filed and becomes part of the public record. Section 523a of the code provides that the following types of debts are *not* discharged in a Chapter 7 case:

▬ Property taxes, employer's withholding taxes, customs duties, excise taxes, and income taxes due for the last three years prior to bankruptcy filing.

▬ Debts incurred (or renewed) through fraud or false pretenses such as the providing of inaccurate credit information.

▬ Debts based on materially wrong financial statements that the creditor can show he or she relied upon.

▬ Debts not listed or scheduled by the debtor in time for the creditor to file a proof of claim.

▬ Debts arising from fraud, embezzlement, larceny, or defalcation of a fiduciary. (A fiduciary is a person to whom property is entrusted such as the executor of a deceased person's estate, or the legal guardian of a child or of an incompetent elderly person.)

▬ Alimony, maintenance, or child-support obligations between former spouses or to a child, arising out of divorce decrees or separation agreements.

▬ Debts based on willful or malicious injury to a person or property.

▬ Debts less than three years old that are payable to a governmental unit for fines, penalties, or forfeitures (other than taxes).

▬ Student loans, except in cases of undue hardship such as extraordinary medical expenses.

▬ Debts based on liability incurred as result of the debtor operating a motor vehicle while legally intoxicated.

▬ Debts from a prior bankruptcy in which the debtor waived discharge or was denied discharge, for example, by failing to schedule the debt.

A Chapter 7 debtor can receive no more than one discharge each six years. Being granted a Chapter 7 discharge does not preclude the debtor from *filing* again within six years of a prior filing, thus getting the protection of the Court and securing an orderly sale and distribution of assets. But no discharge can be granted in the second case.

ADJUSTMENT OF AN INDIVIDUAL'S DEBTS: CHAPTER 13

Chapter 13 is often referred to as wage-earner bankruptcy, although any *individual* with a regular income—such as the sole proprietor of a business—can come under this chapter. There is a requirement that income must be received predictably enough for the debtor to make regular payments. For example, a Social Security recipient can take advantage of Chapter 13.

There are no involuntary petitions under Chapter 13. The debtor initiates this type of bankruptcy proceeding by filing a petition. This petition operates as an order of relief and brings about an automatic stay of collection efforts by creditors.

Chapter 13 allows a debtor to propose a *plan of debt adjustment* that will provide for repayment of creditors. In the plan the debtor lays out a schedule showing how he or she is going to pay off creditors. The court will appoint a trustee to oversee operation of the plan.

Prior to approval of the plan, the court will hold a hearing in which the plan will be presented by the debtor or the debtor's lawyer. The judge will ask for the trustee's recommendations and will listen to comments by the creditors. On the basis of the hearing, the court will confirm the plan or ask that the plan be modified.

While the court-approved plan is in effect, creditors are prohibited from garnisheeing, levying, foreclosing, or otherwise putting additional pressure on the debtor. The time period is usually three years but can be extended by the Court as long as five years.

The idea behind this chapter originated in the economic depression of the 1930s: Give the debtor time to pay and the creditors will collect more.

Generally, creditors are better off having a debtor use Chapter 13 than if they filed an involuntary petition under Chapter 7. The payoff will be slower under Chapter 13, but it will be higher.

For eligibility, the debtor's unsecured debts (whether single or joint with a spouse) must be less than $100,000 and secured debts less than $350,000. A debtor will not be eligible for Chapter 13 if, at any time within the preceding 180 days, the debtor had a bankruptcy case dismissed for willful failure to follow court orders, failed to appear in court to follow through on the case, or filed to obtain voluntary dismissal of the prior case.

The plan that is approved by the Court will not satisfy all creditors because it will call for partial payment of many debts and the discharge (forgiveness) of debts that won't be paid. Unsecured creditors will have no right to object to the plan as long as they would receive at least the amount they would have received under Chapter 7 liquidation.

Since Chapter 13 plans call for payments over time, rather than immediate payment, you as a creditor must factor in the time value of money (interest) in deciding whether you will receive "at least" the amount you would have received in the case of the debtor's liquidation. Pay attention to the interest rate applied to the payments, sometimes called a discount rate. For example, if you feel that the debtor's liquidation would bring you $4,000, and that the appropriate interest rate is 8 percent, this is the equivalent of three annual payments of $1,552, or $4,656 in total. If the interest rate used is 12 percent, the payments should be $1,665 each for a total of $4,995.

There are three alternative ways that a secured creditor can be treated in an approved plan:

1. The secured creditor may approve of his or her treatment under the plan.

2. The debtor may transfer the secured property to the creditor.

3. The secured creditor will retain the lien on the property until the debt is paid, and payments under the plan will be equal to the present value of the property.

If you should find yourself in the position of a secured creditor, you will have to figure out the method that is most likely to give you the best return. Some secured creditors might be willing to "take the security and run," that is, take their chances with selling or finding a use for the property (method number 2). If you aren't familiar with the market in which the property is traded (so that you can accurately forecast how much you'll receive for it and how long it will take to sell), method number 2 may not be wise. All in all, method number 3 is likely to be the most satisfactory, but you, the debtor, and the bankruptcy trustee may have to negotiate about interest rates or the value of the collateral.

Generally, plans that conform to requirements of the Bankruptcy Act, that appear to be workable, and that the court feels are proposed in good faith will be approved by the court. Once a plan is approved by the court, it binds the debtor and all creditors, even the ones who objected.

The debtor has the option of converting to a Chapter 7 liquidation or a Chapter 11 reorganization if the plan can't be followed through. Creditors, on the other hand, cannot force the debtor into liquidation once Chapter 13 has been elected by the debtor.

After the debtor has completed all payments under the plan, the court will hold a discharge hearing. The debtor must attend.

Remaining debts will be discharged (with some exceptions). Filing and discharge may take place as frequently as the debtor wishes. There is no six-year rule such as in a Chapter 7 liquidation.

You can protect yourself against a debtor's right to use Chapter 13 over and over again. Request a credit report from each credit applicant. Pay attention to what it says about bankruptcy. If the debtor is currently paying off creditors under a Chapter 13 plan, decide whether you want to chance giving credit to someone who is probably already fully burdened with payments.

The law provides another protection. The debtor may not receive a second discharge in a case begun within six years of the date the petition in the first case was filed *if* the first case involved a Chapter 13 discharge in which the debtor paid less than 100 percent of the allowed unsecured claims or less than 70 percent of those claims and if the court decides the plan was not the debtor's best effort or was not proposed in good faith. A discharge can also be set aside within one year if a creditor can show fraud on the part of the debtor.

There are several differences between Chapter 7 and Chapter 13 liquidations. We'll point out the important ones. These differences, plus the ones we've already pointed out, are important to understand when you and other creditors are trying to decide whether to force an individual into Chapter 7 when he or she could be counseled to file voluntarily under Chapter 13.

The automatic stay under Chapter 13 is broader than under Chapter 7. The stay applies to attempts to collect from anyone who is jointly liable for the bankrupt's debts. This second person need not have filed for Chapter 13. Only if the debtor's plan proposes to pay less than the full amount of the debt can creditors apply for relief from this stay. If relief is approved, creditors can then try to collect from the codebtor. This expanded type of stay applies only to consumer debts—those incurred for personal or household purposes.

When Chapter 7 liquidation is taking place, all nonexempt property is included that was owned at the time of the petition. Under Chapter 13 wage-earner bankruptcy, there is added to the petition-date property any *additional property acquired during the period of the plan*. Thus, more property will be available to carry out the plan of debt adjustment.

The Bankruptcy Court will issue an "Employer Deduction Order" to any person or business that is a source of the debtor's funds. It's not only the debtor's employer who receives such an order, but also the Social Security Administration, county welfare office, Aid to Dependent Children . . . any source that provides regular payments to the debtor. These sources pay into the trustee, who then pays the creditors.

A Chapter 13 discharge is broader than a Chapter 7 discharge. The only debts not discharged are those for alimony, maintenance, child support, and debts with a due date longer than the length of the plan—for example, real estate mortgage debts. The reasoning for the broader discharge is this: By the time of completion of the plan the debtor has paid all the debts he or she has been able to pay.

CHAPTER 11: REORGANIZATION

Chapter 11 provides for reorganization and continuation of a business. After debts are discharged, the business continues as a going concern. Either a voluntary or an involuntary petition can be used to put a business into Chapter 11.

The Bankruptcy Court will appoint one or more committees of creditors, depending upon the number and size of debts. A committee of unsecured creditors is required. Ordinarily, the holders of the seven largest claims will constitute that committee.

The committee or committees investigate the operation and financial structure of the debtor, consult with professionals such as accountants, and negotiate and counsel the debtor over the best ways to carry out the reorganization. A trustee may or may not be appointed, depending primarily upon whether assets will be sold. On the request of one of the creditors, the Bankruptcy Court may appoint an examiner to look into allegations of fraud or other misbehavior by the debtor.

After the court issues an order of relief, the debtor is given 120 days to file a plan for reorganization. After that time creditors can file their own plan.

To be approved by the court, a plan must:

▬ Identify classes of creditors and other interests, including those that are "impaired" (to be paid less than the full amount of the claim).

▬ Specify the treatment of impaired claims.

▬ Provide for equal treatment within a class.

▬ Set out workable means for carrying out the reorganization, for example, selling certain assets and extending maturity dates on debts.

▬ Be consistent with the interest of creditors, stockholders, and public policy.

In order for a plan to be confirmed by the court it must be accepted by any class of creditors whose claims have been impaired. A majority of the members of a class who have claims totaling two-thirds of the dollar amount of claims must accept. (Acceptance is not necessary if the claims of the class have not been impaired.) Once a *class* accepts the plan, it is binding on all members of that class.

There are provisions for court confirmation, in some cases, despite nonacceptance by an impaired class of creditors. This is referred to as "cram-down." (Still, no creditor can be forced into a plan who would thereby receive less than under a Chapter 7 liquidation.)

Once a plan has been confirmed, it is binding on all parties, such as creditors, stockholders, and the debtor. Confirmation ordinarily works as a discharge of all debts, unless provided otherwise in the plan.

The plan can provide that specified claims and interests not be discharged. If a debtor is unable to adhere to the plan, a Chapter 7 liquidation can still be carried out.

CHAPTER PERSPECTIVE

Without credit most businesses would have to close their doors. By extending too much (or too little) credit a business can put its future in jeopardy. Once a firm or an individual is in financial trouble, the bankruptcy code offers relief not only to the debtor but also to the creditor.

Leasing and Buying

You will need a location to carry on your business. You may need furniture and equipment. You will have to make a choice whether to *lease* or *buy* land, buildings, furniture, cars, computers, or other equipment and fixtures needed by your business. In this chapter we will discuss the pros and cons of buying versus leasing. Because of its importance as a means of acquiring the use of business property we will concentrate mainly on leasing.

After studying the material in this chapter:

━ You will be able to decide whether leasing rather than buying is the way to go.

━ You will know how to find a lessor to provide the equipment and real property you need.

━ You will be able to interpret a leasing contract and negotiate its contents with the lessor.

━ You will understand the legalities of acquiring real property.

━ You will know when you need to see a lawyer.

To lease property—whether real property such as land and buildings or personal property such as furniture and other equipment—means to rent it from the owner. While the terms *rent* and *lease* are sometimes used interchangeably, the former more frequently refers to a short-term arrangement. A *lease* generally refers to an arrangement lasting longer than a year, sometimes many years, in which the *lessor* (who owns the property) allows the *lessee* to use the property as freely and openly as if it belonged to the lessee.

There is an important distinction between a lease of real property—that is, land and buildings—and a lease of other business property, such as equipment and furniture. First of all, we have to clear up a bit of confusing legal terminology.

In a legal sense, there are two kinds of tangible—touchable—property: real and personal. Either can be used for business or for personal activities. That is, you can use a room in your home (real property) as a bedroom (personal use) or as an office (business). Similarly, you might use an automobile (personal property) to drive to the store for groceries (personal use) or to visit a client (business). When we refer to personal property in this chapter we mean *business use, non-real property*. Let's now take a look at leasing this personal property.

PERSONAL PROPERTY

The decision to lease equipment and other personal property is usually based on economic factors, not legal ones. The major advantage of leasing is that it gives you the use of the property with the least money paid up front. In the long run buying may appear to be cheaper, but you may find yourself owning equipment that has become outdated. Let's take a look at all of the true advantages that can be put together for leasing of personal, business use property.

■ Initial costs ("down payment") will be less than if the property were bought.

■ Payment terms can be more flexible, tailored to the pattern of cash flow of your business, with payments rising over time as your business becomes more successful, for instance.

■ In some cases there will be no adverse effects on your financial statements; accounting rules may allow the full debt obligation to be left off your balance sheet.

■ Experienced and highly specialized leasing service firms can advise you on equipment and put together packages to meet your needs. It will be easier and quicker to lease than to buy.

If you have already begun to take a look at leasing, you'll realize that the above list does not include two aspects usually stated as benefits of leasing. The first of these is a benefit related to taxes.

Tax Considerations

Beware! Federal income taxation is a complicated subject. Leasing salespeople have been known to take advantage of this complexity by talking vaguely about the tax advantages of leasing, hoping that the customer (lessee) will be fooled. The fact is, that in a business lease of personal property there are *not* likely to be substantial tax benefits to the lessee. Here are the reasons.

The cost of use of business equipment is tax deductible whether you lease or buy. If you lease, you can deduct the lease payments that you make to the lessor. If you buy, you can deduct depreciation and the interest cost you incur if you buy the asset "on time" or if you borrow to finance it. If your use of an auto is 60 percent of the time for business and 40 percent for pleasure, only 60 percent of the cost is deductible for taxes, *regardless of whether you lease or buy*.

Lease payments may be greater than depreciation plus interest. This is a tax benefit, however, only if you believe that having higher expenses is good because you get to deduct more on your taxes than if you paid less.

Before the Tax Reform Act of 1986 there was a tax benefit, called the investment tax credit, that could be shared between the lessor and lessee. But this tax benefit no longer exists, no matter what any leasing sales representative says.

On the other hand, there is still a tax advantage if *land* is being leased. If you own land, you can't deduct depreciation for it because land doesn't wear out. But you can deduct the payments you make to lease land. We are, however, talking about personal property. Later in the chapter we'll deal with real property.

Obsolescence

The other supposed benefit of leasing is the avoidance of obsolescence. That is, the lessee doesn't have to be concerned about technological changes because the equipment is returned to the lessor at the end of the lease. At that point the lessee can enter into a lease for more modern equipment, and the lessor is left holding the bag.

There are several problems with viewing leasing as a cure for obsolescence. First of all, many leases are written to give the lessee ownership of the property at the conclusion of the lease. Second, it is unrealistic to believe that a lessor is ignorant of the danger of obsolescence. In all likelihood the danger of obsolescence is just another cost that the lessor builds into the amount of the lease payment. Third, obsolescence might occur so quickly that the lessee would be stuck with outdated equipment, unable to get out of the lease without paying substantial cost penalties.

Disadvantages

Now, let's look at some of the problems of equipment leases.

1. At the end of the lease term you retain no economic value. Your payments, in a sense, are going down the drain. (However, you can usually tailor the lease so that you assume ownership of the equipment—if you wish.)

2. It will be costly, perhaps very costly, to get out of the lease prior to its termination. For example, if a proprietorship or partnership goes out of business, the owners will be personally liable for continuing to pay the costs of the lease.

Economic Factors

We have left out of our analysis a summation of the *cost* of leasing versus buying. But, as we said earlier, the decision to lease equipment *should be based on economic factors*, not legal ones.

Among the economic factors that must be considered are interest rates, income tax rates, the expected residual value of the property at the conclusion of the lease (and who owns this value), and who pays for the costs of maintenance, property taxes, and insurance. Your CPA is the best person to analyze the economics of equipment leasing. (Don't rely on the lessor!) Tell your accountant that you want a present value analysis, also called a discounted cash flow analysis, of the benefits of leasing versus buying the asset. With this important tool you will be able to make an objective decision on which way you should go.

BUYING REAL PROPERTY

Since so many persons are already familiar with the basics of buying real estate we are going to make this section short and to-the-point.

Entrepreneurs starting up a new business will be unlikely to buy land or land and buildings. Cash is needed more to pay for inventory, salaries, and operating costs than for a down payment on property. Also, ownership of real property—with mortgage and tax payments—increases the risks of being in a small business. Not only do you have to find the cash to buy inventory and to pay salaries, utilities, and other expenses, but you also have to make mortgage and tax payments. In other words, try to separate the two issues: buying real estate and being in business. Further, be wary of buying a business in which real estate is a major part of the purchase. Sometimes sellers try to build up the prospects of their businesses so they can get an inflated price for the real estate.

You may feel you *must* have the business, yet you realize you would be wiser not to own the real estate. In this case it may be possible to work out a sale of the real estate to an investor from whom you can lease the business premises. Discuss it with the seller's real estate broker. Try making a proposition to a business acquaintance. Mention it to your accountant and attorney. You could try running an ad in the newspaper, too.

Suppose you believe the real estate is a good investment. If you have adequate cash for a down payment and if you can arrange financing, it might make sense to buy the real estate in the name of your children (or in your personal name if the business will be run as a corporation). By keeping the real estate separate from the rest of the business assets, you will stand a better chance of retaining it if the firm fails. In addition, it would be partially paid for with lease payments from your corporation. There are tax advantages, too. You can take a deduction for depreciation on your personal tax return, and your corporation can deduct the lease payments from the corporate income reported on the tax return.

How Real Estate Is Bought

The first step in a real estate purchase that has significant legal consequences is the signing by the buyer and the seller of a *contract for sale*. Ordinarily, the buyer will make an offer to the seller to purchase the property on terms that the buyer drafts into a proposed contract for sale. The buyer will accompany the offer with a payment to bind the deal, referred to as an *earnest money deposit*. When the seller accepts the offer and signs the contract, the deal is made.

The contract for sale contains the terms of the transaction from which lawyers for the two parties will draft up the deed, mortgage, closing statement, and any other necessary documents. At an agreed-upon time—referred to as the *closing*—the buyer and the seller (or their legal representatives) will meet to complete the transaction. The seller will furnish to the buyer a deed that will be recorded at the county courthouse. The buyer is responsible for paying the balance that is due, or for having arranged for a financial institution or other lender to do so. In cases where the seller is providing all or part of the financing, the papers relevant to this deal will be included with the other closing documents.

The sales contract does not, by itself, transfer title to the property, but it *binds* the buyer and the seller in important ways. Thus, even though some buyers and some sellers do not bring their attorneys into the transaction until later, it is wise to seek legal advice prior to the signing of the sales contract. Otherwise, you must be *very* attentive to what you are signing.

In the heat of back-and-forth negotiation, however, it may be difficult to consult an attorney before the contract is signed. We will go over some of the details of the contract to point out potential problem areas.

If, after a contract has been signed, the seller tries to back out, the buyer may be able to enforce specific performance of the contract, that is, may be able to force the seller to go through with the sale. On the other hand, if the buyer attempts to back out, the seller's recourse will be limited to a recovery of damages. The contract should specify that the earnest money deposit paid by the buyer constitutes the agreed-upon damages, and the buyer should make the deposit as small as the seller is willing to accept. (It is not necessary to go along with the real estate agent's statement as to what the seller is likely to accept.)

The buyer can be further protected by making the offer contingent upon events that will be resolved later, such as approval of the terms of the deal by the buyer's attorney or the buyer's partner, a satisfactory report by a real estate inspector of the buyer's choosing, termite inspection, or securing financing at a rate and on terms specified by the buyer in the contract. Contingencies such as these must be used with restraint. Otherwise the seller will object to them as being what they really are—loopholes through which the buyers can escape if they have a change of heart.

The contract should require the seller to provide a title report, abstract of title, or a title insurance policy to the buyer within a stated number of days. If any defects in title (doubts about ownership) are revealed, the seller can be given additional time to pay off liens, get quitclaim deeds, or otherwise clear up the clouds on the title.

Once the contingencies specified in the contract have been satisfied and it appears that the seller can deliver marketable title, the buyer is obligated to pay the purchase price. However, there is generally a period of several weeks between the first examination of the title and the date, after closing, when the deed is recorded. During this time it is possible that the seller may have mortgaged the property or sold an option to another person to purchase the property; in addition, there may have been recorded against the property tax liens or liens arising from lawsuits. The buyer's interests must be protected against these possibilities.

One method of protection for the buyer is to consummate the transaction "in escrow." The buyer's purchase moneys and the seller's deed are together deposited with an escrow agent. The escrow agent (in some communities called an escrowee) is an independent third party who takes responsibility first for seeing that no cloud has appeared on the courthouse records of title before recording the deed, and second that the funds are released to the seller. Where a mortgage is involved, the mortgage funds will also be placed in escrow. Title companies and banks offer escrow services for a small fee.

A second method of protection for the buyer is a title insurance policy covering the "gap" period between the initial title examination and the recording of the buyer's deed.

DEFINITIONS SIGNIFICANT TO REAL ESTATE TRANSACTIONS

Assignment transfer of property rights from one party (the assignor) to another (the assignee). A lease might be assigned by one lessee to another, giving the second lessee the same rights held by the original lessee.

Convey legalistic way to say "transfer" or "sell."

Deed formal document evidencing the transfer of title (ownership) to real estate from the grantor to the grantee. In a warranty deed the grantor makes certain warranties or guarantees—for example, that the property is free of mortgages except as noted in the deed. Quitclaim deeds are used to clear up the ownership of a disputed piece of property. A quitclaim deed makes no warranties. In it the grantor says, in effect, "I convey to you the grantee whatever interest I own in the land (which may be none)." To be binding on other persons, a deed must be recorded at the county courthouse.

Deed restriction a deed may contain a clause or clauses that restrict the buyer's freedom of use of the property—for example, to sell liquor or to maintain a used car lot.

Easement an interest in land that involves use but not occupancy of the land. For example, a utility company might hold an easement to string electric lines across a property, or some neighbors might hold an easement to cross a property in order to gain access to their property.

claim against property that remains a claim until paid. A mortgage is one kind of lien, but there are also mechanic's, judgment, tax, and other types of liens.

Mortgage type of lien against real property. A purchase money mortgage is a conveyance of an interest in the property to the person or institution who loaned the buyer the funds to make the purchase. Mortgages will be recorded at the courthouse. If you buy property that has been mortgaged, you own that property "subject to" the mortgage. This means someone else—the mortgagee—also owns an interest in the property. A buyer who expressly agrees to accept responsibility for paying the mortgage is said to have assumed the mortgage.

Power of attorney legal document gives someone else the authority to carry out business transactions of the person who grants the power. The person holding the power need not be an attorney. The power should be recorded at the courthouse, since it includes the authority to transfer real estate.

Survey chart or picture drawn up to show boundaries and buildings. It's a good idea to get a survey of land you are buying.

Title ownership of real estate, the evidence of which is a deed recorded at the courthouse. An attorney or title company must carry out a title search to determine if the seller is able to convey marketable title, that is, title not likely to result in litigation over actual ownership. An abstract of title is a document prepared to show all the deeds, inheritances, mortgages, and so forth by which the prospective buyer (or the buyer's attorney) can determine the marketability of the title.

Zoning laws regulations enacted by most municipalities to govern the use of land, usually restricting the operation of certain kinds of business activities to certain areas of the city. Unfavorable zoning can *seriously* affect the value of land.

CHAPTER PERSPECTIVE
To buy or to lease is a business decision, a financial decision, and a legal decision. None of these considerations should be given short shrift, and professional advice is important.

Insurance

Business insurance mixes a variety of business and legal considerations. Your state's laws may contain some cut-and-dried requirements for workers compensation insurance, for example, while such things as inventory and liability insurance can take a multitude of forms.

There are no fill-in-the-blanks forms to provide you with a list of the appropriate insurance for your business. And there is no "right" amount of insurance. Insurance needs can be determined only after a detailed analysis of your particular business . . . and your ability and need to pay for protection.

Insurance professionals can assist you in making these determinations. However, beware of insurance "packages" that have not been specifically tailored to your particular situation.

After studying the material in this chapter:

━ You will approach insurance as one tool of your business's overall risk-management plan.

━ You will be able to set priorities in terms of the kinds of insurance policies you purchase.

━ You will understand the basic concepts of insurance.

━ You will appreciate some of your obligations and rights as a policyholder.

━ You will be able to recognize some of the standard forms of insurance policies.

RISK MANAGEMENT THROUGH INSURANCE

Insurance is a system whereby you can pay a fee, or premium, to someone who agrees to share various risks with you. This is a form of risk management intended to lessen the impact of setbacks or potentially catastrophic events to your business.

The insurance contract comes in the form of a policy between you (the insured) and the insurance company (the insurer). As a result of passage of the federal McCarran-Ferguson Act, regulation of these contracts has been left to the states, resulting in a wide range of controls and requirements. So, keep in mind that insurance laws and regulations vary from state to state; there are no national guidelines.

State laws deal with such things as classes of risks, procedures for determining premiums, and minimum training requirements for brokers and agents. In some cases, they stipulate language to be used in insurance documents.

Most states have established insurance commissions or boards whose job it is to regulate insurance companies and ensure that they are financially sound and operate ethically and in a manner to protect the public interest. If you have questions or concerns about a particular policy or company, check directory assistance in your state capital for the telephone number of the state insurance regulatory agency.

When you see references to "domestic" companies, those are companies created in your state. "Foreign" companies are out-of-state companies doing business in your state.

Planning to Control Risk

The small businessperson learns quickly that ample opportunities exist for spending money on insurance premiums: life insurance, property insurance, auto insurance, professional liability insurance, health insurance, key employee insurance, product liability insurance . . . and on and on. Since some risks covered by such insurance policies are potentially lethal to the health of the business, the temptation to buy policies to cover all these risks can be quite strong.

For example, the small company that engages in high-volume manufacture and distribution of novelty items might be ruined by a warehouse fire just before the Christmas buying season without adequate property and inventory insurance. Or the consulting firm whose success depends on the business development acumen of its founders could be permanently derailed by the death of a key principal without key employee insurance.

Running a business enterprise is like any other human endeavor: It has risks that cannot be totally eliminated. The insurance contract is intended to spread those risks—for a fee—to avoid the kind of business disasters just described. However, businesses, like individuals, cannot afford to eliminate all risks.

As with other aspects of your business, your insurance needs must be analyzed and then factored in to your overall budget and plan. To arrive at an idea of adequate and affordable coverage you need to determine the following:

━ The potential events that could seriously injure or even wreck your business. Try to be as specific as possible in constructing this list.

━ The likelihood that these risky events might occur, and how much it is worth to you to avoid absorbing the entire risk.

━ The various alternatives for controlling the risks, including the use of insurance contracts, self-insurance, and risk reduction measures.

When you put together the list of risks, do not include all the things that might—but almost surely won't—happen; on the other hand, make sure you take account of events that are possible and would be critical to your business. Remember the citrus growers in Florida with their frozen oranges when you think some possibilities might be awfully remote. Or the destroyed businesses and homes in Charleston, S.C., after Hurricane Hugo.

When you estimate the likelihood of events occurring, make two lists: (1) events that need occur only once to be devastating to your business (for example, a fire destroying your warehouse) and (2) those events that would be damaging but not devastating (for example, a flooded basement in your store). Then try to estimate the worth of sharing the risk of these events by obtaining insurance coverage.

As the final step in evaluating and trying to plan for controlling the risks in your business, consider the alternatives available. Naturally, insurance is a major tool. However, you should also consider the following:

━ Higher deductibles (the amount you pay before the policy payments kick in) can significantly lower your premiums.

━ Making certain safety improvements (for example, installation of a fire sprinkler system or secure storage of certain hazardous materials) can also lower your premiums. Reputable insurance companies have representatives who can help you plan these improvements.

━ Self-coverage for certain small losses might be less expensive than paying insurance contract premiums, and you might want to budget regular payments into this self-coverage account.

In addition to insurance policies, there are two other possibilities for controlling your risks, subcontracting and redundancy.

Subcontracting. You can avoid certain risks by engaging others to perform tasks that involve those risks. For example, if you are a consultant or an engineering company conducting environmental assessments, you might want to subcontract any work that involves testing or handling of hazardous materials, an activity for which insurance might be prohibitively expensive or virtually impossible to come by at all. Specialists in such fields are often able to use their superior equipment or experience to get the job done at a lower cost.

Redundancy. This term refers to backing up materials or information critical to your business. For example, with the unprecedented reliance on computer media, many companies on a daily basis place "back up," this is, duplicate computer media, in secure, off-site storage facilities. Those firms that cannot afford even a short down time because of fire or other disaster might also establish or rent an off-site "hot" computer facility to allow them to get back in business immediately after what otherwise might be a fatal event to their ongoing business.

Importance of Good Advice

A natural question that arises during the course of putting together your insurance plan is what kind of professional advice to get. The first point is to be sure to seek that advice. But it's up to you to decide whether to go to an independent broker, who sells insurance products from various insurance companies, or an agent who represents only one company.

The argument for the independent broker is that you will get recommendations for the products that suit you best, regardless of the company selling it. Of course, brokers may get more favorable commissions from some companies than from others. The argument for the single-company agents is that they will be experts in the details and nuances of the various insurance products sold by their respective companies, thus making them better able to tailor the products to your business.

Before making a final decision, do some reconnaissance among your business colleagues—especially those in firms similar to your own—before you make a decision. Advice and recommendations from people who have already gone through the experience of purchasing insurance can be invaluable—provided that you evaluate them in light of your own circumstances.

Risk Management Checklist

Before completing the plan for your insurance and risk management program, answer the following questions. If you are not able to answer yes to each question, further action is necessary.

1. In constructing your insurance/risk management plan, have you carefully considered all potential events that constitute risks to your business?

2. Have you differentiated between those risks that would devastate your business and those that would be injurious but not fatal?

3. Have you calculated your ability to pay insurance premiums for the coverage you have decided you need?

4. Have you examined ways of obtaining coverage but reducing premiums through such measures as higher deductibles?

5. Have you considered other measures besides insurance for managing your risks—subcontracting, redundancy, installation of safety improvements, and so on?

6. Have you sought advice about companies, brokers, and agents from others in your field, and have you retained a reputable insurance representative to help you?

7. Is your insurance plan tailored specifically to the operations of your firm?

THE INSURANCE CONTRACT

Keep in mind that an insurance policy is a contract between you (the insured) and the company (the insurer), thus is subject to some formal contract requirements.

This does not mean that the policy should be in legalese and reduced to Lilliputian-size type. Buy only from insurance brokers or agents who can and will explain *all* aspects of the policy, and don't hesitate to ask questions. Note also that some states require "plain-English" insurance policies. In claims disputes, courts are likely to interpret against the insurance company if the language is blatantly ambiguous or misleading.

The insurance contract must have these elements:

- Offer
- Acceptance
- Consideration
- Legal purpose
- Capacity to make the contract

You make the offer when you complete the application and tender your check. However, there is no contract (or coverage) until the insurance company accepts the offer, that is, approves the application for the policy.

An agent handling an application for life insurance typically has no authority to approve the application; that approval usually comes from the company's home office. With other kinds of insurance, such as auto or fire, agents may be authorized to issue "binders," which make the policy effective immediately, prior to home office issuance of the policy. These binders are temporary contracts.

In some circumstances, issuance of a policy might actually be a counteroffer instead of an acceptance. For example, if the physical examination generally required for key employee life insurance turns up some questionable findings, the company might decide to issue a policy different from the one for which you had applied. If you agree, then you have in effect accepted the counteroffer.

Consideration sometimes is referred to as a bargained-for exchange or an exchange of promises. In the case of an insurance policy, you promise to pay the insurance premium, and the company promises to cover you if some specified event (death, a fire at the plant, etc.) occurs.

The requirement of a legal purpose is fairly self-explanatory. No court is likely to enforce a contract in which you agree to pay a hired killer; nor is it likely to smile on an insurance contract on illicit goods, such as a marijuana crop.

The requirement for an insurable interest is to make sure that such contracts are consistent with public policy. Here are two examples of contracts that would not be consistent with public policy: (1) someone you don't know, with no interest in your business, obtains a fire insurance contract on your store; (2) a member of your civic club, otherwise unknown to you, obtains a life insurance policy on you. The people in both these examples do not have a valid insurable interest, thus the insurance contracts would be void and contrary to public policy.

Some legal commentators note that this requirement is an infringement on a person's freedom to make contracts, but the purpose is to remove the temptation to do wrong or harm to someone else for monetary gain.

With regard to insurance on property, it is not necessary to own the property in order to have an insurable interest. If you rent your store building, for example, you would suffer a loss if the building burned; therefore, you could have an insurable interest in the building as well as in the contents. Both the mortgagor and mortgagee of property have an interest, too, and both may insure their proportionate shares.

With life insurance, you might also have an insurable interest in another person's life. For example, a partner or key employee central to the successful operation of the business is often insured to provide compensation for the business loss in the event of that person's death.

Cancellation, Misrepresentation, and Other Issues

Once you obtain the insurance contract, obviously you expect the company to continue sharing the risk with you and to pay off in the event of a loss covered by the policy. So be alert to some pitfalls inherent in insurance contracts.

Insurance laws vary from state to state, so do not rely on knowledge or experience gained elsewhere. If you encounter a problem or question, confer with an attorney familiar with the insurance laws in the state in which you operate.

Cancellation might occur for several reasons: nonpayment of premiums, material misrepresentation of facts in your application, or concealment of material (important) information, for example. Be aware, however, that you might have a strong case to reverse the cancellation decision, depending on the facts in your situation.

Typically, once a policy is in effect you have a grace period past the due date in which you can pay the premium without cancellation. Some states require that notice be given before an insurance policy is canceled to avoid having critical coverage for such things as fire damage and auto liability suddenly disappear.

It is important in completing insurance applications to be accurate, honest, and forthcoming with material information. Otherwise, you may be paying for coverage that could be voided for a number of reasons. Some policies incorporate your application as a part of the contract.

Misrepresentation of material facts is one mistake that could void your policy. Information in the application is used by the company to determine both whether it will issue a policy and what the policy premiums will be. Some inaccurate statements might be immaterial, that is, they would not logically be expected to affect the company's decision one way or another. For example, you might say that your warehouse is painted red when on closer observation the color is orange.

One example of material misrepresentation of facts would be where the insurance company requires a smoke and heat alarm system before insuring a warehouse; in addition, the company significantly reduces premiums if there is a working sprinkler system. You report on the application that the warehouse has both the alarm system and the working sprinkler system, whereas in fact it has neither. You have given the insurance company two reasons to cancel your policy. Of course, they may not do so . . . until there is a fire and the subsequent investigation reveals that the equipment was not in place.

The flip side of material misrepresentation is concealment of material information. Again using the warehouse example, if you are aware of a subterranean seam of coal underneath your warehouse that has been burning for some months, and if there has been a recent buildup of methane gas in the vicinity, you have a sure recipe for an eventual explosion and fire. Not informing the insurance company of this condition is concealment of clearly material information.

In some instances, you might be able to argue that the insurance company has waived its rights under the contract. Taking again the example of the requirement for an alarm system and working sprinkler system, assume that you operate the warehouse for a time without them, then decide that it would be good practice to install them. After doing so, you tell the insurance company agent. He informs you that, since the policy requirements are now being met, the policy will remain in force. The company has probably waived its right to cancel for that particular misrepresentation. But, again, be reminded that insurance laws and decisions vary from state to state.

If you have a loss covered by insurance, be aware that timely notice is required by policies, and you must provide proof of loss. Check your policy for the specific requirements. If you and the insurance company do not agree on the amount you should be paid, check for a section in the policy that would provide for arbitration of the dispute.

Subrogation is an insurance term that means that you give your rights to sue a third party to the insurance company. For example, if someone hits and ruins your truck, the insurance company might pay you full damages, then sue the third party in order to recover its payment to you.

Over- and Underinsuring

A note of caution is appropriate when it comes to determining how much insurance to carry on a given risk.

With regard to overinsuring, your recovery is limited to the value of the loss, no matter what figure you put on the insurance policy. Had you insured your destroyed truck for $200,000 and it was worth $20,000, you will recover $20,000, the total of your insurable interest. Breaking even is the best you can do.

What about underinsuring? You may be subject to a coinsurance clause. These clauses typically provide that you may recover up to the face value of the policy provided that the property is insured for a certain percentage of the full value, usually 80 percent. If you insure for less than that percentage, you may become a coinsurer, that is, you share the cost with the insurance company.

Insurance Contract Checklist

In reviewing your insurance contract, you should be able to answer yes to the following questions:

1. Does the policy conform with the requirements that you have an insurable interest for a legal purpose?
2. In completing the application for insurance, have you been accurate and honest regarding the facts reported?
3. Have you reported all material facts, even though they were not specifically requested?
4. Have you taken care to carry the appropriate amount of insurance, in order to avoid over- and underinsurance problems?
5. Do you understand the terms of the policy, and have you asked questions when in doubt?

TYPES OF INSURANCE

As noted at the outset of this chapter, there seems to be insurance for just about anything for which people or businesses are willing to pay a premium. Some types of insurance coverage are basic, and operating without them can be folly (fire insurance, for example). Others may be appropriate only in certain circumstances or with some businesses (key employee insurance, for example).

Following are various types of business insurance that may be important to your company.

Fire Insurance

Fire insurance is intended to protect you from loss from a hostile fire that is the immediate or proximate cause of the fire.

A hostile fire is one that is uncontrollable or intentionally set. Proximate cause means that although the fire may not have directly inflicted the damage, it set into motion the events that inflicted the damage. Keep in mind the coinsurance provisions when obtaining such coverage.

Fire insurance is fairly standardized in the U.S. and typically covers three basic contingencies: fire, lightning, and losses to goods removed from the property because of the fire. Typically, special coverage (at additional cost) is necessary to protect against other losses such as failure to protect property after the fire, theft, and so forth.

Auto Insurance

The two primary types of insurance here are liability and collision.

Liability insurance provides protection for the owner or driver from the claims of third parties, in the event of injuries or damages caused by the negligence of the driver.

Collision insurance provides protection for the insured party's own vehicle, regardless of which party is held liable. The insured party is obligated to cooperate fully with the insurance company with regard to claims, and the insurance company is obligated to defend the insured party against suits that might come under the policy's coverage.

Some states require no-fault insurance, which requires payment when the insured party is injured without regard to fault. Comprehensive insurance covers a variety of physical loss other than that covered under collision insurance.

Be aware that you may be liable for accidents involving the vehicles of others, such as employees and vendors, if they are acting in some capacity on your behalf.

Life Insurance

Life insurance provides compensation in the event of death. You may need to provide life insurance for the families of employees in order to be competitive in hiring good people. Some group policies will be deductible as a business expense.

Another use of life insurance, as discussed earlier, is to provide compensation to the company in the event of the death of a key employee.

Life insurance comes in many shapes and sizes, ranging from simple term policies (death benefits only, with no cash buildup) to life insurance annuities that can be used to provide pension benefits to your employees.

Health and Disability Insurance
The continually rising costs of health care can be devastating, and many employees now consider health and disability insurance more important than life insurance.

In addition to basic medical and hospitalization insurance, major medical insurance, which is intended to cope with catastrophic illnesses or injuries, is frequently offered. Some companies also include in their employee coverage dental and eyeglass insurance. Another type of coverage, disability insurance, pays employees a portion of their salary during temporary or extended illnesses.

Other Policies
As stated earlier, you probably can find an insurance policy for any risk or eventuality if you are willing to pay the premium. Here are some examples.

Umbrella liability insurance is intended to cover exceptionally large claims that exceed your basic liability policies.

Business interruption insurance pays you for losses suffered when you have to shut down as a result of major disasters, such as the 1989 San Francisco earthquake and Hurricane Hugo.

Transportation insurance supplements that provided by common carriers since those carriers typically are not liable for all possible losses.

Errors and omissions insurance is a form of malpractice liability coverage favored by such businesses as engineering consultants, professional service corporations, and other consultant groups.

Owners, landlords, and tenants insurance is intended to protect the policyholder from any liability arising from ownership, use, or maintenance of property.

Product liability insurance is intended to cover businesses whose products injure someone because they are defective or unsafe.

Glass insurance might constitute a separate policy if the business premises have large areas of plate glass.

Employee theft and misconduct insurance is self-explanatory.

Checklist on Types of Insurance

In evaluating your insurance coverage, you should be able to answer yes to these questions:

1. Have you matched your insurance policy coverage to the actual risks and needs of your particular business?

2. Have you coordinated your insurance coverage to assure that you are not paying for overlapping coverage and that there are no gaps in your coverage?

3. If you have special risks or considerations in your business, have you assured yourself that these are adequately covered by your insurance, even to the extent of having special-purpose policy coverage?

4. Does insurance for your employees make your benefits competitive with other businesses of your type?

CHAPTER PERSPECTIVE

Insurance is a basic tool of risk management planning for your business, but it should be incorporated into an overall plan. Avoid off-the-shelf packages, and make sure that your coverage is specifically tailored to the needs of your business. Guard against overlapping coverage and gaps in your policies. Above all, make sure that you are protected against any potential event or loss that would put you out of business.

Patents, Copyrights, Trademarks, and Trade Secrets

This chapter deals with what is often referred to as "intellectual property"—certain kinds of ideas reflected in products, processes, writings, symbols or names.

Although this kind of property is different in kind from, for example, real estate, the property rights are real, and they can be valuable. If you own those property rights, it is important that you know how to identify and protect them. If someone else owns those property rights, you need to avoid infringing on those rights.

This kind of property is not solely the concern of large companies, either. A small company may have a unique product or process that should be patented, or may be relying on a "new" product or process that has already been patented by someone else. In these and other instances the business owners must make an effort to protect themselves.

Various issues covered elsewhere in this book are governed by local, state, or federal laws—or various combinations thereof. Federal law governs patents and copyrights. In addition, there are various patent and copyright laws in foreign countries that may be applicable.

After studying the material in this chapter:

▬ You will be able to identify intellectual property that can be valuable and deserves protection.

▬ You will know how to exercise care so as not to infringe on the intellectual property rights of others.

▬ You will understand the complexities and technical procedures for protecting inventions via the patent process.

▬ You will know how to identify copyright, trademark, and trade secret opportunities, as well as the proper procedures for preserving rights in these areas.

PATENTS

A patent is a property right granted by the U.S. government through the Patent and Trademark Office. Such rights apply in the United States and its territories and possessions. Anyone who qualifies for a patent for an invention receives the grant for 17 years, conditional upon payment of so-called maintenance fees. Design patents for ornamental devices are granted for 3½, 7, or 14 years, as the applicant elects.

This property right has an important subtlety: The patent holder is not granted a right to make, use, or sell anything. Instead, the right is one "to exclude others from making, using, or selling the invention." Take an example: You may obtain a patent on a new assault weapon. This excludes others from making, using, or selling that weapon without permission, or a license, from you. However, if such assault weapons are outlawed, then you are also excluded from making, using, or selling the weapon.

On the other hand, if you obtain a patent for a new automobile transmission, there likely would be no restrictions on making, using, and selling that product. Others, however, would be excluded by your patent rights.

A "patent pending" notice simply informs the public that a patent application is on file in the Patent and Trademark Office. The law imposes a fine on anyone using this term falsely to deceive the public.

Patent rights have historically been seen as an incentive to invention and innovation. Indeed, the U.S. Constitution contains a patent provision: "Congress shall have power . . . to promote the progress of science and useful arts, by securing for limited times to authors and inventors the exclusive right to their respective writings and discoveries."

Before getting into the subject of what can be patented, three general guidelines should be noted:

1. Always assure yourself that you are not infringing upon an existing patent when you make, use, or sell your product.

2. Seek patents for your own inventions in a timely fashion, and provide for the assignment of patents to your company by persons in your employ.

3. Consider the commercial value of inventions before going through the sometimes lengthy and costly process of securing and defending a patent.

What Cannot Be Patented

Not just anything can be patented. The following areas are outside the boundary of patent protection:

■ An idea (as opposed to a mechanical device or product growing out of that idea).

■ A method of doing business. Example: The assembly line system would not be patentable; a particular piece of equipment or innovative device on the assembly line could be.

■ Printed materials (this falls under copyright protection).

■ An inoperable device.

■ A slight variation or slight improvement on a product that is obvious. Example: Using stronger plastic lenses to replace glass on auto taillights (although the chemical compound for making the new lenses might be patentable.)

National security issues also affect the ability to patent. An application for a patent on processes or products for producing fissionable material can be filed with the Patent and Trademark Office. However, such an application might be withheld if it is judged that national security could be affected.

What Can Be Patented

Although the subject of patents initially appears to be quite technical, there are some general guidelines that can be followed.

First, any new, useful, and unobvious process (usually industrial or technical), machine, manufacture or composition of matter (generally chemical compounds, formulas, etc.), or any new, useful, and unobvious improvement of the above.

Second, any new and unobvious original and ornamental design for an article of manufacture, such as for a pleasure boat or an automobile.

Third, any distinct and new variety of plant, other than tubes-propagated, which is asexually reproduced. (Asexually propagated plants are those that are reproduced by means other than from seeds, such as by the rooting of cuttings, layering, budding, grafting, and inarching.)

Obviously, these definitions are fairly broad, leaving room for a lot of judgment and subjective decisions to enter the process. How different does something have to be to be substantially different from "prior art"? How unobvious does an unobvious improvement have to be?

The dominant theme running through the definitions of what is patentable is *novelty*. It is important to be able to express this novelty explicitly, in writing and in illustrations. Furthermore, novelty has a short shelf life in the eyes of the Patent and Trademark Office—one year. These criteria should be used in testing the invention for novelty:

■ Was the invention known or used by others in this country before the invention by the applicant?

■ Was the invention patented or described in a printed publication in this or a foreign country before the invention by the applicant?

■ Was the invention described in a printed publication more than one year prior to the date of application for a patent in the United States?

■ Was the invention in public use or on sale in the country more than one year prior to the date of application for a patent in the United States?

Note: Even if the invention for which a patent is sought is not *exactly* the same as in previous products or processes, a patent may still be refused if the differences would be obvious or insignificant. Example: Making minor changes in the materials of a boat design. It's a good idea to conduct or arrange for a patent search prior to expending money and effort preparing a patent application of your own.

In addition to the requirement for novelty, an invention must be *useful* in order to be patented. This means that the invention must have a useful purpose, and it must be operable. Although there might be some debate about the useful purposes of some products, there is less room for debate about whether or not they work.

If the inventor describes the invention in a publication or uses the invention publicly, or places it on sale, he or she must apply for a patent before one year has gone by. Otherwise, the opportunity to obtain a patent has passed.

Ownership of Patents

The inventor applies for, obtains, and owns the patent. Having said that, some explanation and qualifications are required.

Only the inventor is the proper applicant for a patent. Spouse, financial backer, lawyer, or best friend cannot obtain the patent for your invention. However, if you die before obtaining the patent, the legal representatives of your estate may apply for the patent. If you are mentally incapacitated, your guardian may apply for the patent. If you refuse to apply for a patent and have a co-inventor, that person may apply for the patent.

In the case of two or more co-inventors, they may jointly apply for a patent. Joint ownership can occur in other forms, too, and without carefully drawn agreements, there is the potential for misunderstandings and disputes.

A patent is a form of personal property, thus can be partially or wholly sold to someone else; it can also be mortgaged, rented out (called licensing in the case of a patent), and passed to the owner's heirs at death.

When the owner of the patent transfers all or part of the ownership to someone else in writing, that transfer is called an assignment. Assignments can take various forms. They can limit the degree of transfer of ownership—one-fourth, for example. They can also specify certain limitations, such as use of the patent only in certain geographical areas or for specified uses or products.

CAUTION: It is dangerous to assign a part interest to someone without a specific agreement between the parties as to the extent of their respective rights and obligations. Otherwise, a partial owner may be able to make, use, and sell the invention for profit, without regard to the other owner, as well as sell the interest or grant licenses to third parties to make, use, and sell the product. *Carefully drawn conditions should accompany any assignment of patent rights.*

The patent owner may also grant or sell licenses to others. Remember that a patent *excludes* others from making, using, or selling the invention without permission. A license is that permission.

No particular form of license is required, so the patent owner should be careful to specify the rights granted under the license.

One question of ownership remains in a gray area that sometimes requires some subjective judgments. This has to do with a business or employment relationship from which a patentable invention grows.

Take these scenarios, for example.

Scenario One: You run a small company where everyone works in harmony in producing a widget for which you hold a patent. The business is successful and grows. One of the employees, during the course of work, also develops significant improvements on your widget, which you begin to market successfully. Then the honeymoon ends. The employee who invented the improved widget leaves, sets up a company, and begins to manufacture and sell the improved widget. You complain—and learn that he has already obtained a patent on the improved widget. He writes you a letter demanding that you stop manufacturing and selling the improved widget.

Scenario Two: You run a small company that employs Jane Scientist and Joe Accountant. Jane's job is to invent and develop new products for your company. Joe's job is to track accounts receivable and other financial matters. During the course of their work, both invent novel, useful products—Jane's as an expected part of her job, Joe's because he is not just a bean counter but a very imaginative fellow. You manufacture and sell both products. Jane and Joe both leave your employ and claim that the patents rightfully belong to them.

Both scenarios leave you with a problem because of poor planning. You have to fight for your rights in situations where you think you deserve the patent and, thus, the right to exclude others from making, using, or selling the widgets.

One approach to dealing with these potential scenarios is to have all employees sign agreements that they will assign patent rights to you as long as they are in your employ. Even the receptionist and secretaries? Remember Joe Accountant, whose job description did not include inventing.

The agreement might require the employee to actively pursue the patent (although the company would agree to pay the expenses), then assign those rights to the company.

As with any agreement, it has to be reasonable or the courts will throw it out. If Joe Accountant invented his products in his basement on weekends, that likely would be found unreasonable.

But if Joe Accountant invented the product at the office and later obtained a patent, you still might have a "shop right"—the ability to use the invention despite Joe's patent.

Although it rarely happens, a complicating factor for establishing ownership of a patent might be what is called interference. This refers to a situation where two or more persons apply for a patent on what seems to be substantially the same invention. These issues are settled by a board of examiners that examines evidence submitted by the parties. Each party will submit evidence to support the claim that it was the first to conceive of the invention. Lacking such evidence, the board will use the date of filing the applications to settle the issue.

Infringement of Patents

Protecting your own patent rights is one issue. The other issue is taking care not to infringe on someone else's.

The person holding the patent has two courses of action available in cases of possible infringement: Getting an injunction to make you stop infringing, and claiming damages for past infringements. You might want to work out a license agreement with the inventor to make, sell, or use the product if it is important enough to your business . . . but you will still be liable for damages for past infringements.

What if someone infringes on your patent? The conventional response probably would be to sue to stop the infringement. However, some lawyers might advise you that your patent is merely a "fighting interest in a lawsuit." What they mean is that you may well get hit with a countersuit claiming either that the patent is invalid, that you have committed antitrust violations, or both.

All patents have disclosures about your invention and a set of claims. What the patent protects are those precise items covered by the claims. In a countersuit the other party might allege that your claims are too narrow to cover his activities or too broad to be a valid patent.

In short, get some good legal advice about the pros and cons of pursuing a patent action.

Getting the Right Advice

A generalist lawyer or even your corporate lawyer is not the right person to pursue a patent for you. Patent law is considered to be an area of precise specialty, and lawyers or agents not recognized by the Patent and Trademark Office are not permitted by law to represent inventors.

The Patent and Trademark Office keeps a register of approved attorneys. Registered attorneys are required to comply with certain regulations, be of good character and repute, and demonstrate legal, scientific, and technical qualifications. An examination is required.

You can obtain a roster of registered attorneys from the U.S. Government Printing Office. Also check the yellow pages in your telephone directory for patent attorneys (most metropolitan areas have such attorneys).

For general background concerning patents, the Patent and Trademark Office publishes a booklet called "General Information Concerning Patents," also available from the U.S. Government Printing Office.

Patents Checklist

Before pursuing a patent, it's a good idea to make sure that you can give a Yes answer to the following questions:

■ Have you determined that the invention has real commercial value and is worth protecting and defending?

■ Does your invention meet the tests of novelty and usefulness?

In addition, the following questions relate to the general state of your business procedure in the patents area.

■ Have you conducted a patent search on products that you make, use, or sell to avoid a claim of infringement?

■ Do you require your employees to sign agreements assigning patents to your company?

■ If you license parties to use your invention, or if you assign a part interest in your invention, do you carefully and specifically restrict their uses of the invention?

■ Do you use a registered patent attorney for patent advice?

■ Before suing to protect your patent, have you determined that it is really worth it from a business standpoint?

COPYRIGHTS

At first glance, the copyright laws may seem less pertinent to your company than patent laws. But if you are in the business of publishing catalogs or newsletters, for example, or if you have started a public relations or advertising agency, copyrights will be of considerable interest to you. Likewise, if you are in the business of creating computer software . . . or if you are using someone else's without permission.

Copyright protection derives from federal law, and it gives the owner of the copyright the exclusive right to do, and to authorize others to do, these things:

■ Reproduce the copyrighted work in copies or phonorecords.

■ Prepare derivative works based upon the copyrighted work.

■ Distribute copies or phonorecords of the copyrighted work to the public by sale or by other transfer of ownership, by rental, by lease, or by lending.

■ Perform the copyrighted work publicly, in the case of literary, musical, dramatic, and choreographic works, pantomimes and motion pictures, and other audiovisual works.

■ Display the copyrighted work publicly, in the case of literary, musical, dramatic, and choreographic works, pantomimes, and pictorial, graphic, or sculptural works.

Term of Copyright

Under the old 1909 federal law, copyright became effective on the date of publication (or on the date of registration for unpublished works) and lasted for 28 years; it could be renewed for another 28 years.

Copyrights have been extended under a new law for works created on or after January 1, 1978. These works are now protected from the time of creation for a term lasting for the author's life, plus an additional 50 years after the author's death. For works for hire (defined later in this section), the copyright is good for 75 years from publication or 100 years from creation, whichever is shorter. These time spans are more in line with international copyright agreements.

An important distinction exists between ownership of a patent and a copyright. Whereas obtaining a patent can be a lengthy and costly process, you have to do nothing to obtain a copyright. Copyright protection comes into existence automatically at the moment the work is created in fixed form. (However, there may be advantages to registering a copyright, and these will be discussed later.)

A work is considered created when it is fixed in a copy or a phonorecord for the first time. Copies are material objects from which a work can be read or visually perceived, either directly or with the aid of a machine (videotapes, for example). Phonorecords are material objects that contain sounds (audio tapes, for example). A piece of music can be fixed both in a copy (sheet music) or phonorecord (audio tape).

Work for Hire

Copyrights differ from patents in another respect. Whereas only the inventor can apply for a patent, if an author is working for hire, the employer and not the employee is considered the author and can rightfully claim copyright.

A work made for hire covers:
■ Work prepared by an employee within the scope of the employment agreement.

■ Work specially ordered or commissioned, as long as the parties expressly agree in writing that the work is for hire.

Work Protected by Copyright

What copyright protects are "original works of authorship" that are fixed in a *tangible* form of expression. The fixed expression may be communicated with the aid of a machine, such as a tape player. Copyrightable works include:

Literary works

Musical works, including the words

Dramatic works, including music

Pantomimes and choreographic works

Pictorial, graphic and sculptural works

Motion pictures and other audiovisual works

Sound recordings

What if your company subscribes to a monthly publication and you routinely photocopy one of the publication's columns and distribute it to your employees?

Although the publishers of that publication would prefer that you buy additional subscriptions for your employees, you are probably protected by the "fair use" doctrine. This is an area that still involves subjective judgment, but the law now takes into account whether the copying is for commercial or educational purposes; the nature of the copyrighted work; the amount copied in relation to the whole; and whether the copying has any effect on the market for the copyrighted article.

Work Not Protected by Copyright

To establish the boundaries of what is covered by copyright, first look at categories *not* covered by copyright protection:

▬ Works that have not been fixed in a tangible form of expression. For example, if you have been whistling a wonderfully creative tune for the past year, but have not fixed it in writing or by recording it, no copyright applies.

▬ Titles, names, short phrases, slogans, familiar symbols or designs, mere variations of typographic ornamentation, or listings of ingredients or contents.

▬ Ideas, procedures, methods, systems, processes, concepts, principles, discoveries, or devices, as distinguished from a description, drawing, or explanation.

▬ Works consisting entirely of information commonly known (for example, a calendar . . . although artwork on the calendar could be copyrighted).

Notice and Registration

Giving notice of copyright is optional for works first published on and after March 1, 1989, although the Copyright Office recommends it. Giving notice was mandatory before that date, and failure to give such notice risked loss of the copyright protection.

Even under the new law copyright registration does have some advantages:

▬ It establishes a public record of the copyright claim.

▬ It is necessary before a copyright infringement suit can be filed.

▬ If done within three months after publication of the work or prior to an infringement, statutory damages and attorney's fees will be available to holders of copyrights (otherwise, only an award of actual damages and profits is available).

▬ It reduces the opportunity for a defendant to claim "innocent infringement" (which, if successfully argued, can lessen damages levied against the defendant).

The copyright notice contains three elements:

1. The symbol: ©, the word "Copyright," or the abbreviation "Copr." For phonorecords the symbol would be ℗.
2. The year of first publication of the work: The date may be omitted from pictorial, graphic, or sculptural works, with accompanying textual matter, when reproduced on greeting cards, postcards, stationery, jewelry, and other articles.
3. The name of the copyright owner.

Another distinction between copyrights and patents lies in the notice requirements. Unlike patent notice, which requires formal approval, the copyright owner requires no such approval before giving notice.

Full information regarding copyrights both in the United States and in other countries can be obtained from the Register of Copyrights, Copyright Office, Library of Congress, Washington, D.C., 20559 .

Copyright Checklist

▬ Does your business produce any original materials that deserve copyright protection?

▬ If so, do you give appropriate copyright notice? Do you register the copyrights?

▬ Are you careful to avoid infringing the copyrights of others?

▬ If you use free-lance or employee writers, artists, or others who create materials for you, do you have agreements with them by which the copyrights on their work for you are assigned to you?

TRADEMARKS

In the business world we are inundated by trademarks and service marks—words, names, symbols, devices, or any combination of these calculated to distinguish one company's goods or services from everyone else's. The trick seems to be finding something new and memorable, and a whole industry (advertising and public relations) has moved in to help fill that need.

Historically, trademarks were a kind of consumer protection device: If a merchant or manufacturer sold defective goods, the mark affixed to the product allowed the purchaser to trace it back. Now, they are seen as a competitive advantage and a way of raising one's product above the crowd.

Trademarks can be registered with the Patent and Trademark Office. However, substantive trademark rights come only through *use* of the trademark. Assume for the moment that you sit in your office and design a dozen trademarks—interesting, unique, and attractive designs, with distinctive names. If you don't actually use those trademarks in the conduct of business, however, you have established no trademark rights.

Does this mean you may have to spend a lot of money designing and then using a trademark before you can register it? No longer. The Trademark Law Revision Act of 1988 made it legal to apply for a trademark prior to use, so long as you state a bona fide intention to use the mark in commerce. The new law also reduces the term of registration and renewal from 20 years to 10 years, in order to clear out some of the "deadwood" of unused registered trademarks.

As we use the term trademarks here, they encompass service, certification, and collective marks. However, whereas trademarks are used to identify goods and products, service marks refer to services. For example, your local Sears store (service mark) sells Sears jeans (trademark). Certification marks refer to product characteristics ("union label"). Collective marks refer to membership in a group.

One more twist: A trademark is not necessarily the same as a company name. Jones Hardware (company name) may sell its own equipment, Tuffest Made (trademark) and provide house call service under the name HouseCalls Repair (service mark).

Not just anything is eligible for trademark protection. For example, "Beans" is not a valid trademark for your product; it is simply a generic term for a common product. "Kodak" and "Exxon" are fanciful terms meaning nothing that are used as trademarks. Some trademark names evolve into generic words and become available for common use; "aspirin" is an example.

The more fanciful and arbitrary your trademark is, the better your chance is of defending it. The more generic it is, the less your chances.

Although registration is not necessary, it does have advantages:

■ It allows the use of the ® mark in conjunction with the trademark, which may warn others not to use the mark.

■ It constitutes evidence of the registrant's right to exclusive use of the mark.

■ If used long enough, exclusive use of the mark may become incontestable.

Trademark Checklist

■ Do you produce goods or provide services that would benefit from a distinctive mark?

■ Have you checked to make sure that you are not infringing on someone else's trademark rights?

■ Is your mark distinctive, or it is more generic or descriptive?

■ Is your mark actually used in order to protect your rights?

■ Have you registered your mark?

TRADE SECRETS

You could be in a business that owns no patents, unique products, or copyrighted materials, yet still possesses valuable intellectual property.

Take the example of a textile company that makes men's underwear. The company purchases the same chemicals as everyone else and sells in the same market as the competition. But the company consistently does better than the competition because of one of the following reasons:

■ It has quietly bought and installed new machinery that allows a significant reduction in the use of salt in the dyeing process.

■ It has negotiated an extremely favorable long-term trucking agreement for distribution of its products.

■ Pay and benefits for employees are a notch below the competition, and the company has discovered a valuable trade school source for new employees not generally used in the industry.

■ It has discovered some new, small suppliers that deliver material, equipment, and services at a cost lower than that offered by the competition.

■ It has focused its marketing efforts on customers with a record of quick paying, significantly improving the cash flow position of the company.

The company is whipping the competition because of its use of trade secrets—information that can be defined as: (1) giving its owner a competitive advantage; (2) treated by the owner as confidential information; and (3) is not generally known in the trade or industry.

Materials used in the dyeing process are the same as those used by the competition; however, the process by which those materials are mixed and used in combination with the new equipment is not generally known and provides a competitive advantage. Both the pay scale of the employees and the supplier list allow the company to underprice the competition in key markets. The marketing efforts are driven by the list of the best-paying customers, a list developed through experience and good intelligence-gathering by the company.

This company is doing well because of *how* it is doing business. These are the company's trade secrets.

If trade secrets are important to your company, they are worth protecting. Here are some examples of protective measures:

■ Require employees to sign nondisclosure agreements.

■ Require suppliers and vendors to sign nondisclosure agreements (for example, you may not want the competition to know how much salt you use in the dyeing process, so make sure the vendor understands that). Make the agreements detailed and specific to impress upon them that this is important to you.

■ Establish the confidentiality of information such as mailing lists, vendor and customer lists, formulas, etc., by restricting and controlling access to the information.

■ Where practical, establish procedures that prevent any single employee from learning all aspects of a piece of information that you would regard as a trade secret.

To avoid being accused yourself of lifting someone else's trade secrets, be wary of accepting unsolicited information from persons outside your employ, or from new employees who have come from a competing company.

Trade Secrets Checklist

■ Have you identified information or ways of doing business in your company that you would consider trade secrets?

■ Have you taken steps to identify that information as confidential? Have you taken steps to protect the confidentiality of that information?

■ Do you require employees to sign nondisclosure agreements with regard to trade secrets? How about vendors and suppliers?

CHAPTER PERSPECTIVE

Many businesses own or produce intellectual property—patents, copyrights, trademarks and trade secrets—that deserve the same kind of care and consideration as other kinds of property, such as real estate. In addition to protecting their own property, businesses need to exercise care to avoid infringing on the intellectual property rights of others.

Retirement and Deferred Compensation Plans

INTRODUCTION

This chapter discusses retirement plans and other methods a business can use to put aside money for future use, for example to motivate executives to stay with and work exceptionally hard for their employer. The Internal Revenue Code allows significant tax breaks for certain of these arrangements.

Accountants and financial planners are fond of illustrating how valuable it is to start saving early for retirement. "The miracle of compound interest," they call it. But that's not the only purpose for retirement and deferred-compensation plans. The importance of these plans to a business enterprise is that they contribute to a stable work force and can provide strong incentives to exceptional performance by top executives.

This chapter first discusses retirement plans, including Social Security, corporate pension plans, and plans for the self-employed such as Keoghs and SEPs. (We will not discuss IRAs because there are so many better deals for people in business and because IRAs are thoroughly covered in other publications.) Then, we will take a quick look at plans designed not so much for retirement as for wealth-building and for their motivational effects.

After studying the material in this chapter:

— You will understand the tax benefits of qualified retirement and deferred compensation plans.

— You will know the characteristics of the most common types of plans.

— You will understand why Keogh and SEP plans are attractive for small businesses.

— You will be able to evaluate which plans might be best for *your* business.

— You will be familiar with techniques for rewarding executives for good performance.

SOCIAL SECURITY

Social Security is a federal program designed to provide workers and their dependents with retirement and other benefits. The law setting up the Social Security system is called the Federal Insurance Contributions Act (FICA). There are four types of FICA benefits:

1. Benefits for workers who are retired and for their spouses and dependent children
2. Survivor's benefits paid to a deceased worker's spouse, minor children, and dependent aged parents
3. Disability benefits for a worker who is unable to carry on gainful employment as a result of sickness or injury
4. Medical insurance, called Medicare, for retirees and for workers who are receiving disability benefits.

Social Security is financed by taxes paid by employers and employees on wages paid in cash or "in kind." ("In kind" refers to meals, lodging, clothing, and services provided to employees.) Social Security taxes are also payable on employees' tip income. Sole proprietors and general partners—who are not considered to be employees—have to pay their own form of Social Security tax, called the self-employment tax.

The employer's portion of FICA taxes is a deductible expense. An employee's taxable income does not include the amounts for FICA that are deducted from his or her paycheck. Self-employed taxpayers can deduct one-half of the self-employment tax they pay. Generally, Social Security benefits received are not subject to federal income taxation except in the case of higher income taxpayers.

Although debate has raged about the financial strength of the Social Security system, recent reforms have convinced most analysts that the system can be counted on to pay the benefits that are promised. Workers interested in estimating their Social Security benefits can receive information by phoning 1-800-937-7005.

QUALIFIED RETIREMENT PLANS

A retirement plan is said to be "qualified" if it meets IRS requirements and those of the Employment Retirement Income Security Act (ERISA). A qualified plan conveys four significant tax benefits to employer and employees:

1. Both the employer's and any employee's contributions to the plan are tax deductible

2. Investments held by the plan accumulate earnings tax-free

3. Participants in the plan aren't taxed until they withdraw their benefits

4. Distributions paid at the retiree's option in a lump sum at retirement are taxed as if they were received over a several-year period, thereby reducing taxes.

Endorsement by the IRS and ERISA comes at a cost. This cost can be broken down into two parts. The first part consists of the expense of fulfilling complex record-keeping and reporting requirements. In addition, retirement benefits can't be provided to executives and other highly paid or stock-owning employees unless similar arrangements are made to cover and pay for retirement for other employees. (In some cases part-time, temporary, and younger workers can be excluded.) To fail to include all eligible workers will bring about the loss of the tax benefits.

Plans that are unqualified are easier and less costly to administer, but they forfeit many of the tax breaks. On the other hand, unqualified plans convey certain advantages. (We will discuss unqualified plans later in the chapter.)

Qualified plans have certain common features. The employer contributes money into a fund called a trust (or to an insurance company) during a worker's years of employment. In some plans—called contributory plans—employees can choose to have part of their pay set aside. In a contributory plan the employer holds back, through salary reduction, some of the compensation the employee would otherwise receive (and have to pay tax on) and deposits it into the trust.

If funds are contributed to a trust, the manager, called a trustee, invests them to produce earnings. The assets and accumulated earnings in the trust provide a fund from which workers are paid when they retire. Pension trustees are held to high standards of conduct, referred to as fiduciary duties, and they must be bonded by an insurance company. Violation of their fiduciary duties can make trustees (or their bonding companies) liable for losses. They are not liable, however, for bad judgments made in the management of the investments.

Funds paid into an insurance company instead of to a retirement trust are used to purchase annuities. A retirement annuity is an insurance contract that promises to pay an income (ordinarily for life) to the retiree and the retiree's spouse.

All qualified plans must meet antidiscrimination standards. Only indirectly do these standards protect women and minorities. Their purpose is to stop business owners, officers, and highly paid employees from structuring retirement plans to benefit themselves while leaving other workers high and dry. To detect this kind of discrimination, complex dollar and percentage formulas are built into the law. The penalty for plans that fail the tests is loss of tax benefits.

Caution: When investigating the reasonableness of a corporate employee's pay—a topic discussed in greater length in Chapter 7—the IRS also considers retirement contributions. The *total* compensation package, including retirement and any other benefits, must be reasonable in order to be deductible as a business expense.

While retirement plans for employees appear to come in a mind-boggling variety, they are mostly combinations of a few basic types: defined benefit plans, defined contribution plans, profit-sharing plans, stock bonus plans, and contributory plans.

Defined Benefit Plans

These plans specify ("define") in advance the amount of income promised to an employee upon retirement. For example, a plan might be set up to provide for each worker an annual retirement income equal to one-half of the worker's highest three-year average earnings. These plans are commonly found in the very largest of corporations but could also be used by a sole proprietor. When the term *pension plan* is used, most people are probably thinking of a defined benefit plan.

During the worker's years of employment it is up to the company to compute and to contribute to a trust (or insurance company) whatever amount is necessary to produce the promised level of retirement income. Contributions must be made even in unprofitable years.

Defined benefit plans tend to be expensive to set up and operate, partially because the services of pension experts, including actuaries, are needed both when the plan is established and annually in connection with reports that must be filed with the federal government. The cost of using these plans is increased by the necessity of conforming to a maze of rules for accounting and reporting.

In some cases defined benefits can be the plans of choice even for small, unincorporated businesses. Here's why. Since older employees have fewer years to work before retirement, actuarial calculations will show that larger amounts must be contributed on their behalf. Since owner and executives tend to be older than other workers, larger amounts will tend to be set aside for them. Of course, the antidiscrimination rules must still be followed.

Defined Contribution Plans

These plans specify the amount the employer must pay in, not the amount of retirement income. For example, a defined contribution plan might obligate an employer to contribute each year an amount equal to 10 percent of each worker's pay. The employee's exact retirement benefit can't be determined in advance; it depends upon how much money is set aside over the years and how successful the trustee is in managing the investments. A money-purchase plan is a type of defined contribution plan designed to be used to purchase an annuity upon the participant's retirement.

Profit-Sharing Plans

Profit-sharing plans are another variety of defined contribution plan. They are flexible in that the employer has discretion to adjust each year's contribution contingent upon profits. No money need be paid in if the company's board of directors decides that profits aren't adequate.

Stock-Bonus Plans

Distributions from stock-bonus plans ordinarily are made in shares of the corporate employer's stock. A popular form of stock-bonus plan, called an Employee Stock Ownership Plan (ESOP), is designed to invest its assets primarily in the employer's stock. The corporate employer may contribute stock instead of cash to the ESOP, thus conserving cash for other uses.

ESOPs convey unique tax breaks, set up because Congress decided that it was a good idea for employees to share in the ownership and growth of the corporations that employ them. A corporation can take a tax deduction for the value of its own stock it contributes into the ESOP trust. Cash dividends that the corporation pays on its stock held in the ESOP are tax deductible, too, while in ordinary circumstances corporate dividends are not deductible.

Another tax advantage: If the ESOP buys securities for the trust, the sellers can elect not to be taxed on any gain if they reinvest the proceeds of the sale in other securities. If the seller of the stock is the estate of a deceased stockholder, the taxable value of the estate can be reduced by 50 percent of the proceeds of the sale to the ESOP.

In exchange for these tax breaks comes a high degree of complexity in conforming to tax laws. Also, since securities (stocks) are being issued by the corporation, federal and state laws must be considered. The advice of an expert is essential!

Unless the worker chooses a later date, distribution of money or stock from the plan begins not later than one year after the participant separates from service with the corporation because of reaching normal retirement age. Workers can also get their money out if they leave the corporation for another reason.

An ESOP can broaden the base of stock ownership, making the small business owner's shares more easily tradable. But ESOPs are not without their drawbacks. Shares owned by the ESOP reduce the percentage of control exercised by the present owners of the business, because the shares are voted by the ESOP trustee (or by the employee participants, in certain instances such as mergers with another corporation or sale of substantial amounts of assets). Also, employee participants may feel cheated if the value of the employer's stock held in the ESOP declines.

Contributory Plans
While most other types of plans can require or allow contributions by employees, so-called 401K plans are particularly popular. These are salary-reduction plans set up to complement profit-sharing or stock bonus plans. They are also referred to as cash or deferred arrangements (CODAs) because each worker can choose whether to receive cash (and be taxed on it) or to have the funds set aside for retirement benefits.

KEOGH PLANS
Keoghs are plans for self-employed people whose income is earned primarily by providing personal services. Since they are qualified plans, they provide the four tax advantages we have already listed for other qualified plans. Keoghs are for unincorporated small-business owners, partners, and professionals such as physicians, auctioneers, writers, lawyers, self-employed mechanics, designers, accountants, and free-lance consultants of all types. Inventors and artists also, even though they get their earnings from selling a product, can open a Keogh. An employee covered by a corporate retirement plan at work can set up a Keogh if he or she has a sideline business earning income from

personal services. For the unincorporated, self-employed person Keoghs are often the preferred choice in qualified retirement plans.

A Keogh works like an umbrella under which a defined benefit or defined contribution plan can be sheltered. A popular and useful arrangement pairs together two different types of defined contribution plans: profit-sharing and money purchase plans. Generally, the owner-employee or the partnership that sets up a Keogh must cover all full-time employees who have one year of employment and are at least 21 years old.

The amount you can deduct for contributions to a Keogh each year is determined by law and depends upon what kind of plan you maintain. The overall maximum for defined contribution plans, however, is 20 percent of earnings (calculated before the Keogh deduction), or $30,000, whichever is lower. (Sometimes you will see this limit stated as 25 percent of *net* earnings calculated after subtracting the Keogh deduction. Both computations result in the same dollar amount.) You must cover your eligible employees by contributing that same percentage of their salaries.

If you choose to set up a defined benefit Keogh, the contribution limit is that amount of money that has to be set aside now to provide you with a lifetime income at retirement. (At this writing there is a limit of approximately $95,000 on annual retirement benefits; both this figure and the $30,000 limit mentioned in the previous paragraph are adjusted for inflation.) In any case, the actual deduction needed to fund this amount of retirement income depends on actuarial computations based on your age.

All of the contribution made to a Keogh on behalf of employees must be made by the employer. This can be expensive, increasing payroll costs by perhaps 20 percent. You must weigh the benefits of increased morale and stability of your work force against the increased payroll cost. Annual reports to the IRS must be filed, taking perhaps from several hours to several days of work, depending upon the type of plan and the number of covered employees. Penalties are severe if you fail to file these reports.

You can get information on setting up a Keogh by contacting a bank, insurance company, investment brokerage firm, or mutual fund. Most of these firms will be able to provide you with a ready-made Keogh plan, called a prototype, that will gain IRS approval.

SIMPLIFIED EMPLOYEE PENSION (SEP)

Even simpler than a Keogh is a SEP, a form of defined contribution plan. A SEP is sometimes referred to as a SEP-IRA because the employer makes deductible contributions to an individual retirement account (IRA) owned by an employee.

SEPs constitute the least complicated way to provide retirement benefits for owners and employees of either incorporated or unincorporated businesses, including proprietorships, partnerships, and corporations. At present no annual reports on a SEP need be filed with the IRS or with any other government agency.

Contributions that you make on a worker's behalf (up to 15 percent of an employee's earnings) are excluded from the worker's taxable income. In addition, employees can choose to make their own contributions via salary reduction, but only if you have no more than 25 employees and more than half of them choose to contribute. The total amount set aside in any year can't be more than $30,000.

It's easy to establish a SEP: Decide what percentage of each worker's and your own pay you will set aside. A uniform percentage must be contributed for each worker. Then fill out and sign Form 5305-SEP and give a copy to each employee. This form is a model designed by and accepted by the IRS. (It is not necessary to file the form with the IRS or with any other agency.) Most banks, mutual funds, and other financial institutions will give advice if the SEP funds are invested with them.

Employees will have to set up a SEP-IRA account into which the employer's contributions will be deposited. If an eligible employee fails to do so, the employer will have to set up the account.

The chief advantage of a SEP is its simplicity: no approvals, no formal plans, no annual reports. This means minimal expense. Yet, contributions to a SEP are tax deductible by the business; not even Social Security tax need be paid on the contributed amounts. Earnings on the investment accumulate tax free just as they do in the more complex plans. Another advantage: The contribution percentage can be changed each year or even skipped at the employer's discretion.

The most important disadvantage of a SEP is that every employee earning more than about $315 who is at least 21 years old and has worked for the company (even if only part-time) in three out of the last five years must be covered and contributions made to his or her account. Antidiscrimination provisions apply to SEPs.

HOW TO SET UP A QUALIFIED RETIREMENT PLAN

With the assistance of a stock broker, insurance agent, banker, or mutual fund representative you can set up your own Keogh or SEP plan. These persons have off-the-shelf "prototype" plans that meet IRS requirements. On the other hand, these persons are selling a product, and you might want to seek advice elsewhere before making a final decision.

You should check with a pension consultant if you are interested in a defined benefit pension, corporate profit-sharing, stock-bonus or ESOP, or a salary-reduction plan. Also check with an expert if your goal is mostly to benefit a small group of owners, executives, or other high-paid workers. At the end of this chapter we give tips about where to find an expert.

NONQUALIFIED DEFERRED PLANS

Many business owners and managers are unaware of the advantages of unqualified plans, those that are not designed to achieve all of the tax breaks of qualified plans. Nonqualified plans can be focused to attract and reward highly skilled executives.

Warning: There have been instances in which a plan thought by an employer to be nonqualified has been held to some of the rigorous IRS and ERISA rules. A pension or benefits expert should be consulted.

Employee Stock Options

The holder of an option has the right to buy at a favorable price the property that is the subject of the option. Stock options can be granted to employees to encourage them to work hard for the corporation that employs them. If the company's stock price climbs, the holder of the option will still be able to buy the stock ("exercise the option") at a predetermined and probably lower price. Ordinarily, the option will not be exercised unless it can be used to buy company stock at a lower-than-market price.

There are no direct tax benefits to a corporation that grants an incentive stock option to its employees. No tax deduction is allowed, but neither is the company laying out any cash. The possible tax benefit to the employee is that profit on sale of the stock bought by exercising the option is taxed at long-term capital gains rates. This can give tax savings whenever current law provides lower tax rates for such gains than for ordinary income.

Incentive stock options are hedged about with numerous legal restrictions, such as requiring that the employee not dispose of the stock within two years from the grant date, that he or she not own more than 10 percent of the corporation's stock, that the option be nontransferable except upon death, and that stockholders give their approval. Because achieving favorable tax treatment is conditional both upon there being favorable capital gains rates and upon conforming to all the restrictions, incentive stock options are not as popular as they once were. Other types of stock option plans have been devised that avoid most of the restrictions.

The tax treatment of these nonqualified plans depends upon whether the option, when granted, has a readily ascertainable fair market value (FMV). (If the employer's stock can be bought and sold in the open market, the option will generally have a FMV.)

If the nonqualified option granted to an employee has a FMV, an employee must report that value as ordinary taxable income; by the same token, the corporation has a tax deduction on the date the option is granted. If there is no FMV, the income and the deduction are postponed until the first date at which the option can be exercised. This delay can provide a few months or years of tax deferral, while motivating employees in the meantime.

Nonqualified stock options having no fair market value serve as rewards and incentives for employees, yet no cash need be paid out by the employer. As a matter of fact, if the option is exercised, the corporation's cash flow is increased because employees must pay into the corporation to buy its stock! (On the other hand, stock that has no fair market value is stock that is not publicly traded, and such stock may appeal only to employees who look to the future growth of the company.)

Nonqualified stock options should be considered seriously by any business owner who sees advantages in granting employees a share in stock ownership and profits. It may even be advisable to incorporate a proprietorship or partnership to be able to offer these benefits.

Unfunded Deferred Compensation Plans

Highly compensated employees who already receive and are taxed on enough income to provide them a satisfactory life-style may prefer to have additional income, such as a bonus or a raise, deferred to a future date. There are no tax consequences to either worker or employer until the compensation is finally paid.

To be assured that the employee is not taxed currently, a legal tangle must be gotten through: Generally, the promise that the employer makes to the employee to pay compensation in the future must be either forfeitable (e.g., if the employee leaves the company) or it must be "unfunded." To be unfunded means that no funds have been transferred to any account for the employee's benefit and that the employer's promise is not evidenced by a promissory note. There are exceptions to these rules, however. Agreements to defer compensation in order to have it taxed at a future date should not be attempted except with the aid of an expert who can advise on the tax ramifications of the plan.

Restricted Property Plans

These plans are used to attract and reward key executives. The employee is given a property right in the form of an ownership interest (property) in the corporation, but he or she can't transfer it to anyone else, and it must be subject to a risk of forfeiture. If these conditions are met, the employee is not taxed (and the employer receives no deduction) until either the risk of forfeiture no longer exists or the interest is transferable.

An example of this type of plan is a corporation that grants 500 shares of its common stock to the executive vice-president. She and the corporation agree that the stock is nontransferable for, say, four years and that she will forfeit her rights to the stock if she leaves the company in that time. At the end of four years she will be taxed on, and the corporation will get a deduction for, the value of the stock at that time. The executive now may choose to sell or to retain all or part of the stock.

HOW TO GET ASSISTANCE

Because of the myriad of regulations that are involved in setting up and maintaining retirement plans, you should probably seek expert advice unless you are setting up a Keogh or SEP for fewer than perhaps 25 employees. Consultants are listed under the heading "Actuaries" or "Pensions" in the yellow pages of a city telephone directory. Larger firms of CPAs, attorneys, and business consultants ordinarily have pension, benefits, and compensation specialists. The American Association of Attorney-CPAs provides a referral service at 1-800-272-2889.

The IRS offers several publications on this subject:
560 Self-Employed Retirement Plans
575 Pension and Annuity Income
590 Individual Retirement Arrangements
1048 Filing Requirements for Employee Benefit Plans
The Small Business Administration has a booklet, *SEPs—What Small Businesses Need to Know.*

CHAPTER PERSPECTIVE

There are legal ways of avoiding taxes and providing for retirement. Business owners should take advantage of retirement and deferred compensation plans both for themselves and for their employees.

Real Estate Considerations

INTRODUCTION

Real estate selection is one of the most important considerations for a small business. Real estate is used not just to house a business: It is a place to meet customers, it provides a form of advertising, and its cost can be a significant component of capital and operating expenses. Real estate decisions require some knowledge of location strategy, finance, law, taxation, insurance, and management.

After studying the material in this chapter:

▬ You will know the importance of location in selecting business property.

▬ You will be able to evaluate the financial aspects of business real estate.

▬ You will understand the differences between buying and leasing, and will know how to evaluate which is best for you.

▬ You will be able to evaluate the impact of the costs of real estate—including insurance and tax considerations—on your business enterprise.

WHERE YOU SHOULD LOCATE

The main consideration in selecting a location for most businesses is the need to be convenient to customers. Put simply, the majority of customers frequent the business most convenient to them. Of course, service counts in developing a business and so does merchandise pricing policy. But what good is a business with the greatest service and pricing policies if it is too remote for customers to trade with?

There are exceptions. Some raw material extractors thrive by being near their source of raw materials rather than their customer. Some service businesses in today's rapid communications age need only a fax machine and a computer terminal with a modem—they can locate wherever there is a phone line. But these exceptions are infrequent. Most businesses need to be close to customers or have an outside salesman who can efficiently reach customers.

Location considerations for a business include the number of prospective consumers within the trade market area, amount of traffic (vehicular or pedestrian), traffic speed and visibility, nearness of competitive and complementary businesses. There are national and local sources of information to provide decision-making data.

CACI in Fairfax, Virginia and NDS of Encinitas, California are national companies that adapt census data to provide information on the number of consumers within any given distance (radius) of virtually any spot in the United States. They provide further information on family size, the size of each age group, income level in the area, and area growth or decline.

Local information sources include utility companies (telephone, water, gas, electric), chamber of commerce, building department, and lending institutions. A planning department, found in most cities, has information on traffic counts of its thoroughfares.

Most businesses prefer to be on busy streets as that provides visibility, (which has advertising value) and generally indicates convenience to a large market. Some other factors to be considered include current and proposed traffic patterns, proposed changes in main arteries and street widening, and ingress and egress of the site. Nearness to public transportation is an important consideration for businesses in many cities.

Nearness to competing businesses can be important. Instinctively, some businessmen want as little nearby competition as possible—but for some businesses the proximity of competition helps draw traffic. For example, automobile dealers in a given market tend to cluster together, as do restaurants, banks, jewelers, physicians, and others. This nucleus provides a form of gravity—the greater the mass, the larger are crowds drawn to that area for a given purpose. So don't rule out a location just because there are already several in your line of business at that place—such is the sign of a successful location, and one more business of that type might further enhance that location's drawing ability.

Nearness to a complementary business may also be a plus. You will often see a ladies dress shop next to a ladies handbag/shoe/hat boutique; a florist or pharmacy near a hospital;

auto parts stores locate near repair shops. Complementary uses provide synergy which enhances all businesses that are connected.

If the location preferred is in a shopping center, as contrasted with a free-standing store, there is a wide choice of shopping center types. These range from a convenience (strip center) to a neighborhood center (typically anchored by a grocery chain store), a community center (with a junior department store) to a regional mall (several department stores).

The business owner must decide on the type of center to be in—does it offer the type of merchandise that customers typically go distances to get and combine with other shopping, or something most consumers need frequently and they want stores to be within 3 to 5 minutes driving time of their home.

PHYSICAL CHARACTERISTICS OF SPACE NEEDED

The size, shape and other physical characteristics of land can be important to a business. A rectangular parcel of land that is relatively flat is easier to work with for a commercial building with parking. Parking requirements vary with each type of business. The Urban Land Institute, Washington, D.C. offers rules of thumb for parking and other requirements of various businesses. For each type of retailer there is usually a standard ratio of parking to building area, such as four to one.

A good businessman will have some idea of the amount of space needed for the scale of operation. A small retailer may need under 1,000 square feet of space, moderate sized 2,000 to 10,000, and a grocery chain may need more than 50,000 square feet of interior space for a supermarket. Department stores often exceed 100,000 square feet.

When starting a business one may not know exactly what size is right. It may be better to err on the safe side, that is keep overhead low, by initially choosing a place which is smaller than expected. If the business is successful there is an opportunity to expand at that location or move to another. If the business should fail it will probably not be caused by the burden of too much space.

Most businesses require space for its principal business activity (manufacturing, retailing, etc.), and for storage and office use. For most businesses, it is not necessary for storage and office use to occupy space at the same place or cost as its principal business activity. The proportion of space devoted to each use should be maintained with an understanding of the needs that each require. The business main activity is what generates income—other activities must be accommodated because they are essential—but they should not use space that is more valuable for other purposes.

HOW MUCH WILL SPACE COST

The price for commercial and industrial real estate is generally quoted on a per square foot basis. The amount will vary widely among major cities and even within a city based on the quality of space and the lease terms. For example, good retail space in Manhattan will cost upwards of $250 per square foot to buy or $50 per square foot per year to rent. By contrast, retail space in Houston Texas can be bought or built for under $75 per square foot, including land, or rented for under $15 per square foot. But within either city, retail space can be found at double the typical amount, or half the amount, mainly depending on the location and quality of space.

For some businesses there are norms as to the typical percentage of sales that is spent for rent by a successful business. While this varies widely, a range might be from 2 to 8 percent of sales. The lower figure is for high volume stores such as a supermarket, with the higher percentage for stores that need little interior space, such as a jewelry store.

The Urban Land Institute, Washington, D.C., bi-annually publishes *Dollars and Cents of Shopping Centers*. It discloses average rents for different retail businesses in various sized shopping centers in several regions of the U.S. The *Office Exchange Report*, published by the Building Owners and Manager's Association, Washington, D.C., provides rental rates and operating expenses by category for urban and suburban office buildings in most major U.S. cities. These provide valuable reference data.

Building costs for various sorts of buildings are described in Marshall & Swift (Los Angeles), Boeckh (Milwaukee), and Dow or Dodge Cost Services (New York). These services publish books that are constantly updated, and on-line computer services to estimate the cost of just about any kind of building.

BUY OR LEASE ANALYSIS

A key decision facing a business is whether to buy or to lease. Buying generally means tying up capital in real estate—capital that could otherwise be used in the business operations, such as to finance receivables, inventory, and payrolls. In addition, with real estate owned the business also becomes burdened with the headaches of ownership—controlling and paying property taxes, hazard and liability insurance on the building, repairs and maintenance to the building and parking, and so on. There is also the leasing problem of excess space, and the disposition problem if the business terminates or needs to move to another location, or to enlarge or downsize.

In ownership's favor are control, known costs, and residual value. When leasing, another party (the landlord) may exercise control over repairs and maintenance, use of the property, selection of other tenants (without regard to compatibility), and lease renewal terms at the expiration of the existing lease. A business owner who owns the real estate exercises control over these matters. Most of the capital costs are known in advance and there is no concern of being evicted when the lease expires. Many businesses with good locations have found that their real estate offers a high residual value that provides most of the money received on resale or retirement. This value increment may be caused by inflation or simply increased demand in that area. Consequently, the future investment value of the property is an important consideration.

A long-term net lease with renewal options at established rents may satisfy a business owner of fair treatment and allow adequate control. Basically, an investor will buy the property, likely aided by mortgage financing, then lease it to a business for 20 or 30 years, perhaps with renewal options. The rent is set in the lease and may be allowed to rise at predetermined intervals in accordance with some index or a reappraisal of the property. The tenant must pay operating expenses and keep the property insured and well maintained. Thus, the business (the tenant) exercises control and responsibilities similar to ownership, but does not tie up its capital.

In recent years there has been a large number of municipal revenue financings of privately used buildings. For example, a city or political subdivision, in order to increase employment opportunities of its residents, sells a 20-year bond issue to raise money. The money is used to build a building to the specifications of, and leased for 20 years to a credit-worthy private company. Because the bond is issued by a municipality at tax-free interest rates, it bears a low interest rate. Rent payments from the company to the city are virtually identical to the city's bond payment requirements, so the company's rent is used just to service the bond debt. The city itself is not liable on the bonds—they must pay interest only if they receive the rent. After 20 years the bonds are retired and the company purchases the property from the city for a nominal amount, as part of the lease agreement.

LEASE RENT

A *gross* lease is one where the landlord pays all of the operating expenses: utilities, property taxes, insurance, and repairs. A *net* lease is where the tenant pays all of those expenses. In practice, most leases are hybrids where certain expenses are paid by the landlord and others by the tenant. Terms such as "triple-net" have been coined to describe a lease where the tenant pays all expenses.

Long term leases of single-tenant buildings tend to be net. The tenant can control and incur expenses to suit itself. The tenant should be required to prove to the landlord it has paid tax assessments and insurance. Short term leases of multi-tenant buildings usually are gross. Common management and mainte-nance of the building serves the tenants better than if each were to arrange its own repairs and maintenance.

A typical lease requires *base rent* paid each month at the beginning of the month. Especially with a long-term lease there may also be additional rent based on changes in price levels, operating expense or tax stops, and maintenance costs. Percent-age leases, discussed below, are typically required of retail tenants.

Leases for multiple years without rent adjustments for infla-tion may impose hardships. In recognition of a lengthy lease term, a cost-of-living adjustment may provide for additional rent based on some published index.

The index, frequency of adjustment and amount of adjust-ment are negotiable. The CPI, published by the Bureau of Labor Statistics of the U.S. Department of Labor, is typically used as a basis for adjustment because of its frequency of computation and widespread publication. A lesser-known local index tied to rental rates, operating expenses, or real estate values may be satisfac-tory but may introduce an element of instability or potential manipulation with possible litigation.

Adjustments may be made once a year or less often. The period between adjustments should be short for a gross lease but may be extended when the tenant pays most of the operating expenses. The degree of adjustment need not be the full change in the index selected; instead it may be a percentage of the change. For example, if 50 percent of the index were selected as the multiplier and the index rose by 20 percent, the rent would increase by 10 percent. This provides some protection to the landlord (who bought the property with pre-inflation dollars), but does not inflict the full brunt of inflation on the tenant.

Although a lease can require either the landlord or the tenant to pay ad valorem taxes, it is frequently appropriate for the tenant to pay such expenses for a single-tenant building. A compromise would use a *stop* (or escalation) *clause* whereby the tenant pays the increase in taxes over a base year amount, and the landlord pays the base year amount annually. A net lease or a tax stop clause obviates the need for frequent rent adjustments in cost of living indexes and the use of short term leases.

There should be some penalty for a late rental payment, charge for attorneys fees to cure delinquencies, and a landlord's lien on the property of a tenant who is delinquent in rent.

In an absolute net lease the tenant is responsible for maintenance, repairs, alterations, replacements, and improvements. This includes ordinary or extraordinary repairs whether structural or nonstructural, interior or exterior. However, even net leases require the landlord to be responsible for matters of structural integrity, such as the roof, exterior, and supporting walls, while nonstructural repairs and problems caused by a tenant's negligence are the tenant's responsibility. No tenant should pay obligations of the landlord—income, gift, inheritance, franchise, or corporate tax; or a tax on the rental receipts of the landlord.

The landlord should be required to remedy any malfunctions in the original building, including the heating, ventilation, and air conditioning system (HVAC), plumbing, and parking area. Curing any defects in the original construction should be an expense of the landlord. Manufacturer's warranties for appliances, especially the air conditioner compressor warranty length, should be specified in the lease as agreed by landlord and tenant. If the tenant does work on the building because of a defect that the landlord did not cure within a reasonable time, the tenant should be allowed to deduct the costs, plus interest, from future rent requirements.

Of utmost importance is the need to specify the obligations of each party. Litigation is the typical result of a failure to do so.

PERCENTAGE LEASES

Leases with retail tenants are frequently percentage leases. They require either a fixed minimum rental or a percentage rent based on gross sales, whichever is greater. For example, rent for a

10,000-square-foot building may be $100,000 per year, plus 5 percent of sales above $2,000,000. Therefore, percentage rents are imposed only when sales exceed $200 per square foot of floor area, and a successful business will pay 5 percent of sales as rent. Guidelines of typical sales per square foot for that retail business are used as the base rate in the formula.

The advantage of a percentage lease to the tenant is a fair base rent and additional rent if the business volume justifies it. For the landlord, the percentage lease provides a reward for additional business due to location. This gives a landlord incentive to maintain a superior facility.

Different types of businesses have different percentage rates. A firm selling luxury items such as jewelry tends to have a high markup and low inventory turnover compared with a grocery or discount store, which has a small profit margin but a high volume of sales. Smaller stores tend to pay a higher percentage than large national department stores which are needed as anchor tenants before the center can be financed. Publications from the International Council of Shopping Centers and the Urban Land Institute provide a wealth of information regarding leasing and operating costs.

Certain lease provisions are necessary to assure fairness to both parties in administering a percentage lease. Monthly and/or annual sales reports may be required, and the landlord may have the right to hire an auditor, whose fee is paid by the tenant if sales have been understated.

TYPICAL PERCENTAGE RENTS
Percentage Lease Rates in Neighborhood Shopping Centers For Various Types Of Businesses*

Firm Type	Percent
Automotive	2.0 to 5.0
Bakery	4.0 to 6.0
Books and stationery	2.5 to 6.0
Cameras	2.0 to 6.0
Cards and gifts	5.0 to 8.0
Computers, calculator	1.0 to 5.0
Drug store	2.5 to 4.0
Food specialty	2.0 to 6.0
Furniture	2.0 to 6.0
Hardware	2.5 to 6.0
Health food	1.5 to 6.0
Jewelry	4.5 to 5.0
Ladies specialty	4.0 to 7.0
Liquor and wine	1.5 to 5.0
Menswear	3.0 to 6.0
Paint, wallpaper	2.0 to 6.0
Pet shop	5.0 to 8.0
Records, tapes	3.7 to 7.0
Restaurant	4.0 to 7.0
Shoes	3.0 to 6.0
Sporting goods	3.0 to 6.0
Supermarket	1.0 to 2.0
Variety store	2.5 to 5.0

FOOTNOTES

* *Adapted from Dollars and Cents of Shopping Centers: 1987 Urban Land Institute.*

LEASE PROVISIONS
Anything legal may be written into a lease. Common lease provisions for commercial tenants follows.

Date and Parties. The lease states the date of the agreement, when the lease is valid, and the names and addresses of the parties. The lessor is typically referred to as the "landlord"; the lessee is the "tenant."

Premises is the property being leased. They consist of land, buildings, and other improvements that exist or will be built. An exhibit or supporting schedule may describe the premises in detail to avoid a misunderstanding about the property.

Term. The duration of a lease is its term. For commercial property that must be financed, permanent lenders look to the length and strength of the lease. While the term of a lease and that of permanent financing need not coincide, having the two reasonably close to each other makes it easier to finance.

Alterations. An alteration clause may obligate the tenant to obtain the landlord's permission and approval of plans. The tenant must maintain insurance for the work and hold the landlord harmless for claims arising from construction.

Insurance. In a long-term commercial lease, the tenant typically provides insurance to protect the landlord from all claims. These include liability and hazard insurance. The tenant is required to show the landlord policies bearing the minimum amount of insurance required by the lease.

Taking. Commercial leases typically provide for termination if a substantial portion of the building is condemned or if some portion (20 percent or more) of the parking is taken, unless the landlord substitutes other nearby parking.

Assignment is transfer by the tenant of all rights in the property. *Subletting* occurs when the tenant retains some of the property or at least some rights. Typically, the original tenant is not released from the lease.

Subordination. A subordination clause in a lease allows the landlord to arrange a first mortgage. However, the tenant rights should not be affected by any mortgage while the tenant is not in default under the lease.

Fixtures. Most commercial leases allow tenants to install their own fixtures, and require the fixtures to be approved by the landlord in advance, and be removed at the end of the lease term.

Destruction. In the event of total destruction, either party should be allowed to terminate the lease. If a partial destruction, the landlord is allowed to rebuild, with exceptions when the damage is extensive or the remaining term of the lease is brief. Rent abatement during reconstruction is negotiated.

Default. Types of tenant default must be listed in the lease. Examples of tenant default include being late in rent, becoming bankrupt or insolvent, or vacating the premises.

Surrender. Upon termination of the lease, the tenant should return the property in good condition, allowing for normal wear and tear or damage resulting from the landlord's neglect or negligence. Generally, fixtures that have become part of the realty remain, while trade fixtures are to be removed.

Arbitration. Some leases call for a specific arbitration board to settle disputes, which is less costly than litigation.

Brokers. Specifies the brokerage firm who negotiated the lease and commissions payable.

Encumbrances. The property is delivered to the tenant without liens.

Estoppels. Requires tenant to provide a certificate stating that the tenant is properly occupying and using the property and is not in default, and requires tenant to certify other reasonable requests.

Notices. Requires notices to be sent, often by registered mail, with return receipt, using the last known address.

Quiet Enjoyment. The landlord will not interfere with a tenant who abides by the lease.

Signs and Awnings. Allows a tenant to install signs with the landlord's advance approval.

Waiver. When either party does not strictly require lease performance, that party's rights may or may not be waived.

THE PURCHASE DECISION

Before buying a business property you may get an appraisal of the property. Sometimes the current owner has a recent one that you may photocopy and read. However, it may not be impartial. Consider who requested it, paid for it, and who appraised the property and its assumptions.

Appraisers of real estate used in a business may have the designation MAI, SREA, SRPA, ASA, FASA, and others. The MAI is awarded by the American Institute of Real Estate Appraisers, Chicago. It is perhaps the best recognized appraisal designation. Other highly coveted designations include the SREA and SRPA, awarded by the Society of Real Estate Appraisers, Chicago. The ASA and FASA are awarded by the American Society of Appraisers in Washington, DC, and the IFA by the Independent Fee Appraisers, St. Louis. The National Society of Real Estate Appraisers (NSREA), headquartered in Cleveland offers the MREA and CREA designations. Most NSREA members are minorities and are well acquainted with urban properties. Some other organizations offer appraisal designations, and some offer identical three- or four letter descriptions, but requirements vary widely. Engaging an appraiser should be like employing any other professional. It is good to get recommendations and to review work products and credentials.

If the business decides to buy a building it should have an attorney be involved in preparing the contract. It will also face a financing decision. Mortgage financing might be available from savings and loan associations, commercial banks, or possibly insurance companies, to cover 50 to 75 percent of its cost. If the business is large and highly creditworthy, that percentage may be increased to nearly 100 percent by a second mortgage or sale-lease back. A commercial mortgage banker may be consulted to determine the best source of financing for the property and business.

With most financings, including sale-lease-backs, the business must report both the asset and liability (in leases the liability is for the future rental payments) on its balance sheet. For many businesses, the various ratios of assets to liabilities that creditors review is adversely affected by a purchase. Therefore, many businesses would prefer to lease, provided the space and lease terms are suitable.

If the space is bought (or the equivalent through a lease) the business must set up controls and policies over its physical and financial management concerning taxes, insurance, maintenance and repairs.

Two major types of taxes are income and property. As to income taxes, commercial buildings are presently depreciable over a 31.5 year life. This allows an income tax deduction of 3.17 percent of the building cost each year, with no payment of cash. The deduction is allowed even if the building appreciates in value. However, when the building is sold, there may be a large tax to pay as the gain is measured by the difference between the selling price and the adjusted tax basis (cost less accumulated depreciation).

As to property taxes, they are assessed locally. The assessments may be reviewed periodically to be sure there is no mistake and the property valuation is consistent with neighboring properties. Some municipalities provide tax abatements to new businesses, even when they are small businesses. Determine if you qualify.

Insurance for real estate includes a one-time purchase of title insurance when the property is first acquired, and on-going hazard and liability insurance to protect against damage to the property and to others, respectively. Even a small business owner should carry large amounts of liability insurance to guard against the possibility of an accidental injury on the premises.

Proper maintenance is essential for a building to retain its value. The facilities should be inspected periodically and any repairs needed performed to prevent a minor problem from becoming major. Expenses for utilities—oil, gas, electricity, water—and maintenance should be monitored regularly. Compare each month's expenses to the previous month and to the same month of the previous year. Any large increases should be followed-up to seek explanations, before any expense gets out of control.

Finally, periodic appraisals may be arranged to assure that the investment in the building is being used wisely. Opportunities to refinance or sell the property or to expand should be considered.

CHAPTER PERSPECTIVE

The real estate decisions of a small business are among the most crucial. Of paramount importance is to choose a location where there is a demonstrated need. This may mean going to a market that is not being served by that type of establishment, or going to an area where the need is proven by a concentration of that type of business.

The amount of space and its cost can be crucial to the success of a business, and the owner must evaluate needs carefully. Finally, the decision to buy or lease is important. Buying ties up capital and brings more responsibilities, but gives the owner more control. If the leasing option is selected, the rent and other terms of the lease need careful evaluation.

Afterword:
Doing Business with
the Federal Government

INTRODUCTION

Doing business with the federal government can take one of several forms: Obtaining financial assistance; conducting business under special governmental waivers or provisions; or landing a federal agency as a customer or client.

Regardless of your party politics or philosophical orientation, the reality is this: Business and government are inextricably intertwined in a multitude of ways. You will probably be regulated by various governmental agencies, you will pay taxes to various governments, and you will be answerable to governmental entities if you defraud or injure your customers or clients.

On the other hand, you may also have positive, profitable, and constructive relationships with governmental agencies as a result of various programs. In such event, you will still need to negotiate a significant thicket of rules and regulations. So pay close attention to the rules and requirements, and ask questions when in doubt.

THE FEDERAL GOVERNMENT AS CUSTOMER

Some of us think only of ther private businesses as potential customers or clients. The federal government through its General Services Administration (GSA) urges us to think otherwise for this reason: The U.S. government is a consumer that buys more goods and services than any other customer in the free enterprise system.

You will need marketing skills and quality products to compete in this special marketplace, but you also need knowledge concerning (1) how to market in the federal structure; (2) how to obtain necessary forms and papers; (3) how to bid for the opportunity to sell goods or services.

Think of the huge governmental market as two market segments: The so-called general segment and the mission-oriented segment.

The General Services Administration (GSA) is the main purchasing agent for the general segment. GSA buys thousands of items used in any business operation: computers, paper, janitorial supplies, construction materials, and everything else.

GSA also makes efforts to spread the business around among various business segments and geographical areas. GSA also operates a Business Service Center (BSC) program, where businesses can get advice and information concerning contract opportunities with the government.

The mission-oriented segment is best illustrated by the military, which needs specialized supplies and services.

Do not count yourself out as a potential government contractor just because you are a small business or just starting. Several programs provide set-asides for businesses, and you may find one to fit your own operation. Among those preferential programs are the following:

Small and disadvantaged businesses. Federal agencies are required to promote participation of such firms in government procurement.

Small business set-asides. Federal law requires agencies to set aside certain contracts for qualified small businesses. The Small Business Administration determines eligibility.

Socially and economically disadvantaged businesses. SBA also certifies firms eligible to participate in these contracts, and it may also provide management and technical support for the firms. Contracts may be awarded on a noncompetitive basis. At least 51 percent of the company's stock must be owned by one or more socially and economically disadvantaged individuals. The law identifies blacks, Hispanics, native Americans, and Asian-Pacific Americans among those who qualify as socially and economically disadvantaged.

Labor surplus area set-asides. When these set-asides apply, only firms that agree to perform most of the contract work in areas having higher than average unemployment may compete for contracts.

Women-owned businesses. Federal agencies must make special efforts to advise women of business opportunities.

Vietnam Veterans. Federal agencies actively encourage Vietnam veterans to seek government contracts.

Mandatory source programs. If workshops for the blind and severely handicapped offer goods or services at competitive prices, federal agencies must purchase from them.

The U.S. Department of Commerce publishes the *Commerce Business Daily*, which lists proposed government procurements, subcontracting leads, contract awards, sales of surplus property, and foreign business opportunities. It is published Monday through Saturday and can be obtained from the Superintendent of Documents, U.S. Government Printing Office, Washington, D.C. 20402.

SMALL BUSINESS ADMINISTRATION

You may have heard that one of the greatest lies is, "We're from the government, and we're here to help you." Your first business encounter with the Internal Revenue Service may reinforce this view.

Many small business owners just like you, however, swear by the Small Business Administration (SBA). Anytime you need financing or technical help—and who doesn't?—it may be an agency worth checking.

The agency and its programs are accessible. SBA has more than 100 offices around the country. Additionally, it enhances its ability to assist small businesses through a variety of public-private initiatives. Some of these are cosponsored projects with private companies, colleges, and universities and volunteer programs such as the Service Corps of Retired Executives (SCORE).

The telephone directory in any major urban area should lead you to an SBA contact. Alternatively, phone 800-368-5855 (202-653-7561 in Washington, D.C.).

SBA's mission is to help small business through the following areas:

—Business development: management assistance through information, counseling, training, and conferences.

—Financial assistance: loan guarantees, bonding assistance, and other direct and indirect financial support.

—Contract assistance: helping small businesses obtain government contracts.

—Advocacy: representing small business interests before Congress and other federal agencies.

You cannot consider SBA your regular business banker, but you should think of the agency when you need capital. The SBA is a backup resource; by law, you must first seek financing from a bank or other lending institution before you can get SBA loan assistance.

SBA can provide two basic types of business loans: SBA guaranteed loans or SBA direct loans. Direct loans are difficult to obtain. They have a ceiling of $150,000 and are available only to applicants unable to secure an SBA-guaranteed loan.

Although direct loans are made infrequently, they are sometimes available—and they're good deals if you qualify. If you plan to locate your business in a high-unemployment area, or if you are handicapped, a Vietnam-era veteran, a disabled veteran, or one of certain low-income persons, you should definitely look into the direct loan program.

Guaranteed loans, on the other hand, are made by private lenders, usually banks. They are guaranteed by SBA for up to 90 percent of the amount of the loan. (If your loan is smaller than $155,000 the SBA can guarantee up to 90%. The maximum guaranty percentage of loans exceeding $155,000 is 85 per cent. The SBA can back loans up to $500,000. Average loan size is $125,000.) The guarantee reassures the lender that the loan will be repaid even if your business fails. The lender, therefore, is motivated to make the loan. The lender is also required to state that the borrower couldn't get a loan on reasonable terms without the guarantee.

SBA guarantees are not giveaways. Unless you fall into one of a preferred list of applicants, your credit will have to be good and you may have to put up collateral (such as a lien on your business property or a second mortgage on your home).

To some extent interest rates are negotiable but are based on the prime rate plus a maximum two and one-quarter percent for loans of less than seven years, two and three-quarters for longer loans. A loan-guarantee fee of two percent must be paid to the SBA.

Normally repayment periods for loans for working capital run one to three years but can go a maximum of seven. For machinery and equipment, three to five years, maximum ten; for real estate, fifteen years, maximum twenty-five.

If you set your hopes on an SBA-guaranteed loan, begin the application process as soon as possible. The red tape is tangled and banks and the SBA seem to take forever. We're talking *months* from the time you start on the paperwork until you receive your check. (Certain "preferred" or "certified" banks can speed up the process.)

Be sure to contact your local SBA office early on. They can name the banks that most frequently work with the guaranteed loan program. They may be able to put you in touch with an "old hand" at filling out SBA papers who works with SCORE or with a small business development center.

Caution: You can create tangible products, but not ideas or opinions, with an SBA loan. Ineligible for loans are such businesses as newspapers, magazines, nontechnical schools and businesses engaged in speculation or investment in real estate.

Just how small is small for purposes of an SBA loan? General size standards include these.

Manufacturing. Maximum number of employees may range from 500 to 1,500, depending on the type of product.

Wholesaling. Maximum number of employees may not exceed 100.

Services. Annual receipts may not exceed $3.5 to $14.5 million, depending on the industry.

Retailing. Annual receipts may not exceed $3.5 to $13.5 million, depending on the industry.

Construction. General construction annual receipts may not exceed $9.5 to $17 million, depending on the industry.

Special Trade Construction. Annual receipts may not exceed $7 million.

Agriculture. Annual receipts may not exceed $500,000 to $3.5 million, depending on the industry.

Small Business Administration Checklist

In reviewing your financial and technical needs, ask yourself these questions to determine whether SBA assistance might be appropriate.

—Does SBA provide technical assistance that addresses the needs of your company?

—Have you checked all the publications available through the SBA office?

—Does your business fall within the dollar eligibility requirements for an SBA loan?

—Have you selected and talked to a private lender?

—Have you prepared the materials necessary to apply for a loan?

—Do you fall within any special favorable category that might make you eligible for an SBA direct loan?

ENTERPRISE ZONES

Enterprise zones are the product of a socioeconomic concept designed to revive run down neighborhoods (or communities) while at the same time providing jobs for the residents of such areas or who are in an.???

From a public policy standpoint, government reshuffles the deck of programs, incentives, and regulations to make certain areas more attractive for investment. Instead of offering a single program or incentive, the intent is to create a general economic climate of opportunity in these areas.

From your standpoint, there may be some aspect of the enterprise zone program that will help jump-start your business. Since programs differ widely, you have to consider each one separately; there is no standard for enterprise zone programs.

Start by checking out the program in areas where you are interested in doing business. A good place to start is the local chamber of commerce, which should have a directory of programs. Other checkpoints are: the local government economic development office; the state economic development office or department of commerce; the local office of the U.S. Department of Housing and Urban Development (HUD).

Other countries have used the concept of special incentive zones for a long time, but the idea was never seriously considered by the U.S. federal government until the early 1970s. However, even so, all the interest, discussion, and debate has led to a program that designates federal enterprise zones but so far has offered few incentives. The federal program mostly *encourages* such things as tax incentives at the state and local levels; specific actions to reduce, remove, simplify, or streamline governmental requirements at all levels; and improved local services.

This is mentioned, however, because of wide state and local interest in being designated a federal enterprise zone in anticipation of future additional benefits in locally designated zones—and because of programs already started in the zones by state and local governments. Thus, while Congress has discussed, state and local governments have put together a variety of benefit packages.

These are examples of state-designated enterprise zone benefits as outlined in case studies prepared by HUD:

—Reduction of city inventory taxes.

—Preferential treatment for water and sewer hook-ons and reduced building permit fees.

—Industrial revenue bond financing.

—Eligibility for other city-assisted loans.

—Construction of various infrastructure projects.

—Inclusion of companies for special clean-up programs.

—Establishment of special zoning regulations to expedite business change and expansion.

—Special agreements negotiated with unions (e.g., building trades) to establish moratoria on work stoppages and construction disruption.

—Provision of incubator facilities.

—Provision of state- or city-assisted job training.

—Building permit waivers.

—Provision of "development expeditor" to streamline all code, permit and licensing transactions.

—Availability of venture capital.

—Exemption from vehicle usage tax.

—Exemption from various state sales and use taxes.

—Writedowns of available land.

These examples are weighted toward manufacturing operations, but benefits are also clearly available to some office and service businesses.

Even if you find an appealing mix of enterprise zone benefits, keep in mind that if location is a critical element of your business, you must keep the benefits in perspective. Enterprise zones serve a social purpose and may be in areas you (and your customers) consider undesirable.

Index